Living in the Word

—

The Four Gospels

Living in the Word

A Devotional Commentary On The Four Gospels

Edited by Frederick Coutts

AUGSBURG PUBLISHING HOUSE
MINNEAPOLIS, MINNESOTA

Preface

Augsburg is pleased to publish *Living in the Word:* A Devotional Commentary on the Four Gospels. This is the American edition of the same book published in England under the title *The Armoury Commentary: The Four Gospels*. These devotional comments first appeared in *The Soldier's Armoury*, a Bible reading plan with a daily commentary published every six months in England since 1955. More than 50,000 copies of each issue are distributed for personal, family, and group use.

Frederick Coutts has edited the comments on the Gospels and organized them in this useful volume.

In his review of the book, Sherwood E. Wirt, editor of *Decision* magazine, says, "I like a devotional commentary that is faithful to the gospel, that brings light to the text, that draws upon a wide range of illustrative material, and that speaks to my condition today. *Living in the Word* has all of these characteristics, and I am delighted to recommend its use."

Alvin N. Rogness, well-known writer of devotional books and seminary president, says, "This warm and concise commentary will enrich both heart and mind. It is devotional reading, and it is instructional reading, and both of high character. The rich meaning of the Gospels will come alive as you read."

We offer *Living in the Word* to our Christian friends of all denominations as a resource for Bible study and prayer.

THE PUBLISHER

Contents

THE GOSPEL ACCORDING TO MATTHEW

Is Not This The Christ?

INTRODUCTION

Though not the first of the four gospels to be written, that of
Matthew is well placed at the beginning of the New Testament
for it provides the strongest link with the Old by its presentation
of Jesus as Messiah, the One in whom the prophecies of the Old
Testament came to pass. 'That it might be fulfilled . . .' is a
recurring theme.

Jesus is also presented as Teacher. The compiler of the gospel
has gathered His words into five sections, each of which concludes
in an almost identical manner—7: 28, 11: 1, 13: 53, 19: 1 and
26: 1.

Finally, Jesus is presented as King. From the beginning of the
gospel where the wise men came seeking for the One 'born king
of the Jews' to the mocking inscription over the Cross: 'This is
Jesus, the King of the Jews', here is the Christ to whom 'all power
is given'.

'The son of David, the son of Abraham ... the husband of Mary, of whom was born Jesus' (vv. 1, 16).

A CHILD OF HIGH RENOWN. What this genealogy is saying is that the coming of Jesus, Son of Mary, was no chance event. 'When the fulness of the time was come, God sent forth His Son' (Gal. 4: 4). The line of descent begins with two of the great names in Jewish history—Abraham, through whom 'all the families of the earth were to be blessed' (Gen. 12: 3), and also David—for the Messianic hope centred in one who should be of David's line. We would say—a David come to life again who would restore the kingdom to Israel.

But this genealogy is significant in two other ways—both Jew and Gentile have their place in the list, as do saint and sinner. Ruth was an alien (v. 5) as was Rachab (or Rahab) who is described in Joshua 2: 1 as an harlot. Thamar's story was even more unsavoury (Gen. 38). But we are meant to understand that God can turn even the evil of men to His redeeming purpose—as is shown by the way in which the worst of man's actions, the crucifixion of Jesus, was transformed by God into the means of man's redemption.

The inclusion of Gentile as well as Jew is saying that while Jesus was King of the Jews, His rule is wider than His own race.

> Peoples and realms of every tongue
> Dwell on His love with sweetest song.

So the truth implicit in the opening verses of this gospel is explicit at its close when the disciples are bidden 'go ... and teach all nations'.

'Behold, the virgin shall be with child, and shall bear a son, and they shall call Him Emmanuel (which means, God with us)' (v. 23 Knox).

THE DESCENT OF GOD. The doctrine of the virgin birth does not imply that there is anything inferior about the normal process of human birth. Nor is it, in itself, the foundation of our belief in the Incarnation. This doctrine affirms that the coming of Christ was at God's initiative. The life of Jesus was the result not of human evolution—He was not merely man at his best—but of Divine intrusion. To use spatial terms, the life of Jesus marks both the descent of God and the possibility of the ascent of man.

The full meaning of the name Emmanuel we cannot begin to imagine. We are thrown back upon human but inadequate analogies. At the beginning of this century, a young man who worked at a London bank was spending his Sundays in the common lodging houses. Dressed in his best clothes, and armed with a New Testament, he was surprised at the men's indifference. 'I was enormously impressed at their iniquity,' he said, 'a young man in a frock coat and silk top hat, and they didn't even listen.' One evening he donned the oldest coat he could borrow and with 4d. in his pocket went to a lodging house. 'I sat where they sat,' he later wrote, 'the fleas that bit them bit me. . . . I spent nights in that dreadful chamber listening to their needs and woes. Then at six o'clock one morning when they were getting their breakfast, I began to speak to them without the slightest difficulty. I had understood exactly how dirty they were, how the seas of life were buffeting them, and they were perfectly willing to listen!'

Harold St. John adds these words: 'After forty centuries of dwelling in cloud and thick darkness, God sent His Son to learn the experiences and thoughts of men. . . . He knew hunger, weariness, poverty, sorrow . . . and when He had learned these things, Jesus opened His mouth and the world has been listening to Him ever since.'

MATTHEW 2: 1–12

'There came to Jerusalem from the East scholars who were students of the stars' (v. 1, Barclay).

FOR ALL THE WORLD. As the main purpose of Matthew was to show that Jesus is the fulfilment of Jewish hopes, it is remarkable that his Gospel is the only one that records the visit of Gentiles to Bethlehem. Aspiration after truth was not confined to the Jew. G. E. P. Cox has said: 'There is abundant evidence that, in an age distracted by social disintegration and civil war, the ancient world in general was moved by a spirit of expectancy corresponding to a sense of men's desperate need.'

The importance of all this should not be missed. It points to the universality of Christ's appeal and influence. He was manifested 'to the Jew first and also to the Gentile', and the Christian is convinced that He is the Saviour of the whole world.

The story of the men from the East also points to another vital truth: God begins with men as they are. We may think astrology a false science, but we must not therefore write off the reality of the revelation to those who read the signs of the stars. As W. R. Matthews comments, 'It is not unknown in human friendships that they begin in misunderstanding and end in love.' God has many ways to bring men into truth. Let us not think that the way we travel is the only way. Nor let us forget that He can break into our lives with fuller understanding in new and even startling ways, and through people we may not have considered the instruments of His grace.

MATTHEW 2: 13–23

'Flee into Egypt . . . for Herod will seek the young child to destroy Him' (v. 13, R.V.).

THE WEAKNESS OF FORCE. We sometimes forget that there is more to the Christmas story than music and poetry, romance and beauty. Today's reading should help us to see its utter realism.

Jesus was born in a real stable, surrounded by smelly animals, to a mother who felt that neither Baby nor herself was wanted, except by the understanding Joseph. He was born in Palestine—'occupied territory'—and directly associated with His coming is this story of tyranny and bloodshed we call the 'massacre of the innocents'.

Herod and Jesus represent the two ideals for ever confronting the human race. Tyranny, self-assertion, force; love, self-discipline, peace. Herod appears so strong and effective, Jesus so weak and ineffectual. The fact that Herod failed on this occasion does not alter the fact that he often succeeds. Thirty years later Jesus stood before another Herod, and brute force won the day. But did it? Think of both those Herods, or men like Caiaphas and Pilate—are they not total failures? Were it not for the Christ they opposed, their very names might hardly have been known.

Both Jesus and Herod are facts, and this world is the arena in which the struggle between the two concepts of life they stand for takes place. We are called to identify ourselves with one or the other, and to say 'No' to Christ is to say 'Yes' to Herod.

'This is he that was spoken of by Isaiah the prophet (v. 3, R.V.).

THE CALL TO REPENTANCE. Chapter 2 concludes with the Child Jesus in Nazareth, His home town. Chapters 3 opens with the mission of John the Baptist in Judea, which was to be the signal for our Lord—now a Man of some thirty years (see Luke 3: 23)—to leave the obscurity of His home town and commence His own public ministry.

For centuries devout Jews had been waiting for the voice of an authentic prophet, hence the ready response to the Baptist. His message was that the final crisis had arrived and preparations for it demanded a total change of life. His call was to repentance, and the word used meant 'thinking again'. God's own people had their backs to Him, and they must turn and face Him before they could find their true life.

It has been pointed out that when non-Jews wished to embrace the Jewish faith, a rite of baptism was used as a sign of their new beginning; but baptism for Jews was new and revolutionary. This was an essential part of John's message; the Jewish claim to be a privileged and chosen people is now, in the light of the impending judgment, out of date. This baptism signifies a total renunciation of the past, and a total self-dedication to the future. Thus racial exclusiveness is shattered by John's pioneering axe.

In our repentance it is to our Lord we turn.

'Prepare ye the way of the Lord' (v. 3).

RENEWED OR DESTROYED. It was said of John that he would do his work in the spirit and power of Elijah (Luke 1: 17). In his dress he resembled Elijah and he spoke with the directness of an Elijah (compare with 1 Kings 18: 21, 21: 20). The result was that, whatever their motive, even the Pharisees and Sadducees came to the Jordan to see what was happening.

John may have had cause to be suspicious of them. They represented the 'establishment' of their day. With their faith in race (v. 9) could they have any place in the new order which the Messiah was to inaugurate? The Baptist unflatteringly compared them to snakes scurrying for dear life before a bush fire. These new arrivals would have to prove their good faith by genuine sorrow for their past ways. Real repentance would be known by its fruits and, what is more, their repentance had better be speedy. The fire which would bring cleansing to some would mean destruction to others (compare vv. 11 and 12). All this teaches us that we deceive ourselves if we think we can live on the spiritual capital of our fathers in the faith.

John made it clear that his was a ministry of warning. His baptism was one of repentance—an outward sign of inward sorrow. Only the One of whom he was the herald could impart the power—the power of the Holy Spirit—by whom the repentant man could be born anew. But for such there was this lively hope— as there is for us today.

MATTHEW 3: 13-17

'Leave it like this ... it is fitting that we should ... do all that righteousness demands' (v. 15, Jerusalem Bible).

THE BAPTISM OF THE SINLESS ONE. Why should the One who was sinless submit to a baptism that was 'for the remission of sins'? If, however, we see this in relation to Jesus' purpose in coming to earth, we can understand why. It was a natural act in the positive sense of a total self-dedication to the coming Kingdom which John was proclaiming. He identified Himself with a wayward nation and an alienated world, for that was the only way of redemption. This act 'became' Him (the same word is used in Heb. 2: 10), for He stands in 'the sinner's place, the only place where forgiveness can be offered and received. The Redeemer cannot stand aloof from those He would redeem.'

And in the experience came the divine confirmation. The growing conviction of the silent years in Nazareth suddenly became crystallized. An utter assurance of His vocation came to Jesus, in the combined language of Psalm 2: 7 (Son) and Isaiah 42: 1 (Servant). As the 'beloved' Son He was also to be the perfect Servant of the Lord. Sonship always involves responsibility as well as privilege.

MATTHEW 4: 1-11

'Then was Jesus ... tempted of the devil' (v. 1).

THE TEMPTATION OF THE SINLESS ONE. A Jewish father of Jesus' day might quote a Jewish book of the period 'My

son, if thou comest to serve the Lord, prepare thy soul for temptation' (Ecclesiasticus 2: 1). This the Son-Servant experienced to
the full.

Previous expositors have pointed out that the temptations are
closely related to the baptism which had just preceded them, to
the purpose of our Lord's ministry, and to the special power with
which he was endowed. Here, as so often, the subtlest temptations
come, not as the allurement of what is wrong in itself, but as an
inclination to use what is good in itself for wrong purposes, or to
try and get things which God intends us to have by methods that
He cannot bless.

Let us apply our Lord's temptations to our own.

The first: God does care for the physical needs of His children,
but the selfish desire to get things for ourselves must be resisted.

The second: God does deliver His children from trouble, but
the unreasonable demand that He should protect us no matter
what we do must never be made.

The third: It is God's purpose that His Kingdom shall come,
but we must learn not to snatch at God's gifts. We must grow in
fitness in order to receive them.

MATTHEW 4: 12–17

'From that time Jesus began to preach' (v. 17).

PUBLIC WORK COMMENCES. The imprisonment of John
(14: 3) was a sign to Jesus that this should begin. But not in Nazareth where He was known as Joseph's son (Luke 4: 22). A prophet
was rarely recognized as such in his own country. So He moved
to the lakeside city of Capernaum, in which action the compiler
of the gospel saw a fulfilment of Old Testament prophecy. Yet
this very Jewish way of understanding the ministry of Jesus is
used to describe the commencement of His mission in the 'Galilee
of the Gentiles'—and there 'Jesus began to preach.'

Preaching is a word which has come down in the world. In
some minds today it conjures up the artificial drone of a voice
pitched well above the heads of a body of weary listeners. Yet the
communication of the gospel is the primary task of the people of
God today.

This can be done by word of mouth, which requires personal
fellowship with Him who is the Word, and an overmastering

passion to share with others, the faith that Jesus holds the key to the mysteries of life and death. As F. W. H. Myers wrote:

> Then, with a rush, the intolerable craving
> Shivers throughout me like a trumpet call.

But there is a silent and eloquent preaching by deeds as well. Jesus used both methods in His ministry. And so must we today.

MATTHEW 4: 18–22

'Follow Me and I will teach you to catch men' (v. 19, J. B. Phillips).

EVERYBODY HAS A PART TO PLAY. Though some of the disciples had met Jesus before this incident (John 1: 41, 42), here was the Master's firm call to His side. Having listened to John the Baptist, it could have been that they had thought of Jesus only as One who shared the Baptist's outlook and message. But the authority in this new voice caused these two pairs of brothers to forsake their daily employment and become the nucleus of the Twelve. They left their calling, but not their skills. The same resourcefulness they had shown in catching fish on the Sea of Galilee was now to be dedicated to the work of catching men on the wider and wilder seas of life.

We are not required to be other than the men we are in order to serve both our Lord and our fellows. All the colour was not drained out of the life of the big fisherman by his act of obedience. The fact is that he became more truly himself in the company of Jesus. His weaknesses were mastered, his forthrightness was an inestimable asset in making the gospel known as, like a rock (16: 18), he stood for Christ and helped his fellow believers so to stand.

The calling of these four men illustrates how God can use diverse characters and diverse gifts in His service. Peter and John were of opposite natures, yet we would be hard put to say which of them contributed the most to the life of the church of the New Testament. Enough to agree with the words of an early day Salvation Army chorus: 'Everybody has a part to play in the great salvation war.'

'He opened His mind and heart to them, and this was the substance of His teaching' (5: 2, Barclay).

TEACHING FOR FOLLOWERS. The conclusion of chapter four sums up the Master's early Galilean ministry. Crowds had flocked to hear Him from all parts of the country. There had been preaching, healing and teaching, and now the gospel record gathers together in systematic fashion the sayings of Jesus which are to be found in different settings—for example, in the gospel of Luke.

About the 'Sermon' two things may be said—first of warning. Here we have a series of illustrations—some compressed into a sentence or even a phrase—as to how the principles which Jesus enunciated would work out in real life. But these sayings are addressed to the disciples (5: 1), though it can be added that the whole world has overheard them. Yet though it is sometimes said that the world's woes would end if men but lived by the teaching of chapters five, six and seven, there is nowhere in the gospels any suggestion that men will be able to follow the teaching of Jesus without a personal committal to Jesus and the strong help of the grace of Jesus. We shall only disappoint ourselves unless it is noted that this is Christ's way of life for those who are Christ's followers.

The second is the more encouraging truth, that Jesus Himself is the best example of His teaching. As Hensley Henson once said: 'The founder of Buddhism was no model for normal man; the founder of Mohammedanism was no model for any man ... Jesus alone is able to offer Himself as a sufficient illustration of His own doctrine.' It is this fact which strengthens our faith that we can be doers, and not just hearers, of the word.

MATTHEW 5: 3

'How happy are the humble-minded, for the Kingdom of Heaven is theirs!' (J. B. Phillips).

POOR IN SPIRIT. Jesus did not mean, 'Blessed are the poor,' for slums, starvation and disease, three common signs of poverty, are clearly not conducive to human happiness; and they are always an offence to the spirit of Christ's gospel. He said, 'Blessed are the poor in spirit,' meaning that utter dependence upon God is the secret of blessedness, of inward joy.

The 'poor in spirit' recognize the folly of proud self-sufficiency. This was the idea in the psalmist's mind when he wrote: 'This poor man cried, and the Lord heard him, and saved him out of all his troubles' (Psalm 34: 6); for the poor man, lacking influence and prestige, and in consequence oppressed by men, knew his helplessness, and therefore placed his whole hope and trust in God. 'Self-sufficiency and therefore pride', wrote Brother Roger in *So Easy to Love*, 'are the foundations of all our complications.' Our prosperity tends to make us independent of God, even though our lips continue to pay homage to Him.

The 'poor in spirit' alone are citizens of the Kingdom of Heaven. Realizing their utter need of God, their utter unworthiness and weakness, they gratefully render to Him implicit and loving obedience. They possess the Kingdom because the Kingdom possesses them.

MATTHEW 5:4

'Blessed are the mourners, for they shall be comforted' (Weymouth).

JOY THROUGH SORROW. Those who suffer and sorrow the most are often most aware of the consolation of God. The intensity of their 'mourning' becomes the measure of the divine comfort granted them. 'How happy are those who know what sorrow means (translates J. B. Phillips) for they will be given courage and comfort.' This truth can be applied in two ways.

Blessed are those who mourn over the sufferings of the world. 'If we cannot have Christ's arm', said Alexander Whyte, 'we can have His heart.' In other words, we can weep with those who weep. Paradoxically, only those who are capable of such sorrow know the elation of real joy. Kagawa, who chose to live in a Tokyo slum, was an example of radiant living. Though his heart never ceased to ache over the misery of those in whose midst he lived, his eyes reflected the joy of the Lord.

There is an even more personal application of these words of Jesus—blessed are they who mourn their own sinfulness. Repentance is at the last a joyful experience. Those who confess their sin know the happiness of divine forgiveness. The penitent Psalmist prays that he may know the joy of God's salvation.

'Blessed are the patient; they shall inherit the land'
(Knox).

'Blessed are the humble! they will inherit the earth'
(Moffatt).

'Happy are those who claim nothing, for the whole earth
will belong to them' (J. B. Phillips).

'Happy the gentle; for they shall inherit the earth' (Rieu).

THE MEEK. These four renderings indicate the difficulty of
recapturing the exact meaning of the Greek word translated
meek in the Authorized Version. Meekness certainly includes
patience, humility, self-forgetfulness and gentleness; but even
these qualities do not necessarily guarantee the presence of meekness or dispel the idea in some minds that to be always meek is
to be sometimes weak.

Meekness is strength controlled by love. Some people are never
disturbed because they do not care deeply enough about anybody
or anything other than themselves; others are often excessively
angry (bad tempered) because they care too deeply about themselves, always themselves. Christ's love for people caused Him to
be angry at their wilful stupidity and harmful self-centredness;
but because His anger was unfailingly God-inspired, it was also
God-controlled, which made it an expression of true meekness.

If the meek sometimes lack the things which money can buy,
they possess riches that money cannot buy.

MATTHEW 5:6

'Blessed are those who hunger and thirst for goodness!
they will be satisfied' (Moffatt).

THE POWER OF DESIRE. The people to whom Jesus was
speaking knew, if not from personal experience, then from
observation, the miseries of starvation and burning thirst. They
would therefore readily understand the idea behind these words
of His: God's blessing is for the individual who yearns for goodness as a starving man hungers for food, and a parched man for
water.

In God's Kingdom we find what we seek. 'All that is necessary
to be a saint,' recorded Thomas Merton in *Elected Silence*, 'is to
want to be one. Don't you believe that God will make you what

He created you to be, if you will consent to let Him do it? All you have to do is to desire it.' The trouble is that our 'hunger' for God is frequently more a passing whim than a sustained longing. But still we find only what we seek; for spiritual discoveries can never exceed spiritual desires.

In God's Kingdom we become what we love. Our strongest interests control our lives—whatever opposite impression we may manage to convey. This unalterable law of the Spirit can be a source of comfort, for it means that secret intention counts for more than open achievement, that sincerity of motive is accounted unto us for righteousness.

MATTHEW 5:7

'Happy are the merciful, for they will have mercy shown to them' (J. B. Phillips).

THE QUALITY OF MERCY. Mercy is not patronage, nor is it a form of proud forbearance which parades as a virtue rather than seeking to help a friend in need. It should be remembered that just as justice should be tempered with mercy, mercy should be tempered with justice. Nothing is easier than to display mercy (so-called) in an even vindictive way.

The truly merciful see life through the eyes of those in need of mercy. If to know all is not always to forgive all, it should be to understand all. Far from being sentimental on the one hand, or condescending on the other, sympathy means sharing together. The word 'empathy' has been coined to express this attitude.

The truly merciful know themselves to be in need of mercy. They forgive because they themselves know their own need of forgiveness. Such insight delivers them from the last remains of contempt and expresses itself in loving goodwill.

MATTHEW 5:8

'Blessed are the clean of heart; they shall see God' (Knox).

SEEING THE INVISIBLE. To some people God is obscure, impersonal and seemingly unknowable. The truth is that we can see only that which our heart—or character—allows us to see. It has been well said that 'all true awareness of God is the fruit of spiritual discipline'.

In *Can Human Nature be Improved?* Dr. F. E. England has written: 'Bad feeling distorts vision. If there is bitterness in a man's heart, if he is angry, he will inevitably see things out of perspective or actually distorted. Rancour, contempt, envy spring from a mind vitiated by undisciplined feelings. The judgments and criticisms we pass in our heated moments proceed from our mixed feelings. But when our feelings are chastened, our judgment is clear and our vision sharpened.'

Spiritual vision is impossible without purity of heart. In the Bible the word 'heart' stands for the seat and centre of the human personality—the point at which thought, will and feeling meet. So purity of heart involves purity of motive and imagination and secret desire. This depth of purity belongs to those who know the meaning of worship and who continually—in the words of John 15: 4—abide in Christ.

MATTHEW 5: 9

'O the bliss of those who produce right relationships between man and man, for they are doing a godlike work!' (Barclay).

PEACEMAKERS. Most problems in life originate in strained human relationships. People cannot 'get on' with each other. Even though sometimes sharing the same faith and actually giving allegiance to the same Lord, they nevertheless remain at loggerheads, maintaining at best an attitude of pained tolerance. They are a burden to themselves and a liability to the cause of Christ.

He said that happiness was found in peacemaking. Some people's love of peace makes them little but troublemakers; for their policy of peace at any price, causing them to leave undisturbed unjust situations, and to 'patch up' quarrels without dealing with basic antagonisms, makes harmonious human relationships finally impossible.

Peacemakers, themselves reconciled to God, to their personal limitations and to their circumstances, heal breaches, create a spirit of unyielding goodwill, and make it easier for people to stay united on a basis of mutual consideration and respect. Their happiness is the unsought-for result of their concern for the happiness of others.

MATTHEW 5: 10

'Happy are those who have suffered persecution for the cause of goodness, for the Kingdom of Heaven is theirs' (J. B. Phillips).

PROVING OUR FAITH. Some people have a martyr complex; they imagine themselves to be the uncomplaining victims of innocent suffering, and their persecution mania is often little more than unrealized self-pity. Jesus was clearly not referring to such people when He talked about the blessedness of those who suffer persecution for the cause of goodness. We can perhaps best get to the meaning of His words by pondering two truths that flow naturally from them:

Persecution is never easy, but it is triumphantly bearable if endured for a noble cause. A widowed mother gave her son the opportunity of advanced education by scrubbing other people's floors and taking in other people's washing. Yet she never talked of sacrifice; always of privilege. The reason behind her drudgery was the cause of its transformation. The pain of those who suffer 'for the sake of goodness' (Moffatt) is no less severe, but the cause for which they suffer is great enough to inspire fortitude and to yield the fruit of joy.

Persecution can prove the believer's spoken confession of faith. Henry Hardy, the Anglican priest known as Father Andrew, was once asked for counsel by a younger clergyman. He himself was discouraged to the point of despair, and was considering resignation from the ministry. But he was told to say of such moments: 'This is a wonderful opportunity of proving my love for Christ.' For such a privilege we can 'greatly rejoice' (1 Peter 1: 6).

MATTHEW 5: 11, 12

'Blessed are you, when men revile you, and persecute you, and speak all manner of evil against you falsely, because of me' (v. 11, Knox).

FACING ADVERSITY. Jesus never tried to hide from His disciples the probable costly outcome of their faithfulness. They would be persecuted; and this, He said, should not surprise them, for the human heart's natural instinct is ever to destroy the light that reveals its sinfulness. The Old Testament prophets were persecuted; and for the same reasons of selfishness and bigotry the disciples of Christ would face fierce antagonism.

George Fox was right when he said, 'The light which shows us our sins is the light that heals us.' But what if men do not want to be healed? What if their only aim is to remain undisturbed in the darkness? They comfort their consciences by smothering every source of distasteful self-revelation, sometimes actually in the name of righteousness. When confronted by this situation, the Christian, insisted Jesus, should still rejoice for, as Dietrich Bonhoeffer observed, 'To endure the cross is not a tragedy; it is the suffering which is the fruit of an exclusive allegiance to Jesus Christ.'

The believer should also see his present trials in the light of future glory. This is not the same as trying to escape from life's harshness by thinking of the life to come, nor to allow thoughts of eternal reward to compensate for temporal deprivation. The Christian remembers the reality of the invisible world only as an encouragement to face his responsibilities in this one. Like his Master, for the joy set before him he endures the cross.

MATTHEW 5: 13

'You are salt to the world' (N.E.B.).

INSIPID CHRISTIANITY. Dean Inge once asked: 'What is the difference between holiness and righteousness or moral goodness? Most believers wish to be good, but do not exactly wish to be holy. Holiness for them means a soft kind of goodness, that sort of unworldliness which comes from ignorance of the world. Holy people, they think, constitute a sort of third sex, and they rightly believe that a good Christian man ought to remain a man, and a good Christian woman a woman.'

It is sadly true that some believers do bring discredit upon Christianity by their insipid living. They represent a way of life that is negative and timid and denies the spirit of Christ. He said that His followers should be salt to the world—which comparison suggests two truths.

Christians should be examples of purity. Their presence should be like an antiseptic, attacking corruption and adding fragrance to life. 'Each of your visits', wrote a friend to the Quaker Corder Catchpool, 'has been such a pleasure to us and as refreshing as a walk in the high Alps ... One seems to breathe the mountain air of spiritual heights.'

Christians should be examples of radiant living. Salt gives both flavour and character to food. Without it even otherwise correctly cooked dishes are lifeless and uninviting. So followers of Jesus should add colour and zest to life, which may be one reason why an ageing saint prayed: 'O Lord, keep me living while I'm still alive.'

MATTHEW 5: 14–16

'Let your light so shine upon the world that it may see the beauty of your life and give glory to your Father in Heaven' (v. 16, Rieu).

REFLECTORS OF LIGHT. The house lamp in Palestine was a saucer-like shape filled with oil in which a wick floated loosely. When a householder went out he would, for safety's sake as well as to avoid the trouble of using flint and steel again, place the burning lamp under his earthen bushel measure. Its proper place, however, was on the lamp standard to give light to everyone in the house—and this was the homely practice which Jesus used to illustrate the nature and purpose of Christian discipleship.

A Christian should always make his allegiance plainly evident—most of all by his good works. But by 'good' is not meant the self-conscious charity, cold and patronizing, which is marked more by conceit than by compassion. Jesus intended that the Christian's whole life should be marked by a sensitive helpfulness born of a genuine goodness of heart—though that goodness would never be aware of itself.

This truth led naturally to the next point—that such 'good works' should glorify God. It is sadly possible to parade one's goodness, to turn opportunities for service into occasions for attracting attention to one's own 'unselfishness'. The One who said of Himself, 'I am the Light of the world', said to His followers, 'Ye are the light of the world'—meaning that they were to be reflectors of His light. In this way their service would reveal the source of its inspiration. If our work is to be God-honouring it must be self-forgetful.

MATTHEW 5: 17, 20

'Do not think that I have come to set aside the law and the prophets; I have not come to set them aside, but to bring them to perfection' (v. 17, Knox).

DESTROYING OR FULFILLING? Jesus said that He had not come to destroy the Law—though in some instances He Him-

self seemed to break it, to the indignation of the religious teachers
of His day.

The explanation of this can possibly be found in our understanding of the word 'Law'. To most of our Lord's contemporaries
this included the multitude of scribal comments which were a
well-meaning, but impossible, attempt to apply the letter of the
Law to every conceivable situation. This almost turned them into
a glorified book of rules. Jesus declared that He had come to
fulfil the law—that is, to reveal its true meaning which (said He)
could be summed up in the two great commands, love to God
and love to one's neighbour. That is why Augustine could say—
in his sometimes misquoted sentence—'Love and do what you
will.' For if the love of God is the fount of all goodness, then the
man so motivated will be basically good.

This was Christ's new motive for true religion. As the parable
of the Pharisee and the publican shows, there were those who
deemed themselves righteous if the letter of the Law was observed.
But Jesus called upon His followers to aspire after a goodness
which exceeded that of the Scribes and Pharisees. So that if He
broke the yoke of religious legalism He left no room for moral
licence. What He did was to help men to realize the inwardness
of true religion. In this He fulfilled the hopes of the greatest of
the Old Testament prophets who—in somewhat different language—looked for the day when the laws of God should be
written 'not on stone tablets but on the pages of the human
heart' (2 Cor. 3: 3, N.E.B.).

MATTHEW 5: 21 22

**'Anyone who contemptuously calls his brother a fool
must face the supreme court; and anyone who looks down
on his brother as a lost soul is himself heading straight
for the fire of destruction' (v. 22, J. B. Phillips).**

CONTEMPT AND SLANDER. In teaching the inwardness
of true religion, Jesus emphasized that whereas human judgments
were mostly concerned with what a man did, God's judgment was
concerned primarily with what a man was. This meant that
murderous anger in the heart was as blameworthy in God's sight
as the act of murder itself, though in the first instance the letter
of the Law had not been broken. The truth is that intemperate

language indicates an inner condition that is more perilous to the abuser than to the abused.

There is the sin of contempt. 'Raca' is a transliteration of an Aramaic word which appears as such in the Authorized Version. Scholars differ as to its precise meaning; this may lie more in a tone of voice than in a definable term. But it denotes an attitude of contempt; of harsh insensitivity to another's weakness; and as such stands condemned even though no physical injury may be inflicted.

There is also the sin of slander. 'Whosoever shall say, Thou fool . . .' So to address a man (comments William Barclay) 'was not to criticize his mental ability but to cast aspersions on his moral character. It was to take his name and reputation from him and to brand him as a loose-living person.' Such malicious gossip invited the severest judgment (v. 22).

MATTHEW 5: 23-26

'If then you bring your offering to the altar and there remember that your brother has a grudge against you, leave your offering there before the altar, go and make friends with your brother first, and then come back and offer your gift' (vv. 23, 24, Rieu).

A SPIRITUAL PRINCIPLE. We cannot be wholly responsible for an individual's attitude towards ourselves—he can refuse to be reconciled, but we are wholly responsible for our attitude towards him.

We cannot be in a right relationship to God if we are in a wrong relationship to our fellows. Said the Quaker Rufus Jones, 'It is impossible to open successfully the door of the soul to God if that same door is shut or barred to some human brother. Prejudices, hardness of heart, a grudging spirit, invariably close the eye of the soul and keep the inward life in the shadow of eclipse from God.'

No wonder Jesus said, 'Come to terms quickly with your opponent while you have the chance' (v. 25, J. B. Phillips), for the longer any estrangement lasts the more entrenched it will become. The wound will fester and poison the whole body. To know fellowship with God requires us to maintain a spirit of constant goodwill towards men—even towards those whom we find it hard to like.

'If thy right eye is the occasion of thy falling into sin, pluck it out and cast it away from thee; better to lose one part of thy body than to have the whole cast into hell' (v. 29, Knox).

THE BATTLE FOR THE MIND. Jesus was not here suggesting that every evil thought necessarily indicated either evil desire or evil intention. The best of men have known the experience of alien ideas invading the mind. Here our Lord was referring to the evil suggestion which is deliberately allowed to remain so that it takes possession of the mind. Jesus knew that what men allow to capture their imagination will enter into their lives and the results, though not always immediately apparent, are inevitably disastrous.

This was why Jesus insisted upon the importance of ruthless self-renunciation. His words about plucking out an eye and cutting off a hand are obviously not to be taken literally. For one thing, blind men are not thereby made free of impure thoughts, any more than a thief is cured by having his fingers cut off. There is no doubt that Jesus intended the dismembered figure to be symbolic of the cost of victorious living.

The battle for a man's soul takes place in his mind. Once temptation finds a lodging place there, defeat is only a question of time; and temptation enters the mind through what we see, imagine, and ponder. At whatever cost, we must guard our minds by filling them full of thoughts that are 'holy and right and pure and beautiful and good' (Phil. 4: 8, J. B. Phillips).

'No man therefore must separate what God has joined together' (see Matthew 19: 6, J. B. Phillips).

THE SECRET OF HAPPY MARRIAGE. Divorce in the days of Jesus was widespread and easy. In the presence of two witnesses, the rejected wife was handed a bill of divorcement: 'Let this be from me thy writ of divorce and letter of dismissal and deed of liberation, that thou mayest marry whatsoever man thou wilt.' This brief formality marked the legal dissolution of the marriage.

In the light of this situation Jesus could well have staggered some of His hearers when He declared that marriage was intended by God to be an unbreakable union. Rudolf Bultmann once said, 'He who divorces his wife has not understood that marriage requires of him a complete decision.' True, and neither has he realized, almost certainly, that the union to which Jesus referred was more than legal or physical. It involved mind and heart, the sharing of the whole of life together.

This is what Frances Wilkinson had in mind when she wrote in *Growing up in Christ*, 'In these days of early marriage and short engagements, young couples often think it is sufficient to be "in love". Of course, the initial physical attraction must be there, but John will grow bald . . . and Mary will wrinkle . . . The secret of happy marriage lies first in loving one another a lot, but even more in loving many other things together.'

Believers will not disagree with A. M. Hunter's conclusion that 'marriage in Jesus' view is a God-given institution, having for its aim the life-long union of a man and a woman, and divorce is a declension from the divine will for them.'

MATTHEW 5: 33-37

'Let your word be Yes for Yes, and No for No; whatever goes beyond this comes from evil' (v. 37, Knox).

KEEP YOUR WORD. Behind these words of Jesus was the Jewish thought that words were binding only if God's name was actually mentioned. Though many of the rabbis disliked the taking of oaths, they never forbade the practice, so it was common to swear by Heaven, or earth, or Jerusalem, or one's own head. The comment of Jesus was that every promise was made, or oath was taken, in the presence of God. As T. W. Manson has said, 'Heaven is His throne, earth His footstool, Jerusalem His city and every part of man is God's handiwork. It is He who governs our lives so that the hair which is black in youth is white in age.'

The believer's word should be his bond. Whether on oath or not, his interest should be in the truth, the whole truth, and nothing but the truth. He should be so honest and dependable that any form of oath would be seen to be unnecessary.

MATTHEW 5: 38–42

'Do not take revenge on someone who does you wrong' (v. 39, Good News for Modern Man).

TIT FOR TAT? The Mosaic law to which Jesus referred in v. 38 was an endeavour to make the punishment fit the crime—otherwise revenge would know no limit (see Gen. 4: 24). But though the law laid down in Exod. 21: 24, 25 (and elsewhere) was a civilizing influence, Jesus would have His followers return, not evil for evil but good for evil.

We miss the teaching of the illustrations which follow if we take them only literally—though there can be human circumstances in which a literal obedience is the right course to pursue. This would have been so in the first century when a Roman soldier called upon any Jew who might be around to carry some military material. But what Jesus is saying by means of these real life situations is that those who name His name will endure injury rather than inflict it and, if Matthew 5: 12 is kept in mind, will do so cheerfully.

'I must have no hatred or bitterness towards any one,' said Edith Cavell on October 12th, 1915, when facing the final injustice of death. And many another believer, while recognizing the lofty and difficult standard required of the followers of Jesus, has agreed with its demands. 'I do not see how one can fight for life', wrote Leslie Tizard, 'unless mind and spirit are purged of bitterness and resentment, for they are destructive things akin to death and not to life.'

MATTHEW 5: 43–48

'You must be perfect as your heavenly Father is perfect' (v. 48, Moffatt).

THE HIGHEST AIM. This call to achieve perfection is based on three grounds. First of all, this is the attitude of God who, in the natural order, causes the sun to shine and the rain to fall with complete impartiality upon the evil man and the good man. On this score He makes no distinction between men. In the second place, the disciples of Jesus are expected to behave more generously than the ordinary man. Even he likes those who like him. Last of all, to be godlike is the goal of every true worshipper.

Three other observations may be helpful. Jesus is not saying that we must show the same feelings towards all and sundry that we have say, for members of our own family. While each of the disciples was His special care there was one who was known as 'the disciple whom Jesus loved'. Again, the word 'love' in this setting has more to do with the will than the emotions. It has well been described as unconquerable goodwill, the spirit which persistently seeks the other man's good whatever the difficulties in the way. Finally, it is in this sense that we shall be 'perfect' for, as God shall help us, we shall be endeavouring to fulfil the purpose for which we were created—to reveal the divine likeness in our human lives.

MATTHEW 6: 1–4

'They have had all the reward they are going to get' (v. 2, J. B. Phillips).

THE RIGHT THING FOR THE WRONG REASONS. We have not learned our spiritual alphabet unless we have discovered that we can do the best of things from the worst of motives. The very natural desire for self-display can find expression in ostentatious 'Christian' service.

The giving of alms was rightly regarded as an important part of a Jew's religious life, but Jesus said it should be done unobtrusively. To publicize one's piety merely shows that the old self-regarding motives—that are to be expected in the worldling—are still operative, even though cloaked by a religious profession. On this point Jewish thought was at one with Jesus, for the rabbis taught that alms were wrongly given if the object was to bring kudos to the giver. He was not laying up treasure in heaven whatever he might be doing on earth. He had all the reward he was ever going to get—the brief publicity of the moment. T. W. Manson has pointed out that the relation of the right hand to the left is used in the oriental world as a type of closest fellowship. We can therefore understand Jesus as saying that even our bosom friend was not to know about our charities.

The perils which attend giving are typical of all forms of Christian service. It is said that there was once a saint who desired to reform the world without his existence being known. William Barclay has rightly observed that 'the rewards of the Christian life are rewards which are rewards only to a spiritually minded person.' When John Newman was made a Cardinal he declared: 'I tremble to take this great honour lest I should be taking out my reward on earth.'

MATTHEW 6: 5–8

'When you pray go away by yourself, all alone' (v. 6, Living New Testament).

CHRISTIAN PRAYER. Jesus taught that even prayer—that most personal and intimate exercise of our religious life—can be used for the purpose of self-display. In *Father and Son*, Edmund Gosse described the rigid upbringing he had to endure. Of his narrow-minded father's prayers he wrote: 'I cannot help thinking that he liked to hear himself speak to God in the presence of an admiring listener. ... He was not displeased with the sound of his own devotions.'

In our approach to God, we must have only God in our thoughts. Jesus' teaching, both here and elsewhere, drives home the truth—unpalatable to all hypocrites—that every kind of conduct gets its reward on the plane of its motive, and even the beautiful exercise of prayer can be marred by being used for the purposes of the old self-life.

'Love makes no parade, gives itself no airs, is ... never selfish' (1 Cor. 13: 4, 5, Moffatt). A. M. Hunter has written:

'The secret of religion is religion in secret. The true man of prayer will seek a quiet place for his communion with God. Nor will he, like the pagan, bombard the unseen world with empty babbling as though the virtue of prayer lay in sheer verbosity, but will rest in faith on a Father who knows all His children's needs already.'

In one of His parables Jesus said that the Pharisee 'prayed with himself'. He was so self-centred he never escaped from himself. Only too well aware of his fellow-men watching his religious devotions, he was unaware of the fact that God was an absentee.

MATTHEW 6: 9, 10

'After this manner therefore pray ye' (v. 9).

THE MODEL PRAYER. The plan of the model prayer is simple—though instead of being called the Lord's prayer it could well be entitled the disciple's prayer, for Luke (11: 1) describes how the prayer was given by Jesus in response to a request from one of His followers. But the order of the prayer is straightforward enough and the first three petitions have to do with God and His glory. We sometimes mistakenly give priority to the second three petitions.

Wrote Bede Frost in *The Art of Mental Prayer*, 'The fundamental weakness of Christian life today is largely due to the fact that we are more concerned with self than with God, with the question of saving our souls rather than adoring, praising and serving God ... We do not think enough, contemplate enough, adore enough, God in Himself; our minds are so filled with self that we habitually think of God in relation to our needs and our desires.'

First then must come 'Father'—Jesus' first and last recorded word for God (Luke 2: 49 and 23: 46). Then comes the honouring of His name, and this our lives are required to do in deed as well as word. For the coming of His reign we are to pray, and 'Thy kingdom come' often must mean 'my kingdom go'. The doing of His will is (as Bishop Gore commented) 'a prayer against all self-will and also against all sloth; a prayer for the vigorous co-operation of all rational creatures in furthering the divine order of the world.'

MATTHEW 6: 11-15

'After this manner therefore pray ye' (v. 9).

A PRAYER THAT COVERS ALL OUR NEEDS. Now follow the three petitions which have to do with our personal needs.

Our need of sustenance. While Jesus declared, 'Man shall not live by bread alone' (Matt. 4: 4), He recognized that man cannot live without bread. Here He teaches that God is interested in our daily needs. Moffatt's interpretation of the phrase ('give us today our bread for tomorrow') has found wide acceptance as representing our Lord's meaning. If the material needs of the immediate future are assured, we can the better give ourselves to our tasks, whatever their nature.

Our need of forgiveness. We cannot live without bread; we cannot live without the divine forgiveness. This is one of the 'musts' of life. If, perchance, we have no sense of need we are in a state of grave spiritual danger. Note how that Jesus here repeats the principle underlying the fifth Beatitude, that God deals with us as we deal with others. Verses 14 and 15 are simply an amplification of this. It is not that God is in any way arbitrary in His dealings, but simply that there are spiritual, as well as natural laws. How can we receive God's forgiveness if there is within us an unforgiving spirit? So if we wish to know how the face of God looks toward

us—and ignorance of this is ignorance indeed—we should look at
our attitude to our fellow-men.

Our need of deliverance. Temptation and evil are ever-present
realities, but Christ has sanctified the way of temptation for those
who follow Him, so that through Him we can become 'the master
of every situation'.

MATTHEW 6: 16–18

**'When you fast, brush your hair and wash your face so
that nobody knows that you are fasting—let it be a secret
between you and your Father' (vv. 17, 18, J. B. Phillips).**

NO GLOOMY FACES (Jerusalem Bible). Hugh Schonfield,
a Jewish scholar, has explained that 'the equation of fasting with
penitence was a very ancient one. Fasting was the outward
expression of inward contrition. We have the phrase "fasting for
sins", but it was always emphasized that fasting unaccompanied
by any change of heart was valueless.' Some devout men had
forgotten this; hence the observation of Jesus.

Jesus was not against the principle of fasting. 'When you fast',
He said to His hearers. We could understand this as referring to
self-discipline. Wrote Thomas Merton of the spiritual dangers of
over- or under-eating, 'The effects of either of these excesses will
be felt most grievously by the soul. It will lose all its vigour in
prayer if too great abstinence has dulled and brought low the
body. If, on the other hand, the appetite has been over-indulged,
such repletion will be like a leaden weight on the heart and will
prevent it from offering pure and fervent prayer to God.'

Christian fasting is concerned with more than food, but with
the need for Christian discipline in every detail of life.

MATTHEW 6: 19–24

'You cannot serve God and Money (v. 24, N.E.B.).

GOD VERSUS GAIN. Is Jesus here setting His face against
all possessions? Surely not. Money itself is not evil, but the love
of it (1 Tim. 6: 10). But it must be admitted that Jesus always
regarded wealth as spiritually dangerous because it tended to
distract a man from his 'chief end' in life, which is to 'glorify God
and enjoy Him for ever'. Man belongs to eternity and anything
that binds him to earth is a snare. Elsewhere Jesus asserted that
'a man's life consisteth not in the abundance of things which he

B

possesseth'; it consists of having 'treasures in heaven', which means a right relationship with God.

The 'single eye' means a singleness of purpose and desire. When life is thus controlled 'the eye is the lamp of the body' (Moffatt), its only channel of light. To pay attention we have to focus the eye on one thing at a time. It is a division of interests that causes inward confusion or darkness. So we grasp at shadows and lose the substance—which leads very naturally to the truth that no slave can serve two masters. If material gain dominates our life then God cannot; but if God dominates our life gain will not. He who was 'born a man but died a stockholder' has, like Esau, bartered his birthright for a mess of pottage.

MATTHEW 6: 25-30

'Do not fret over your life' (v. 25, Knox).

'Put away anxious thoughts' (v. 25, N.E.B.).

'Don't worry about living—wondering what you are going to eat or drink' (v. 25, J. B. Phillips).

'Can any of you by fretting add a moment to his years?' (v. 27, Rieu).

WHY WORRY? T. H. Robinson has pointed out that two truths emerge from this passage. One is our Lord's love of nature. He was in line with the Old Testament prophets who drew some of their most powerful illustrations from the world around them. The lily (v. 28) is the field anemone. The fowls of the air (v. 26) are simply the wild birds. When we see the beauty of the one and hear the song of the other, we realize that the best that over-anxious man can do falls far below the least of the works of God.

But only man can be aware of the Father's care. God may clothe the wild flower with a beauty that far exceeds the studied splendour of a Solomon, but the flower can only be its inarticulate self. But man can recognize God as Father and, in the light of that knowledge, trustfully commit himself as to a faithful Creator.

MATTHEW 6: 31-34

'Set your mind on God's kingdom ... before everything else' (v. 33, N.E.B.).

WHAT TO DO AND WHAT NOT TO DO. Here follows teaching which is complementary to what has gone before. We must be careful not to attribute to Jesus what He did not say.

Here is no excuse for idleness. After all, the birds have to build their nests and to search for food. Jesus is not belittling foresight, but He is prescribing a cure for that ulcer—anxiety, well defined as 'suspense, the only insupportable misfortune in life'.

Worry has been called 'the interest we pay on tomorrow's troubles', whereas Jesus has said that 'each day has troubles enough of its own' (v. 34, N.E.B.). What we are to do is, first of all, to live a day at a time. 'I think I have learned at last (said a man near to death while still in the prime of life) to live a moment at a time, which Jesus said was the proper way to live. I wish I had learned the lesson years ago. We give ourselves so much trouble by trying to live in a future which we cannot foresee, to cross bridges before we get to them, to solve problems before the time for action comes.'

The other thing we have to do is to put God's Kingdom first. This means that we are to make God's will the main purpose of our lives. As Edward Wilson of the Antarctic wrote: 'Look at life carelessly . . . It's only real carelessness about one's own will and confidence in God's that can teach one to believe that whatever is, is best.'

MATTHEW 7: 1–5

'You will be judged by the way you criticize others, and the measure you give will be the measure you receive' (v. 2, J. B. Phillips).

WHAT IS SAUCE FOR THE GOOSE! Various sayings of Jesus not always directly related to one another have been gathered together in chapter seven. Today's reading should be taken to heart for two reasons:

Our judgments are based upon incomplete knowledge.
We see:

> The little, catty, criticizing ways,
> The crude self-consciousness she cannot hide,
> The grudging, niggard praise.

But God sees:

> The soul that sometimes seeks Him in the night,
> And weeps slow tears upon His heart like rain,
> And longs and prays and vows to do the right—
> Yet fails, and falls again.

For this reason, Edward Wilson of the Antarctic wrote to his wife: 'Better to say nothing than to condemn, and to laugh with than to criticize, and so much happier.' So often we judge 'according to the appearance'.

Our judgments are tainted at their source. We either look for faults in others to hide our own or unconsciously recognize our own faults in others. As Jesus said, the splinter we see in another's eyes is merely the reflection of the beam in our own. 'He that well and rightly considereth his own work', wrote Thomas à Kempis, 'will find little cause to judge badly of another.'

As General Orsborn wrote:

Save me O Lord,
From vision that distorts;
From words that smite and wound;
From magnifying evil;
From criticizing good.
And make me honest
In clearing my own sight,
Before I even think
To put another right.

MATTHEW 7: 6

'Do not give dogs what is holy' (Jerusalem Bible).

THE MATTER OF COMMUNICATION. At first glance these words may seem out of character with the Speaker—but that only means we must look at them more closely. Dogs are the scavengers of the East; they eat the refuse that lies about the streets and with such they are satisfied. To set before such animals that which is sacred (comments T. H. Robinson) is to degrade it to the level of offal. The footnote in the Jerusalem Bible carries this thought a stage further by saying that our Lord's words apply to the difficulty of 'parading holy beliefs and practices in front of those who cannot understand them'. So that Jesus, far from being offensive, was talking about the task of making the gospel intelligible to those 'inoculated' against it either by godless living or a superficial acquaintance with merely conventional religion.

Said C. S Lewis in a letter to *The Christian Century*, 'Any fool can write learned language. The vernacular is the real test. If you can't turn your faith into it, then either you don't understand it or you don't believe it.' Fair enough—to a point. But there is a still more meaningful presentation of the gospel. William Booth referred to this when writing to his wife: 'God is not glorified so much by preaching, or teaching, or anything else, as by holy living.' 'The blessed gospel none can doubt revealed in holy lives.'

MATTHEW 7: 7–12

'Ask and the gift will be yours, seek and you will find, knock and the door will be open to you' (v. 7, Moffatt).

THREE LAWS OF PRAYER. Some of us pray as if we needed to persuade a begrudging God to come to our aid. Yet Jesus said that if a father would help his child without delay, how much more would our heavenly Father give without stint to His children. This is the thought which lies behind Tersteegen's line, 'You don't need to search for God, you have only to realize Him.'

Yet, though this truth is undoubtedly basic to prayer, Jesus also said that what we receive from God is dependent upon the intensity of our desires. So He uttered what John Oman called three laws of prayer:

Asking is the law of receiving.

Seeking is the law of finding.

Knocking is the law of discovery.

Notice the gradation of desire: to ask is comparatively simple; to seek makes greater demands and therefore expresses growing concern; to knock bespeaks persistence, even desperation, the spirit that refuses to be discouraged. And only those who know this depth of longing pray with any degree of importunity.

Our prayer-life is merely the reflection of our desire-life, which is one reason why, whether consciously or not, we all 'pray without ceasing'; and why our words of prayer are sometimes so artificial. Of this we can be certain—the adventure of spiritual discovery (the third law) is in proportion to the secret yearning of our hearts.

MATTHEW 7: 13, 14

'The highway to hell is broad ... the gateway to life is small' (Living New Testament).

'WARE THE PRIMROSE PATH. The picture of the broad and narrow ways used to feature in many an old family Bible, and more than one solemn address has been based on this contrast.

It is a platitude to say that vice seems more attractive than virtue. Swinburne was not the first—and he has had many imitators since—to contrast 'the raptures and roses of vice' with 'the lilies and languors of virtue'. Numerous writers have agreed that it is easier in a work of fiction to depict a 'baddie' than a 'goodie'. The followers of 'the pale Galilean' are often judged to have come off second-best in that argument. It is not hard to caricature goodness.

But for all its superficial attractiveness the line of least resistance is frequently the way to disaster. No one needs to be a heavy-handed moralist to point this out. The drug addict can bear his own unhappy testimony. 'Hooked' can be accepted as the modern equivalent of the old evangelical idiom about the slavery of sin. The addict is 'hooked' and cannot set himself free. Too late he finds that the way of the transgressor is hard.

T. W. Manson has well commented that this utterance of Jesus presents us with death with no hope of life as opposed to life with no fear of death. As with other biblical contrasts, man has to choose.

MATTHEW 7: 15–20

'Be on your guard against false religious teachers, who come to you dressed up as sheep but are really greedy wolves' (v. 15, J. B. Phillips).

NEGATIVE RELIGION. False prophets and teachers were often referred to as wolves. Jesus described them as ravening wolves, for, despite their religious pretensions, their first concern was personal popularity and prestige. 'You may go through life', warned General William Booth, 'with the Bible under your arm, and yet finish up in the bottomless abyss, spending your eternity in Hell reading over and over again the words that might have got you to the heart of God on earth and to the home of God in the skies.'

To serve in the name of religion is no guarantee of being truly religious. General Booth continued: 'It means something more than walking with the forms and ceremonies of religion. Forms and ceremonies there must be; but alas! men and women come to rest in them . . . and rest in them to their doom.'

Jesus Himself was always more concerned with inward attitudes than outward observances. A man, He said, might even dress like a prophet, but his teaching can be trusted only when self-evidently it strengthens him to face the trials of life, and commends itself in his noble character. Nothing angered Jesus more than false prophets whose teaching, concerned solely with outward observance and endless prohibitions, made religion a burden to be endured, not a relationship with God to be enjoyed. But do our harassed lives tend to give unbelievers this same false impression?

MATTHEW 7: 24–29

'Everyone then who hears these words of Mine and puts them into practice is like a sensible man who builds his house on the rock' (v. 24, J. B. Phillips).

STRENGTH OF CHARACTER. A parable has been defined as 'a slice of life seen through the eyes of Jesus'; and He told this one—of the two houses which looked identical until the storm came—to illustrate what so easily we forget—that strength of character depends upon what a man does in his secret life.

People who normally appear to be much the same are often seen to be utterly different when facing unexpected trials; the storms of life reveal the values by which they have lived and in which they have trusted. Jesus named two essentials for stability of character:

We must listen to His words. But in listening, we must also be as near sure as possible that we understand exactly what He meant. Wrote John Baillie in *Invitation to Pilgrimage*: 'Many men criticize and even oppose Christianity without ever having taken much trouble to discover what it is all about.' We can fall into the opposite danger—of taking for granted our belief in the familiar words of Jesus without realizing their searching implications. However, even perfect understanding is not enough:

We must put His words 'into practice'. For the Christian, hearing and doing are opposite sides of the same 'coin'. The ideal must always be translated in experience. Principal John Mackay made this same emphasis of implicit obedience when he wrote: 'Christ can never be known by men who would be His patrons, but only by those who are prepared to become His servants.'

MATTHEW 8: 1–13

'Only say the word, and my servant will be healed' (v. 8, R.S.V.).

THE HEALING MINISTRY BEGINS. The Sermon on the

Mount is an exposition of the Kingdom in words. Today's reading sets forth the Kingdom in deeds. The words of Augustine regarding Jesus Christ merit our attention: 'He was the Word of God; and all the acts of the Word of God are themselves words for us; they are not as pictures, merely to look at and admire, but as letters which we must seek to read and understand.'

What do we see in these two acts? Firstly there is a remarkable combination of compassion and authority. Secondly, they show the breadth of the Kingdom, for they tell of healing coming to a leper and a Gentile, both excluded as 'unclean' from Jewish society.

Behind the centurion's request lies an unspoken doubt, which our Lord's ready response anwers. Would Jesus, a Jew, enter a Gentile's house? He expresses His willingness to do so. But the remarkable expression of faith on the centurion's part makes unnecessary this breach of Jewish custom. Our Lord heals from a distance.

There is yet a further lesson for consideration. The centurion's authority depended upon his obedience to Rome, and we can here perceive that it was Jesus' perfect obedience to God which gave power to His word.

MATTHEW 8: 14–22

'Let me wait until my father dies' (v. 21, footnote, Living New Testament).

POWER OVER DISEASE AND MEN. More miracles follow. We read that Jesus healed 'with a word' (see verse 16 in R.V.).

Some commentators have observed that this is an oft-recurring emphasis in the gospels: Jesus speaks, and mighty results follow. It is the evangelists' way of saying that He shares in the creative and re-creative power of God, who 'spake and it was done'. In the old Genesis story of creation 'God said . . . and there was . . .' Now, in the Person of Jesus, the powers of the new age are operating, and a new creation is taking place. The evidence is to be seen in men and women made whole.

But our Lord's authority is over more than disease; man himself must yield. Too often we fail to sound forth this imperious note in seeking to urge the claim of our Lord. In verses 18 to 22 Jesus reminded a scribe who seemed too easily won, that he might find himself without a home or even a shelter. He then proceeded to

rebuff another would-be disciple with words that have an appearance of hardness, but which indicated the total nature of the
response that He demanded. This would-be follower was really
less than frank for he was trying to fob Jesus off with a phrase. To
this the answer was that the work of the Kingdom could not wait
on any man's personal security—in this instance, the benefits
which might accrue from the death of the head of the family. The
call to service cannot yield place to any human consideration.

MATTHEW 8: 23–27

'Save us, Lord. We are lost! (v. 25, Goodspeed).

'WITH CHRIST IN THE VESSEL WE'LL SMILE AT
THE STORM.' A parallel account of this incident is found in
Mark 4: 36–41. The suddenness with which these short but
violent storms blew up on the Sea of Galilee was known to all who
fished its waters. Nevertheless, on this occasion the disciples
panicked. They thought this trip would be their last. 'Help,
Lord, we are drowning' (Moffatt). It seemed intolerable to them
that they should be in such peril and Jesus be unaware of it.

What are we to learn from this story? Not that every storm
which assails us will be calmed at a word from Jesus. This was not
even what He intended His own disciples to understand. It was
for them to learn that if they shared the faith of their Master they
would not be in such terror for they would realize that they were
in the hands of One who was Lord of the storm and Lord of the
sunshine, the Lord of life and Lord of whatever lay beyond the
gates of death.

One apt comment on this story is that Jesus does not promise
to still all our storms, but He has said that He will always remain
in the boat with us. 'Lo, I am with you alway', is the promise
with which this gospel concludes—and in His company we can
face whatever may happen.

MATTHEW 8: 28–34

'He said to them: Away with you; and they came out' (v. 32, Knox).

THE DEMONIACS OF GADARA. Again Mark (5: 1–20)
gives a parallel but fuller account of this incident, but with
Matthew there are two demoniacs, not one as in Mark.

To begin to understand this story we must keep in mind two

facts—first of all, the superstitious fears which possessed most people in the ancient world—and still possess many today; and secondly, the fact that Jesus met people at their own level. It is, of course, impossible to help people in any other way.

Men believed themselves to live in a world peopled by unseen spirits, most of them evil or malicious. One of Christianity's greatest blessings has been—and still is—to dispel these irrational fears with the assurance that a God of love who cares for His children rules over all.

To Jesus fear and faith were like oil and water. They could not mix. But this was no time for argument—which would have been fruitless, anyway—on the existence and nature of the devils by whom these unfortunate men felt themselves possessed. Their salvation lay in our Lord's demonstration that even devils were subject to Him (Luke 10: 17). In Wesley's line, even 'devils fear and fly'. And today the devils of hate and bitterness, intemperance and unchastity, can be conquered by the power of His name.

MATTHEW 9: 1–13

'I did not come to invite the pious but the irreligious' (v. 13, Goodspeed).

REDEMPTION FOR THE WHOLE MAN. The Psalmist blessed the Lord 'who forgiveth all thine inquities; who healeth all thy diseases' (103: 3). Today's reading gives an example of God doing just that, in Christ. Elsewhere Jesus repudiates the conventional Jewish view that a sufferer was necessarily enduring the consequences of personal wrongdoing (Luke 13: 1–5; John 9: 1–3), yet it is clear that here there was a closer connection between the palsied man's disease and sinful condition. Jesus restored the whole man and today we are learning much of how inner harmony may lead to physical well-being.

Elsewhere it has been noted that the scribes were right in saying that, by claiming the authority to forgive, Jesus was in fact claiming an authority which belongs to God alone. In outward appearance, to say 'Arise and walk' is the more difficult test, since there is immediate ocular evidence of whether the word is effective or not; to Jesus, it is the other way about; the healing is the lower and the less important thing, but the outward is given as a visible sign to authenticate the reality of the inward deliverance.

The palsied man was a religious outcast; Matthew was a social outcast, for he was in the pay of the Roman invader. So both these events illustrate the principle stated in verses 12 and 13. Jesus knew that 'aloofness and pride will win no one'. What we need today is the courage to offer real friendship, in the common things of everyday life, to the spiritually needy—particularly if they are disreputable.

MATTHEW 9: 14–17

'No one patched up an old coat with a piece of new cloth' (v. 16, Good News for Modern Man).

THE NEW VERSUS THE OLD. Our Lord's answer to the question on fasting was audacious indeed. It is either supreme arrogance or ultimate truth. It was as though He said, 'Those who are with Me do not need the conventional means of grace. My presence is sufficient. No one needs any other medium between themselves and God!'

The point of verses 16 and 17 is the same. The Messiah expected by the Pharisees was to add to all the ceremonial requirements, but Jesus said He had come to do a new thing. He could not be bound by the past, and what He was doing could not be used to patch up their traditions (see Hebrews 8: 13). 'Any attempt to put a new spirit into an old institution would lead to disaster ... His Spirit could not clothe itself in a second-hand religion.'

Sometimes it may be a bad thing to abandon the old too readily. On the other hand, to refuse to accept something new can be sadly shortsighted. Our faith must never be afraid to launch out upon new ways of expressing the eternal gospel, as well as new methods of making that gospel known.

MATTHEW 9: 18–34

'It is the prince of devils that enables Him to cast the devils out' (v. 34, Knox).

FOUR MORE MIRACLES OF HEALING—the woman suffering a haemorrhage (Mark 5: 21–43) and the daughter of Jairus is cured; two blind men have their sight restored and a man who was dumb is able to speak once more.

Two points can be noted. In three of the four incidents faith in Jesus is pointed out as playing a decisive part. But the critics of Jesus, while unable to deny the effectiveness of His cures, attributed His power to the devil (v. 34).

There have always been scoffers. There were on the day of Pentecost when some of the onlookers declared that the disciples were drunk (Acts 2: 13). Faithful and his fellow pilgrims met them at Vanity Fair where the judge at their trial was Lord Hate-Good, and the foreman of the jury, Mr. Blind-man, returning the unanimous verdict, said: 'I see clearly that this man is a heretic'. There were scoffers in the early days of The Salvation Army—witness a convert's song:

> My old companions said: He's undone;
> My old companions said: He's surely going mad!
> But Christ has made me glad ...

The only defence against such prejudice is 'when men speak ill of thee, live so that no one will believe them.'

MATTHEW 9: 35-38

'The sight of the people moved Him to pity' (v. 36, N.E.B.).

'EXCEPT I AM MOVED WITH COMPASSION'. Jesus now commenced another tour of Galilee, but, as ever in the days of His flesh, He was the prisoner of time and place. He could not be in two places at once. But this did not prevent Him seeing the plight of the people. He realized His need of helpers. He asked the disciples to join Him in prayer for an increase of labourers. The harvest would not be reaped without consecrated compassionate aid.

It is this sense of the urgency of the occasion which explains the demands which Jesus had made (Matt. 8: 19-22) and which He would still make (Matt. 10: 34-39). The King's business could brook no rival. Moreover the demands which He makes are God's demands. The labourers who are to be sent out are God's labourers. What is God's work must be given top priority.

The prayer for which Jesus pleads (v. 38) is not only one of intercession that others may realize where their duty lies, but that I who pray may also perceive where my duty lies. I cannot pray that others may do the Lord's will unless and until I myself am already committed to that will. I must say: 'Here am I; send me' (Isaiah 6: 8) before I begin to pray that my fellow believers may answer God's call.

'Preach as you go ... Heal the sick, raise the dead, cleanse lepers, cast out devils' (vv. 7, 8 Moffatt).

THE MISSION OF THE TWELVE. The twelve disciples (the word means 'learners') are here called apostles (the word means 'sent forth'). In His high-priestly prayer Jesus addressed God in the words, 'As Thou hast sent Me into the world, even so I have also sent them into the world' (John 17: 18). Jesus' apostles were His representatives, dispatched with His authority to proclaim the Kingdom and to serve in it. They were told to preach and to heal.

For the moment their mission was to be limited to Israel. Matthew was not unaware of the significance of the gospel for the whole world but, writing for Jewish readers, stressed the importance of Jesus for His own people. They must have first opportunity of accepting Him as Messiah.

Living in a crisis situation, the disciples' equipment was to be frugal indeed. They were to travel light and to depend upon the hospitality of those to whom they ministered. Where they were received, they were to respond by announcing the good news of the Kingdom. Where they were rejected, they were to waste no time in recrimination but to press on elsewhere. But before leaving they were to disclaim all responsibility for the refusal of the people of that place to hear them. To 'shake off the dust of your feet' was to proclaim them as no better than heathen and, though Jews, as no part of the true Israel. Their blood was on their own head.

'You must stand trial ... for My sake. This will give you the opportunity to tell men about Me' (v. 18, Living New Testament).

ENDURANCE AND FEARLESSNESS. In the time of the Maccabees (168 to 165 B.C.) the persecutors of the faithful Jews were called 'wolves' and the pious sufferers 'lambs'. In sending out His disciples Jesus warns them that they must not expect better treatment than the godly endured under the tyrannical Syrian dictator, Antiochus Epiphanes. J. A. Findlay's paraphrase of v. 16 says that Christians must be 'clever as the devil and simple as God's Spirit'.

Our Lord taught that His followers must expect trouble,

but that the earlier lessons of trust and refusal to worry must apply throughout. Whatever happened they must endure to the end, for anyone can start a race. They could find the courage to face the worst that man can do. Death itself need not be feared.

There are times when the Christian's duty is to stand, at whatever cost. At other times he should 'flee', that his witness may be given elsewhere. The criterion is 'the furtherance of the gospel'. The manner in which the Early Church took to heart these words of our Lord is seen by the way in which believers who had to flee from Jerusalem carried the gospel with them to Phoenicia, Cyprus and Antioch (Acts 11: 19). Stamp on a fire, the sparks fly—and other fires are started.

MATTHEW 10: 24–33
'The servant will not fare better than his Master' (v. 25, J. B. Phillips).

LIKE MASTER, LIKE DISCIPLE. In this passage Jesus warned His disciples—as He does us today—that the world will not treat them any better than they treated Him. Fair enough! If Jesus was given a crown of thorns His followers cannot expect a bed of roses. Nevertheless the disciples were not to be dismayed, and the truths which they had learned of Jesus in private they were fearlessly to declare in public (v. 27). Such boldness could bring them into danger—even to death itself, but they were not to be terrified of those whose powers were limited to the physical suffering which they could inflict. Whatever happened, the souls of the righteous would be in the hands of a loving God.

Now follows the familiar reference to the sparrows—the cheapest food on the market. An imperial ruling at the end of the third century fixed the price of ten sparrows at a sum equal to $3\frac{1}{2}$d.—say less then 2p. Luke (12: 6) has five for two farthings; Matthew two for one farthing. An odd sparrow thrown in as a makeweight?

Jesus does not say that no sparrow ever falls to the ground—but that it does not happen without God marking the bird's fall. Said a Jewish rabbi: 'No bird perishes without God—how much less a man.' Wherefore, lift up your heart!

MATTHEW 10: 34–42
'To find your life is to lose it, and to lose it for My sake is to find it' (v. 39, Barclay).

A SWORD AND A CROSS. The purpose of Christ's coming

was to bring peace; it was His bequest to His disciples. Yet its effect was to bring division. This is but one of many intriguing paradoxes we find in the New Testament. Light is bound to cleave the darkness, the offer of salvation inevitably brings judgment upon those who reject. So it is that the Prince of Peace becomes the centre and source of conflict, even within the family circle itself. Christ Himself set out upon His public work without the blessing of His kith and kin.

The demands of the Kingdom cut across all the natural relationships of men, and verses 37 and 38 emphasize this in the most uncompromising way possible. But we do well to start by counting the cost. The disciple should early grow familiar with the cross, for this was what awaited his Lord.

The cross, in the Christian sense, has nothing to do with the strains of life which are the lot of all men everywhere, believer and unbeliever alike. 'See what a cross I have to bear', said a man to John Wesley when his chimney smoked. Nothing of the kind! The cross represents what we must accept on account of our total commitment to Christ. But with this demand goes a promise. The most trivial kindness—the cup of cold water—given in the name of Him who bore the Cross for our salvation, will neither be unrecognized nor unrewarded.

MATTHEW 11: 1–15

'Happy is the man who does not lose faith in Me' (v. 6, Jerusalem Bible).

THE WEAKNESS AND STRENGTH OF JOHN. 'Happy is the man who never loses faith in Me,' said Jesus. (This is Phillips' translation of verse 6.) Even John, our Lord's forerunner, had been so 'put off' that he considered looking for someone else (v. 3). Here we see the grave danger of preconceptions. John's own picture of what he expected the Messiah to be and do almost closed his mind and robbed him of the truth. In like manner we can create our own picture of Jesus and worship it—which is a subtle form of idolatry.

But, as has frequently been noted, Jesus is always Himself; He creates His own categories; He Himself gives the light by which He can be known. He was the Messiah, but not the kind of Messiah that anyone had previously imagined; that is why He prefers to call Himself by the mysterious title 'Son of Man'.

Our Lord makes no direct claim but in order to set John's mind at rest points to the fulfilment of the prophetic word of Isaiah 35: 5, 6. The preaching of the good news to the poor was no anti- climax, for nothing is more important than the declaration of the gospel.

Note Jesus' high estimation of John; He declared that none greater than he had ever been born. It has been said that no vacillation or softness marred his witness: he was much more even than a prophet. Nevertheless he stood at the end of an epoch, an epoch which, when compared with the new day now arrived with the coming of Jesus, looked like shadow as compared with reality or half-light compared with noontide blaze.

MATTHEW 11: 16–24

'When John came ... people said, "He has a demon!" Now that the Son of man has come ... people say "... A glutton and a drinker" ' (vv. 18, 19, Goodspeed).

WARNINGS TO THOSE WHO REJECT TRUTH. It was impossible to please Jesus' contemporaries, for nothing suited them. In His humorous illustration our Lord likens them to sulky children refusing to play games. 'John was too funereal, Jesus was too convivial.' There is no pleasing some people. The closed mind can always find excuses for refusing to participate. It takes no skill to say, 'I'm not going to play.' The important thing about the gospel is that all who hear have a responsibility to acknow- ledge its benefits. Too many think that their obligation is fulfilled by criticizing.

Verses 20 to 24 are of interest for several reasons. For instance, we know nothing of Jesus' work at Chorazin (v. 21), which reminds us that our knowledge of Jesus' life is incomplete.

We can discover, also, that out Lord appealed not only to individuals but to communities. J. A. Findlay writes: 'It is not true that His only concern was to save and reform individuals; His appeal to the individual and to the community went together. While social and industrial conditions are what they are very many men and women cannot be expected to understand any spiritual message; it is not enough to say that we must make everybody Christian before we can hope for lasting social better- ment. We must work from both sides, clearing away abuses, keeping the corporate conscience awake, if only to make it more possible for men and women to become Christians.'

'Come unto Me . . . wear My yoke . . . let Me teach you . . . I am meek . . . you shall find rest' (vv. 28, 29, The Living New Testament).

THE MEANING OF MEEKNESS. 'There is no good translation in English for the Hebrew word translated meek', writes W. A. L. Elmsie in *How Came Our Faith*, 'and there ought to be. It is the characteristic of a man who is a man indeed, but does not regard others as worms; who, if great, has no thought that he is a superman and others are beneath him. Persons with this kind of humility are usually towers of strength in whatever walk of life they may be. It does not mean weakly meek, or abjectly humble.'

Meekness is possible only to the spiritually strong. The meek are invincible because they are freed from self-concern in their devotion to God's Kingdom. Instinctively viewing every experience (adversity, injustice, disappointment) in the light of eternal values, they recognize the emptiness and ultimate insignificance of what would otherwise have caused them distress and resentment. The only thing they ask for themselves is the opportunity to go on serving.

Yet, wrote H. R. Mackintosh, 'no one ever lived who accomplished a work so great as that of Jesus Christ. No one ever bore the burden of so tremendous a mission; yet the impression conveyed by His life is one of repose and tranquillity. So deep and unshakeable was His confidence in God whom He knew as Father that He could invite the whole world to come and share His rest.'

He who at Nazareth made yokes for cattle, making sure they did not hurt, tells His disciples that His yoke will enable them to bear life's burden without strain. Hearts can rest in God while heads and hands are engaged below. The gracious invitation is to 'come', 'take', 'learn' and 'find'.

MATTHEW 12: 1-14

'I require mercy, not sacrifice' (v. 7, N.E.B.).

THE DIVINE DEMAND. This chapter provides a selection of incidents which illustrates the continuing conflict between Jesus and the Pharisees. It is worth noting that it is they who attack Him rather than He who attacks them, and this particular dispute had to do with what was allowable on the Jewish Sabbath. The plucking of corn was allowed (Deut. 23: 25) though not on the Sabbath. To the charge of Sabbath breaking Jesus replied by quoting the conduct of David in an emergency (1 Sam. 21: 1–6), and also the scribal rule that 'the Temple service takes precedence over the Sabbath'. That is to say, the priests were allowed to 'work' on the Sabbath so that the Temple ritual might continue without interruption.

The claim of Jesus is that his questioners stand in the presence of a spiritual fact greater even than the Temple—the presence of the Reign of God exemplified in His own person. The old law is amended by the new; the lesser submits to the greater. The reference to Hosea (6: 6) means that the work of God is mercy in action.

The same point is made concerning the healing of the man with the withered hand. Any Galilean shepherd would pull out a sheep that had fallen into a pit, Sabbath or no Sabbath. Was not a man worth much more than a sheep? But the opponents of Jesus were not to be convinced. As they had failed to silence Jesus by fair means, they resolved on foul.

MATTHEW 12: 15–32

'He will not strive, He will not shout' (v. 19, N.E.B.).

THE UNOBTRUSIVELY EFFECTIVE MINISTRY. The first seven verses in this reading describe the spirit of Jesus. Matthew sees His withdrawal in face of the plotting of His enemies (v. 14), not as any sign of weakness but as a planned fulfilment of the Messianic words of Isaiah (42: 1–3), of which a free rendering is given in vv. 18–21. He would not wrangle or shout (Moffatt) but would persist until truth was victorious (Jerusalem Bible).

The Pharisees then renewed their charge that Jesus was in league with the devil (see 10:25). Beelzebub meant 'Lord of the flies' and was the name given to the Philistine god of Ekron (2 Kings 1: 2). The accusation provoked our Lord's strong retort. How could He fight against Satan by the help of Satan? The charge was not even rational. What He did was further indisputable proof of the power of God among men.

The concept of an 'unpardonable sin' must never be divorced from this context. It is not a single word or act, but an established attitude of mind and way of life. How can God do anything for men who deliberately and persistently falsify spiritual facts by calling evil good? The ability to recognize good as good and evil as evil is one of those things that makes a man a man, and if he wilfully corrupts and destroys this part of his nature he robs himself of his eternal hope.

Our Lord is the Stronger who contends with the strong (v. 29), and in this fight we each have our part to play.

MATTHEW 12: 33-42

'For every careless word that men utter they will have to answer' (v. 36, Goodspeed).

THE THOUGHTLESS WORD. Men believed in the power of words both for good and ill. Balak entreated Balaam to put a spell on Israel as if, by some form of incantation, he could halt their progress (Numbers 22: 5 ff.). But it was supposed that until thoughts were expressed in words, there was little to be feared from them.

Jesus took a more searching view. Words were evidence of the state of a man's inner being. 'A man's words are nothing other than the overflow of what is in his heart' (v. 34, Barclay). Obviously speech may conceal thoughts rather than express them. Hence the point of what Jesus said about being judged by our 'idle' words, for these are a reliable guide to character. The premeditated word might be deceptive, but the spontaneous utterance—being the overflow of heart and mind—shows the nature of the inner life. 'Second thoughts' may be best, but first thoughts declare what we are.

Then came the demand for a sign—though the Pharisees had discounted all previous evidence that the Spirit of the Lord was upon Jesus (Luke 4: 18). The point of the reference to Jonah and Solomon is that on two previous occasions in Israel's history the Gentile world had bowed to the authority of a Jew. Nineveh had repented on hearing the message of the prophet Jonah. The wisdom of Solomon had impressed even an Arabian queen. Both events spoke of the way in which the presence and power of the living God had been recognized. How much more should not God's chosen people recognize Him in Jesus—undeniably a greater than either Jonah or Solomon, singly or together!

**'The man ends up by being worse than he was before'
(v. 45, Jerusalem Bible).**

A WELL MERITED WARNING. Once again Jesus spoke
to men in their own terms. What other way is there of getting the
message across? A speaker has to be on his hearers' wavelength.

The dry, or waterless, place—i.e. the desert, was thought to be
the natural haunt of demons. But this particular evil spirit was
not content with so harsh a life—not when he had known the
comfort of the more settled home from which he had been
expelled. So back he went! The place was empty, but had been
cleaned and redecorated for a new tenant. Without further ado
the evil spirit found seven other companions, and whoever tried
to put them out the next time would find the task seven times
harder!

The lesson does not need spelling out. Nature abhors a vacuum.
The man whom God has delivered from the thraldom of sin must
yield himself to the indwelling of the Spirit of God. Where this
happens all things become new, and there is added yet another
member to the world family of which God is Father and Jesus
Christ the Elder Brother (v. 50).

**'He spake to them in parables, at some length' (v. 3,
N.E.B.).**

OUT OF PERSONAL EXPERIENCE. This chapter marks
a turning point in the teaching method of Jesus as He turned
from direct instruction to the use of parables. His disciples wanted
to know the reason why (see below) but it could be that in the
parable of the sower our Lord was assessing the outcome of His
own work.

As Wellhausen wrote: 'Jesus is not so much teaching here as
reflecting aloud upon the results of His teaching.'

Perhaps as our Lord looked beyond the crowds—He was using
a boat as a pulpit—He could see a sower at work. Every sower
must be prepared to see good seed die because of unfavourable
conditions. Knowing that much is sheer waste, he persists because
he also knows the joy of harvest.

Christ is Himself the Seed, so the varying responses of the
different soils is no reflection on what is sown. A man's reaction

to Christ judges the man, not the Saviour. So it is that this parable is not only an analysis of the immediate situation; it is a challenge for all men for all time.

We too are sowing the same seed—Christ, who called Himself 'the Truth'. Much of our sowing may seem to be in vain, and in this we share our Lord's experience. Much of the seed seems wasted, yet we must continue the task. The disappointment of discouragement must not make us 'weary in well-doing'. In Ecclesiastes we read: 'Thou knowest not which shall prosper' (11: 6, R.V.), and so the command remains:

> Sow in the morn thy seed,
> At eve hold not thine hand;
> To doubt and fear give thou no heed,
> Broadcast it o'er the land.

MATTHEW 13: 10–17

'The reason I talk to them in parables is that they look without seeing and listen without ... understanding' (v. 13, Jerusalem Bible).

WHY PARABLES? To continue: this change in the teaching method of Jesus, needs to be seen in the context of His experience.

1. The crowds, with which He was popular, wanted miracles rather than truth. His 'acts of power' were not regarded as signs of a spiritual Kingdom.

2. The nation's religious leaders, with whom He was in conflict, were blinded by prejudice and bigotry.

3. John the Baptist was still in prison.

4. The secrets of the Kingdom were not understood by the 'wise and prudent', so they were to be revealed unto 'babes', the 'little flock' to whom it was the Father's good pleasure to give the Kingdom.

In Matthew 13: 10 the disciples express surprise at this fresh departure, and Jesus' own explanation of it (the rest of today's reading) is illuminating. It seems as though a dividing line had been drawn within the Jewish nation, though not in any arbitrary way, between those who had refused to see and those who had, in a measure, responded to the truth. Jesus was sharing the prophet's experience, whose words He quotes (Isa. 6: 9, 10). His message was destined to fall on deaf ears and the very hearing would increase the responsibility of its rejectors. While disclosing the secret to the 'babes', the parables would conceal it from the closed mind. They demanded an effort on the part of the hearers upon whom they acted as a judgment. They separated the earnest from the merely curious.

MATTHEW 13: 18-23

'Learn what the parable of the sower means' (v. 18, Good News for Modern Man).

FOUR KINDS OF HEARERS. In the explanation of the parable of the sower we have delineated four categories of listeners. (The parable says nothing of the size of each group: it is not dealing with percentages!) There are:

1. *The hard and unimpressionable.* The seed never gets beneath the surface! The Word fails even to penetrate the first defences of the rebellious heart.

2. *The shallow and superficial.* The seed brings forth immediate fruit. The Word calls forth a spontaneous response, but the first onslaught of affliction kills it.

3. *The double-minded who compromise.* The seed grows among the thorns. The Word is welcomed but the heart remains essentially unchanged. Divided loyalty brings confusion and finally evil chokes the good.

4. *The single-hearted.* The seed goes deep and occupies the soil, and brings forth fruit. The Word lays hold of the heart, and the life becomes filled with an abundance of spiritual results. Even here, though, no two people produce the same kind or the same amount of fruit. There are differences of capacity and diversities of gifts. The important factor is the responsive heart.

MATTHEW 13: 24-30

'Let them both grow together till the harvest' (v. 30, J. B. Phillips).

JUDGMENT IS NOT OUR BUSINESS. A problem familiar to everyone in the agricultural community in which Jesus lived was the baffling similarity of tares and wheat in early growth. Not until they were well advanced could they be distinguished and by then their roots were so intertwined that to pull up the tares would also uproot the wheat. Jesus used this fact to convey a fundamental truth. The coming of God's Kingdom is as certain as the coming of the harvest. When men have done their share in sowing the seed they may leave the rest to God. Human interference is positively dangerous.

The parable exposes the error of those who intolerantly judge their fellows. The separation of good and bad is not as easy as we sometimes imagine. 'No man can justly censure or condemn another,' wrote Sir Thomas Browne, 'because indeed no man truly knows another.' We know neither the hidden weakness in the person we admire nor the secret goodness in the person we condemn. Nor do we know the strains and stresses which others have to combat.

Judging others is not merely presumptuous—it is also harmful. C. G. Jung wrote, 'Condemnation does not liberate, it oppresses. I am the oppressor of the person I condemn, not his friend and fellow sufferer.' Even if we do not express our judgment outwardly, it is remarkable how much disapproval can be conveyed in subtle ways. Best to leave judgment to God. Or we are, like the elder son in another of Christ's parables, afraid that God will be too merciful?

MATTHEW 13: 31, 32

'The Kingdom of Heaven is like a mustard seed, the smallest of all seeds' (v. 31, Good News for Modern Man).

SMALL BEGINNINGS. Jesus' listeners might have thought He was making an exaggerated claim when He told this parable. He had gathered around Him only a few followers who, judged by worldly standards, showed little promise as pioneers of a movement symbolized by a tree 'big enough for the birds to come and roost in its branches'. When He left the earth there seemed little to show for His work—a small company of men and women with little influence, wealth or learning between them. Small beginnings indeed! But the movement had life and it would grow, as Jesus said. So it proved. 'Probably the only institution that has survived these nineteen hundred years is the Christian Church,' Hugh Martin observes.

We should not underestimate small beginnings. What had been proved true of the Kingdom of God (of which, we should note, the Church is but an instrument) may be also of our own progress in the life of faith and holiness. While on occasions Jesus rebuked the disciples for the smallness of their faith, on another He said that if they had 'faith no bigger than a mustard seed' they could move mountains.

Yet the small faith of the believer, while in itself valid and valuable, may grow. We may feel we are among those of 'little faith' and therefore of little account. But there is a potential stored within us of which God is aware. We develop as we learn of Christ.

'The Kingdom of Heaven is like yeast' (Good News for Modern Man).

UNSPECTACULAR GROWTH. Like the parable we considered yesterday, the Parable of the Leaven has to do with the growth of the Kingdom of God. In both parables the end is shown to be out of all proportion to the beginning. While yesterday the emphasis was on the extent of the growth of the Kingdom, today it falls on the method of that growth.

About yeast it has been said, 'It influences the particle nearest it, and so its work spreads, until a tumultuous upheaval takes place and all is leavened.' Applying this to the influence of the believer brings an inescapable challenge. How truly do we influence for Christ those nearest to us? It is easy for us to be dazzled by spectacular Christian service; it may also make us complacent. There may be legitimate reasons—family responsibilities, for instance—why we cannot tackle the great and heroic and it might be thought that therefore we are absolved from responsibility for taking any action in the cause of Christ. The truth is that the work of the Kingdom has to be done most often in unspectacular ways.

Though there are times when it is our duty to do and to speak, and when inactivity and silence are cowardly capitulation, the yeast speaks of the effectiveness of a life lived quietly for Christ in the everyday. A Christian man was asked, 'Under whose preaching were you converted?' and he replied, 'Under nobody's preaching; under my aunt's living.'

'Do not think (wrote J. H. Jowett) that we need to be stars in order to shine. It was by the ministry of a candle that a woman found that which was lost.'

'The man who has ears should use them' (v. 43, J. B. Phillips).

GOOD AND EVIL SIDE BY SIDE. As with the parable of

the sower, there is an explanation of the parable of the weeds and the wheat. Why do good and evil exist side by side in a world ruled by a righteous God? What Jesus said by way of reply was couched, first of all, in terms of current agricultural practice and then, in the apocalyptic language of the day.

The weed—the poisonous bearded darnel—was very much like the wheat in the early stages of growth. Fields were frequently weeded but, in this instance, the darnel had grown so thickly that the owner decided it had better be left alone. (As was mentioned in the comment on 13: 24–30, to uproot the darnel would have been to damage the wheat.)

This is an obvious fact of life. Good people, and those not so good, and outright rascals, live side by side—and are dependent on one another. I do not call upon the services of a godly bus driver, or doctor, or dustman only. The world is not, and never has been, a community of saints. The believer has to play his part in our common life along with the unbeliever—and not separate himself from him.

But judgment on good and bad alike is a certainty, though no-one is to attempt any advance excommunication. The harvest will be sufficiently revealing. This is the truth which lies behind the imagery which is employed. And the reality of such truth is infinitely more searching than the figures of speech used to describe it.

MATTHEW 13: 44

'The Realm of Heaven is like treasure hidden in a field' (Moffatt).

UNEXPECTED TREASURE. This parable and the next (vv. 45, 46) form a pair which underlines the same two truths. Firstly, the Kingdom of God is found in unexpected places and, secondly, the worth of the Kingdom is such that he who sees its true beauty and value will gladly forgo all else to possess it. Today we will consider the former idea.

The man was not looking for treasure. He came upon it unawares; he might easily have trodden it underfoot. Concealing his find he bought the field that the treasure might be his. We need not concern ourselves with the question of the man's morality. We may think he dealt dishonestly, but by Jewish law what a man found was his. The point for us, however, is that he came upon the treasure unexpectedly. Similarly, in unexpected places we may find the Kingdom of God.

As has been mentioned earlier, the Church is but an instrument of the Kingdom and not synonymous with it. God does not work only through those who consciously acknowledge His Lordship. In *Change of Address* John V. Taylor asserts that the Holy Spirit 'is uniquely present in Christ and, by extension, in His Church, while universally present through the whole fabric of the universe'. We should expect, then, to see Him at work apart from, as well as within, the Church. And we do. Every expression of the brotherhood of man is an acknowledgment, conscious or not, of the Fatherhood of God. Every deed of mercy, and not only those performed by believers, reflects the divine compassion. We should take care not to undervalue, nor to be slow to acknowledge, every operation of God's Spirit among men.

MATTHEW 13: 45–46

'Again, the Kingdom of Heaven is as if a trader were looking for rare pearls . . .' (v. 45, Knox).

THE LONG SEARCH. The parables of the Kingdom tempt us to seek a simple answer to the question: 'What did Jesus mean by the Kingdom of God?' We tend to equate it with 'being converted' or 'finding Christ'. But Jesus would hardly have used so many diverse parables to illustrate something which He could have defined in a sentence. No, the Kingdom of God is a richly varied thing: both a far-off event toward which the whole creation moves and something immediately present, both individual and social. Dr. Leslie Weatherhead describes it as 'the kingdom of right relationships' and this is most helpful though not intended to be comprehensive. Another writer uses the analogy of the rising sun throwing shafts of light across the sky—the perfect reign of God is not yet, but the world is already touched by its glory.

The labourer, probably ploughing his field, blundered upon treasure—the merchant was seeking it. Indeed, it was only through long experience in trading with pearls that he developed the ability to discern true excellence and the wealth to purchase it. Prolonged seeking, and the increased discrimination this brings, is one way to the Kingdom.

'How can we find the one pearl of great price?' asks Harry Williams. 'Only thus: by refusing to be satisfied with anything less than what is totally satisfying.' In other words, better to remain in the ranks of the seekers than, falsely assuming we have found all there is to find, give up our seeking.

MATTHEW 13: 47–52

'The Kingdom of Heaven is like a net let down into the sea, where fish of every kind were caught in it' (v. 47, N.E.B.).

NO TERROR IN JUDGMENT. This parable, like the Parable of the Tares, shows that the Church, which is the instrument of the Kingdom of God on earth, is bound to include a mixture of all kinds of people. The drag-net would by its very nature bring in not only varieties of fish, but driftwood, shells and useless rocks. Similarly, the Church attracts all kinds of people— the sincere and the insincere; the strong and the weak; the good and the bad. But who belongs to which category is not ours to judge, and we should not presume to do so. There *is* to be a separation, but the time for that is not yet, and man is not the separator, anyway. That is the work of God.

The idea of judgment should not be the unwelcome thought it appears for many people who hope that 'everything will come out right at the end'. Rightly understood, it is only judgment that can give dignity to human life and make sense of man's built-in sense of 'oughtness'. As Paul Hessert has remarked, 'The Christian belief in the last judgment is the conviction that all our achievements are to be seen in the eternal light where right and wrong are finally seen as they are.'

The Christian sees judgment in the context of God's love for mankind. The Judge is Jesus, who never changes. In His life among men He was seen to be caring and compassionate, and He will be our caring and compassionate Judge, even while His kind but searching glance will penetrate any pretence.

MATTHEW 13: 53–58

'In amazement they asked, Where does He get this wisdom from?' (v. 54, N.E.B.).

FAMILIARITY BREEDS CONTEMPT. It was not surprising that Jesus should return to His native village. He did not cease to love the folk at home because His love embraced all men everywhere. Nor was it surprising that He taught in the synagogue. He had taken part in synagogue services before (Mark 1:

21, Luke 4: 16, Matt. 12: 9). In Jewish worship no one person always gave an address. Any visitor might be invited to speak (Acts 13: 14 ff.). But on this occasion when Jesus spoke, incredulity turned to hostility. Having known Him as a boy—'the son of the joiner' (Moffatt)—His neighbours could not accept Him as Messiah.

Older folk sometimes find it difficult to accept instruction—or even suggestions—from those whom they have known as children. This situation can arise in a church or a Salvation Army corps. We find it hard to believe that the boy whom we have known in the young people's band is now mature enough to give strong local leadership. And if he attempts to preach to us . . .

This provides one more illustration of the truth that the worth of a meeting does not depend entirely upon the leader. If a hearer cherishes a feeling of superiority—whether on account of his age or his fancied gifts—then the blessings of that meeting can pass him by. The oldest among us still need to pray: 'O give me Samuel's ear.'

MATTHEW 14: 1–12

'The king was stricken with remorse but . . . granted her request' (v. 9, Knox).

WHO FOLLOWS IN HIS TRAIN? A parallel account of the death of John the Baptist is found in Mark 6: 14–29. Such minor variations as occur in the narrative leave untouched the revengeful plot of Herodias and the fact that Herod's regard for John was not proof against the public promise he had so rashly made. Commented John Wesley: 'Herod murdered an innocent man from tenderness of conscience.'

No two men could be less alike than Herod and the Baptist. The courage of John triumphed over his loneliness. He had not been content to denounce evil in general from a safe distance but had told Herod to his face: 'You have no right to her' (v. 4, Moffatt). (Herod had previously taken as wife the daughter of Aretas, but subsequently married the wife of his own half-brother.) Plainly John was no 'reed swayed by the wind' and, like many another Christian since, paid for his convictions with his life.

But though Herod killed John, he still feared him (v. 2). The thought that Jesus was none other than John risen from the dead frightened him. Conscience can make cowards of us all. The

Baptist may die before Herod, Paul before Nero, Sir Thomas More before Henry VIII, Dietrich Bonhoeffer before Adolf Hitler —but the verdict of God and history has reversed the judgments of man.

'So all ate and were fully satisfied' (v. 20, Weymouth).

'AN ADVENTURE IN FELLOWSHIP.' The feeding of the five thousand is the only miracle story that appears in all four Gospels. In John 6 we read that because of it the people wished to make Jesus their king—it had Messianic significance. The miracle was an acted parable for, later, our Lord likened the Kingdom of God to a great feast (22: 1–14). The multitude had nothing to plead but its own need—and that is how men find their way into the Kingdom. 'Nothing in my hand I bring.'

All that Christ did had a deeper significance than the mere act. J. A. Findlay has commented: He had already invited the working people to share His secret knowledge, now He gives them the opportunity of living with Him for a little while and of seeing for themselves what trustful dependence upon the Heavenly Father can do in an emergency, if His children are willing to share round whatever is available. When He is alone, He will not turn stones into bread; as the Head of the family, He does multiply the loaves—a practical object lesson in the miraculous power of fellowship and trust.'

Only Matthew mentions the women and children. That they should sit down and partake with the men, and actually be served by the disciples, turns the event into what has been called 'a daring experiment in fellowship'. Sex and age do not constitute barriers when Christ is followed and obeyed.

' "Courage," He said, "it is I; do not be afraid." ' (v. 27, Twentieth Century).

'GIVE TO THE WINDS THY FEARS.' William Barclay writes that this story 'is the sign and the symbol of what He (the Lord Jesus) always does for His people, when the wind is contrary, and when we are in danger of being overwhelmed by the storms of life.' Words of George Matheson come to mind:

> I sink in life's alarms
> When by myself I stand;
> Imprison me within Thine arms
> And strong shall be my hand.

Matthew has been called 'the Gospel of the Church', because so much recorded in it had deep significance for the small—though growing—Christian community in the second half of the first century. The Early Church was launched upon a troubled sea indeed, and apart from her Lord nothing but overwhelming disaster might have been expected. Peter, ever the leader of the disciple band, was sometimes carried by his impetuosity into situations in which he revealed a lack of stability and soundness of judgment. But at least he loved his Lord, and the Lord who loved him much, much more was never so far away that He could not speak the steadying and encouraging word. And that goes for us all as well.

MATTHEW 15: 1–9

'Your tradition empties the commandment of God of all its meaning' (v. 6, J. B. Phillips).

VAIN WORSHIP. The legalism of the Pharisees' religion had long been the object of our Lord's criticism. Today's reading admirably illustrates the two entirely different views of religion which He and they represented.

Perhaps an actual case was being discussed. An angry son, following some disagreement with his parents, had formally dedicated to God money that could and should have assisted those who had cared for him through childhood and early manhood. The religious authorities sanctioned and approved the vow, insisting that it must take priority over his parents' needs.

Our Lord's teaching was consistent throughout and laid its primary emphasis on the personal and the spiritual. The Pharisees may have been correct in their interpretation of the letter of the law, but Jesus was echoing the noblest teaching of the Old Testament when, as in this instance, he declared that the care of needy parents took precedence over a sacred gift.

The Pharisees thought of worship in terms of ritual and law; Jesus thought of worship in terms of a clean heart and a life of love. William Temple wrote: 'To worship is to quicken the conscience by the holiness of God, to feed the mind with the truth of God, to purge the imagination by the beauty of God, to open the heart to the love of God, to devote the will to the purpose of God.'

'What comes out of the mouth comes from the heart— and that is what defiles a man' (v. 11, Moffatt).

A REVOLUTIONARY RULING. On v.11 C. G. Monte-fiore has said that whatever meaning Jesus may have intended His words to convey, the rabbis 'could see where they led and could do no other than reject a principle which (to them) had such revolutionary implications'. William Barclay has commented: 'It may well be held that for a Jew this was the most startling thing that Jesus ever said. For in this saying He does not only condemn Scribal and Pharisaic ritual and ceremonial religion: He actually wipes out large sections of the book of Leviticus. This is not a contradiction of the tradition of the elders alone. This is a contradiction of Scripture itself. The saying of Jesus cancels all the food laws of the Old Testament.'

Our Lord here declares that the conditions of true worship are spiritual. External things like food cannot disqualify a man for fellowship with God. What does defile is evil in the heart, that which transpires in 'the dark halls of thought'. Ceremonial cleansing fails to touch the unworthy motive and unclean desire as the following verse recognizes:

> All my best works are naught,
>   Please they not Thee;
> Far past my busy hands
>   Thine eye doth see
> Into the depth of mind,
> Searching the plan designed,
> Gladdened when Thou dost find
>   First of all, Thee.

'Even the dogs take the bits from under their master's table' (v. 27, Basic English).

THE TESTING OF FAITH. The apparent hardness of Jesus to this 'woman of Canaan' may be due to our limited knowledge.

So often it is not so much what is said but how it is said that determines whether a statement is harsh or not. It may have been our Lord's smile that brought the woman's wit into action and called forth her ready repartee (v. 27).

On the other hand, it is necessary to fit the event into its context in our Lord's life. He had escaped from Herod's domain in order to teach the disciples. The opposition of the Jewish leaders was hardening into dangerous hostility. Yet though the word was still 'I am not sent but unto . . . the house of Israel', this incident is one more illustration of our Lord's faithfulness to the spirit of His own teaching. Here was a human need—that is, a need which was greater than any difference between Jew and Gentile. The girl was ill. The mother's faith in Jesus was strong to the point of persistence. Every other consideration must therefore be set aside. The girl was cured.

It could be that our own requests in prayer could benefit from an infusion of this same persistent faith.

MATTHEW 15: 29–39

'My heart goes out to this crowd, He said' (v. 32, J. B. Phillips).

A GENTILE MINISTRY. Mark's Gospel helps us to place geographically the incidents of today's reading (Mk. 7: 31 ff.). They took place in Decapolis, i.e. pagan territory, on the other side of Jordan, in the area which Sir George Adam Smith has well called 'Greece over Jordan'. If this is so, the suggestion of some scholars that the feeding of the four thousand was no more than a 'doublet'—another form of the earlier miracle—loses some of its force. There is a very old tradition, which may go back to the time of the evangelists themselves, that the feeding of the four thousand represents symbolically the calling of the Gentiles into the Kingdom of God, while the feeding of the five thousand represents the calling of the Jews.

This view enables us to assume that our Lord engaged in a Gentile ministry, despite what is said in Matt. 10: 5, 6 and 15: 24. Confronted by the human need of the Canaanite woman (see above), the sick (vv. 29–31) and the hungry (vv. 32–39), He breaks His plans for quiet and the uninterrupted instruction of the disciples. He is true to His own teaching. Confronted with human need there can be no question of ignoring it. The Saviour of mankind overrides those false distinctions that would separate one nation, or one man, from another.

'What is this discussion among you, you men of little faith, about having no bread?' (v. 8, Weymouth).

FAILURES IN UNDERSTANDING. Verses 1 to 4 deal with the failure of the Jewish leaders to understand our Lord; verses 5 to 12 show the disciples trying to take literally an obviously metaphorical remark. More than one commentator has drawn attention to the fact that we are so familiar with the words of the Gospels that we underestimate the difficulty on both sides; Jesus was speaking of things of which no man had ever spoken before, and was trying to add a whole new dimension to human thought.

With all that Jesus had done in expressing the divine love toward mankind, the Pharisees and Sadducees should, surely, have had the penetration to read the spiritual signs. Their further request for a sign that could not be gainsaid was their condemnation. We read that our Lord simply 'left them, and departed'.

But when Jesus tried to turn this encounter with the Jewish leaders to the disciples' profit, they in turn became puzzled and worried. With the recent feeding of the multitude in mind, they thought that Jesus was reproaching them for yet another breakdown in their food supplies! Whereat the Master had to remind them that as their physical needs had earlier been fully met, so would they continue to be. Their first concern should be to guard against any temptation to lose confidence in the mission and power of their Lord and Master.

'Thou art the Christ' (v. 16).

THE WATERSHED OF THE GOSPEL. This incident marks the turning-point in our Lord's ministry. From this time onward the way is clear; He turns to Jerusalem to throw down the gauntlet to the nation in His final challenge.

'Jesus cannot be discussed objectively at arm's length.' Sooner or later the question: 'Whom do men say that I the Son of Man am?' must become: 'But whom say ye that I am?' There is no escape. Let us beware of ascribing to Him high-sounding names

C

that bear no relation to anything in our contemporary lives. The name we give should enshrine our own experience.

F. R. Barry paraphrases Jesus' reply to Peter's confession of faith: 'This is a great achievement of spiritual insight . . . and on the rock of this intuition I will build My church.' As the first to believe in this deeper sense it is fitting that 'the keys of the Kingdom' should be his. The 'key' was the knowledge his own insight had brought, and by using it under the Spirit's guidance Peter opened the door of the Church to the Jews on the day of Pentecost (Acts 2) and some time later to the Gentiles of the household of Cornelius (Acts 10). So the word of our Lord was adequately fulfilled.

The 'gates of hell'—meaning in this context, the 'gates of death'—would prove impotent. The crucifixion itself was the outstanding illustration of this, and the death of God's martyrs— such as Stephen or Peter himself—has always proved a strengthening experience in the supernatural life of the Church.

MATTHEW 16: 21–28

'You are a hindrance to Me. Your outlook is not God's but man's' (v. 23, Moffat).

THE SEQUEL TO THE CONFESSION. Our Lord's task was to teach the true meaning of Messiahship. It is difficult, if not impossible, for us to realize just how intolerable was the idea that God's anointed One had come to suffer and to die. We must try to understand Peter's reaction. A disturbing fact becomes clear: the man who had just given utterance to a truth that was of God can, the next moment, become the agent of the worst of temptations.

M. Goguel wrote: 'Jesus did not believe that He was the Messiah although He had to suffer; He believed that He was the Messiah because He had to suffer. This is the great paradox, the great originality, of the gospel.'

But the road of shame and bitter pain was not for our Lord alone. A. M. Hunter said of those first disciples that they had to 'begin to live as man on the way to the gallows'. The self-denial of the Christian way of life is not the giving up of this or that but the full renunciation of the self.

How true verse 28 has proved to be! Many present must have witnessed in the years which lay ahead the mighty power of the crucified and risen Son of Man. The Cross and Resurrection established the Kingdom on earth, in history. Jesus still reigns from the Tree.

MATTHEW 17: 1–13

'This is My Son, My Beloved. He is My Chosen. Listen to Him' (v. 5, Goodspeed).

GLORY AND SUFFERING. In the experience of baptism the 'Voice from Heaven' confirmed the mission upon which Jesus was then launching out (3: 17). Here, as He set His face towards the Cross, the 'Voice out of the cloud' confirmed the new interpretation He had been giving to the Messianic hope.

From the eternal world came Moses—representing the Law, and Elijah—representing the prophets. But Moses was more than the lawgiver; he was the prophet who prefigured the One still to come to whom the people would hearken (Deut. 18: 15). And Elijah was more than a prophet; he was to be the final precursor of the Messiah.

Moreover, they were both examples of vicarious suffering. Moses, the hero of the Exodus, had identified himself with an enslaved nation; Elijah the hero of Carmel, had identified himself with a faithful suffering minority.

The disciples, however, misunderstood the significance of this supernatural event. Here was majesty and glory such as they had associated with their Messianic hope. 'Let us make this permanent,' says Peter in effect, 'and forget all about those morbid thoughts of suffering and death' (v. 4). But it was of that greater 'exodus'—our Lord's decease—that Jesus, Moses and Elijah talked (see Luke 9: 31). In Kingdom values, suffering and glory are one. It is not surprising that Peter, James and John found this difficult to accept, but there is no excuse for us.

MATTHEW 17: 14–21

'The disciples asked Jesus privately, "Why couldn't we cast that demon out?" "Because of your little faith", Jesus told them' (vv. 19, 20, Living New Testament).

TRAGEDY AND IMPOTENCE. The comparison has often been made between the mountain-top experience and the valley of human need. Undoubtedly it is true that religion must come down from the heights into the vortex of suffering and heartbreak. But if tragedy is one of life's grim realities, so was the impotence of Christ's disciples to effect a cure. Lack of faith led to failure. In spite of their close association with Jesus, they were unable to take their Master's place in His absence.

But let us bring the story out of the past. Every believer is a 'member' of the Body of Christ on earth. Where we happen to be placed, the effectiveness of the Body depends upon the strength in us.

'Why could not we cast him out?' asked the disciples, perhaps querulously. There had been a time when they had cast out devils. But Jesus had no doubt as to the cause of their failure. They did not possess the faith which (as T. H. Robinson wrote) is 'more than a mental acceptance of statements about God and the world. It is the translation of intellectually perceived truth into actual experience, a weaving of the doctrines of the spiritual life into the very fabric of the soul. . . . Jesus did not argue from the world to God, from physical experience to spiritual reality. His processes were the exact opposite of this; He knew God first of all.' To such as share His faith, the greatest physical obstacle or material difficulty becomes surmountable (v. 20).

MATTHEW 17: 22–27

' "Does your Master not pay temple tax?" "He does," said Peter' (v. 24, N.E.B.).

As A. C. Bouquet has written, in external appearance the Jerusalem temple conformed to the pattern of similar buildings in the Mediterranean world save that, as a Roman contemporary of the Apostle Paul observed, 'there were no representations of gods . . . the place was empty'. But the temple ritual with its daily sacrifices, the incense and music, the multitude of priests on call, must have been expensive to maintain—hence the annual temple tax which was roughly equivalent to two days' wages for the average peasant.

The question in v. 24 was probably a loaded one. If Jesus did not pay the tax, this could be the ground of a charge against Him, and Edersheim has pointed out that non-payment could be met by a distraint of goods.

The point of our Lord's remarks in v. 25 is that the Temple was His Father's house, erected to His praise and for His worship. Was a son to be levied for the upkeep of the paternal establishment? Even earthly kings collected their taxes from subject peoples, not from their own. Nevertheless, for example's sake, let the tax be paid—and let fisherman Peter see to it. The duties of a good citizen must not be evaded. Caesar must receive what is Caesar's—though never that which is God's.

MATTHEW 18: 1–6

'Unless you change and become like children, you will never enter the Kingdom of heaven' (v. 3, Good News for Modern Man).

THE KEY INTO THE KINGDOM. Jesus refuses to answer the disciples' question about precedence in the kingdom, pointing out instead the conditions of entrance. It is idle to debate who is greatest in the kingdom of heaven while still uncertain about the qualifications for entry.

Why did Jesus make the child His model of candidateship for the kingdom? Children are so obviously not humble that commentators, especially on the Markan version of the story, have forwarded many other suggestions. Children are more open and unprejudiced, naturally more trustful than adults. Yet in the first Gospel it is humility which is highlighted. To understand this we must transport ourselves from the twentieth century, where the child is the centre of care, concern and study, to the first century where he was utterly without status. Even an heir, while he was a child, had no higher status than a slave (Gal. 4: 1).

With our modern understanding of the child we would stress that, in a good family, the child is sure of love and feels no need to grasp at status. Søren Kierkegaard, the Danish philosopher, stood one evening looking out to sea. 'The power of the sea and the battle of the elements reminded me of my own nothingness,' he wrote, 'and on the other hand the sure flight of the birds recalled the words spoken by Christ: Not a sparrow shall fall to the ground without your Father. Then all at once I felt how great and how small I was; then did those two mighty forces, pride and humility, happily unite in friendship. Lucky is the man to whom that is possible at every moment of his life.'

MATTHEW 18: 7–14

'It is never the will of your Father in Heaven that a single one of these little ones should be lost' (v. 14, J. B. Phillips).

MISSING THE WAY. This simple parable speaks of the

patient, seeking love of God whose will is that no man should be lost. That word 'lost' should be rightly understood. To think, as some are apt to do, merely of 'lost souls', the last judgment and consignment to hell, is to miss the point of the parable. Judgment and the separation of the good from the evil are inescapable realities. But Jesus did not mean here that the lost are those who by their persistent and conscious exercise of their free will have for ever cut themselves away from the outstretched hand. A man is lost when he is not fulfilling the divine plan for his life; when he has not found the fellowship he should be enjoying with God who created him and loves him. He is then outside the Kingdom of Heaven. This is the lostness of which Jesus spoke and it is a condition God is ready and, indeed, eager to heal. Patiently, lovingly, He seeks all who have missed their way. No one is unimportant to Him; just one in a crowd. It is as individuals men are sought and brought into the fold.

This is a challenge to us in our endeavours to bring men to acknowledge the lordship of Christ. As His love reaches to the least and lowest so should ours, and any superior and censorious attitude in our approach to people must bear the divine disapproval. It is also heartening to reflect that our mission is His; our concern for men is shared, in a greatly multiplied way, by God Himself.

MATTHEW 18: 15–22

'Then Peter . . . said, "Lord, how often must I forgive my brother?" . . . Jesus answered, "Not seven . . . but seventy-seven times." ' (vv. 21, 22, Jerusalem Bible).

CHRISTIAN RELATIONSHIPS. Certain aspects of today's reading are difficult of interpretation. Undoubtedly if we knew the way in which Christ said certain things many of our problems would disappear. Whenever we face a difficult saying the only safe thing to do is to interpret it in the light of all we know of Jesus' life and character.

The Christian must always work towards reconciliation. On occasions it may be necessary to point out a man's faults, but this should be done in private. If that fails, the help of a few friends should be solicited, and only if that fails should the whole church be informed. No harshness needs to be read into the final part of verse 17. Pagans and publicans (i.e. tax-gatherers—traitors) may exclude themselves from the Christian fellowship by their stubborn refusal to be reconciled, but Jesus befriended the social and religious outcasts. As Jesus teaches in His answer to Peter, there must be no limit to our willingness to forgive. The believer must never regard any man as 'beyond the pale', even if the man himself does.

Verse 18 is a repetition of words previously spoken to Peter (16: 19) but here addressed to the disciples as a whole. As Dr. Barclay has observed: 'It cannot mean that the Church can remit or forgive sins, and so settle a man's destiny in time or in eternity. What it may well mean is that the relationships which we establish with our fellow-men last, not only through time, but into eternity —therefore we must get them right.'

MATTHEW 18: 23-27

'Then his master was moved with pity for him, set him free and cancelled the debt' (v. 27, J. B. Phillips).

BOUNDLESS MERCY. In Shakespeare's play, Macbeth felt his sin was so grievous that, even if he attempted to wash his guilt away in the ocean, the sea itself would become red with the blood of guilt.

> Will all great Neptune's ocean wash this blood
> Clean from my hand? No, this my hand will rather
> The multitudinous seas incarnadine
> Making the green one red.

A similar assessment of the human situation is hidden in the humorous exaggeration of this story—though without any sense of morbid guilt. We may be sure the crowd laughed when Jesus told of the slave who owed his master 10,000 talents—two and a quarter million pounds! They laughed, but got the point. Our debt is unpayable. The attempt to earn credit with God is doomed to failure. Free forgiveness is our only hope—and that is exactly what is offered.

It is sometimes more easy to believe in the boundless forgiveness of God for others than for ourselves. C. G. Jung has said that Christians remember their Master's command to forgive others but do not always extend that charity to themselves. He wrote, 'But what if I should discover that the poorest of all beggars, the most impudent of all the offenders, the very enemy himself—that these are within me, and that I myself stand in need of the alms of my own kindness—that I myself am the enemy who must be loved what then? As a rule the Christian's attitude is then reversed; there is no longer any question of love or long-suffering; we say to the brother within us "Raca", and condemn and rage against ourselves.' We must not deny ourselves the benefits of God's boundless mercy which we offer to others.

MATTHEW 18: 28-35

'It is thus that My heavenly Father will deal with you, if brother does not forgive brother with all his heart' (v. 35, Knox).

GRACE OR LAW. We noted that some Christians deny themselves the forgiveness which in God's name they offer to others. On the other hand some people deny others the forgiveness they hope to receive. It is to them this parable is really addressed.

We share the callousness of the servant in this story whenever we adopt harsh, calculating attitudes to our fellows. Dare we, who utterly depend upon God's forgiveness, be ungenerous toward others' failings? This parable faces us with a decision: either we choose to live in the realm of grace, both receiving and offering forgiveness; or we opt for relationships based upon law, demanding our dues from others but burdened by our own debt toward God. Failure to forgive others puts us in the hands of the 'torturers', which J. Alexander Findlay likens to 'that hell on earth into which a man is plunged when he is left with his grievances for sole company'.

Willingness to forgive is often the one hope of remedying unhappy relationships. A novel by Morris West penetratingly depicts a family situation made tense by submerged hostility. The father, an elderly lawyer, asks a young artist for her advice. 'Here is my prescription,' she replies. 'Unless you want to end by killing each other, someone has to say the first gentle word. And you are the one who has the least time left.' How many difficult situations, even within the Christian Church, wait for one who will 'say the first gentle word'.

MATTHEW 19: 1-12

'What God Himself has yoked together man must not separate' (v. 5, Twentieth Century).

MARRIAGE AND DIVORCE. The question of the Pharisees

was a trap. Would Jesus agree with the strict school of Shammai or the more liberal school of Hillel regarding divorce? He agreed with neither, but affirmed God's original intention in marriage— i.e. the indissoluble union of one man and one woman. The Mosaic permission for divorce was not intended to encourage the unhappy practice, but was a concession to fallen human nature— it bore witness to man's sinfulness.

The principle declared by our Lord was recognized as an exacting one. The disciples began to wonder if it was not too much of a risk to embark upon marriage if there were no escape route! The fact is that adequately to fulfil the Christian ethic we need the Christ spirit. 'The teaching of Christ demands the presence of Christ.'

In verse 12 we have a saying of our Lord's relating to those for whom, for a variety of reasons, the ordinary course of married life is impossible. Three classes are referred to. Firstly, there are those unhappy people for whom marriage is out of the question because of physical deformity or some strange constitutional factor. The second group have no counterpart in present-day civilization. Thirdly there are those who for the sake of the Kingdom of God renounce marriage, a sacrifice not to be regarded lightly in view of our Lord's lofty doctrine.

Finally, a word of warning. Jesus was enunciating a principle, not enacting a civil law. But those who claim to be His followers are expected to obey His commands.

MATTHEW 19: 13-15

'You must let little children come to Me, and you must never stop them' (v. 14, J. B. Phillips).

PRAYER FOR THE YOUNG. What a blessing that

> When mothers of Salem
> Their children brought to Jesus

our Lord 'saw them ere they fled'.

The parents and friends of the children were right; the disciples were wrong; and Jesus was not slow to take sides in the debate. Nothing must come between Him and the little ones.

A welfare state can look after the education and physical well-being of its children. It cannot ensure that they have the opportunity of direct contact with Jesus Christ. That is the privilege and weighty responsibility of its parents.

Jesus was so much a man of prayer that these parents 'brought unto Him little children, that He should put His hands on them, and pray'. It is to be hoped that they themselves learned the secret of the Master's prayer-life, so that their children in turn might make the great discovery. It is idle simply to tell children to pray; they must see prayer as part of the normal life of their parents. Example, here as elsewhere, is better than precept.

Those who take their babies for baptism or dedication and then regard their obligations as discharged betray a superstitious outlook. Parents must follow up their initial act by a life in which example and precept unite to remind their children of the children's Saviour.

MATTHEW 19: 16–22

'He went sadly away for he had great possessions' (v. 22, Moffatt).

FIT FOR THE KINGDOM. The gospel sets before us who is and who is not. The earlier encounter with small children showed who was; this incident had to do with one who unhappily was not.

A wealthy man is usually treated with respect, not always on account of himself but because of the influence which his money can exercise. In this story the young man himself was acceptable to Jesus. His property was the great barrier. In our Lord's judgment the power which wealth can bestow is a greater danger to its possessor than to those over whom it gives him power. Jesus would have had this well-to-do newcomer give his money away so that he could enter the Kingdom as a man. But no; his 'great possessions' held him in their grip; they stood between him and eternal life.

One of the virtues of this story is the way in which it illumines the meaning of eternal life, which is the kind of life which God himself lives. 'Eternal' does not just mean lasting for ever, for there is no time scale in eternity. Eternal life is that kind or quality of life which belongs to God and is characteristic of Him. It is a life where loves rules supremely and from which selfishness has been banished. The young man 'went away sorrowful' but his sorrow was not greater than that of Jesus at his departure.

'A camel could more easily squeeze through the eye of a needle than a rich man get into the kingdom of God!' (v. 24, J. B. Phillips).

PEDESTALS ARE OUT! Most readers are familiar with the suggestion that a small gate called 'the needle's eye' existed in the walled city of Jerusalem, and that it was to this Jesus here referred. There is no justification for this interpretation. The bringing together of the largest, most ungainly animal, and the smallest possible hole, is simply another example of the striking extremes used by Jewish teachers which we have already noted.

Many rich men have gained access to the kingdom—'with God anything is possible!'—regarding themselves as trustees rather than possessors. Christ's vivid warning applies, not only to those in a particular income bracket, or those rich in money. The danger Jesus pointed out was that we tend to credit ourselves with our possessions—financial, intellectual, social or moral, in such a way as to lose our humanity. We are ourselves plus. Person to person encounter becomes impossible because we insist on carrying around our pathetic little pedestals. As the kingdom is essentially social we have to learn to say 'Just as I am', not only to God, but to our fellow men.

The Church could barely have survived without periodic reminders of the danger of possessions and the virtue of simplicity. John Woolman wore undyed clothes as his witness against luxury, travelled steerage on his last Atlantic crossing and recorded some awkward questions about poverty and wealth in his Journal, adding, 'May those who have abundance lay these things to heart.'

MATTHEW 20: 1-7

'The Realm of heaven is like a householder who went out early in the morning to hire labourers for his vineyard' (v. 1, Moffat).

THE JOY OF LABOUR. Dr. Leslie Weatherhead writes about two young women, both possessing good health, excellent education and the ambition to become missionaries. One quickly achieved her aim, proceeding overseas, marrying a missionary and spending her life in happy service. The other girl was held back because aged parents were dependent on her. Many years passed before, at the age of forty-seven, she was eventually free of family responsibilities. It was then too late for overseas work so she served in London. No doubt the girl who became a missionary sometimes felt weary with her arduous service, but the real burden fell on the girl who had so much to give but was unable to give it.

The parable of the labourers in the vineyard makes a similar point. Forget for a moment the surprise ending, which we will consider below. Imagine the excitement and joy of the grape harvest. Remember that the men standing in the market place (the equivalent of the modern labour exchange) were no loafers. They were anxious workmen who knew their families would go hungry if they remained unemployed.

Labour in God's vineyard may be arduous, but it brings dignity and joy to life. The real tragedy would be to be spiritually unemployed. This need never be for, though some may be frustrated from giving the service they would choose, nobody is precluded from serving in prayer and love.

MATTHEW 20: 8–16

'May I not do what I like with what belongs to me? Must you be jealous because I am generous?' (v. 15, J. B. Phillips).

LAST COME, FIRST SERVED. The 'bolt from the blue' ending to this parable underlines the lesson of the previous comment. Service in the vineyard is a high privilege—being unable to serve is the real tragedy. But the parable also tells us something about rewards in the Kingdom of God.

The master's treatment of his workers was unbelievably quixotic. No wonder it caused unrest. Had he desired to pay all his workers equally, irrespective of length of service, he could at least have paid the early-starters first. But no, 'last come, first served' was his method. The injustice of this only goes to prove that Jesus was not presenting a pattern for employer-employee relationships. He does not say, 'the world of business or commerce is like this'; He says, 'the Kingdom of Heaven is like this'.

The question of carefully calculated rewards does not arise in the Kingdom—the love of God cannot be shared out in appropriate measures according to merit. To be obsessed with rewards shows we have not discovered the joy of work motivated by love.

Meister Eckhart suggests a similarity between the merchants whom Jesus expelled from the temple and those religious people who bargain their 'goodness' for God's favour: 'Lo, they are merchants all who, while avoiding mortal sin and wishing to be virtuous, do good works to the glory of God . . . but do them with a view to God's giving them somewhat, doing to them somewhat, they wish for in return. All such are merchants.'

MATTHEW 20: 17–28

'Whoever would be first must be the willing slave of all —like the Son of Man' (v. 27, N.E.B.).

TRUE GREATNESS. Our Lord's third prediction of the Passion (see 16: 21 and 17: 22, 23) is here followed by an incident that reveals how little the disciples understood their Master. In Mark (10: 35–45) the requests for the best seats in the coming Kingdom came from James and John themselves; here, however, it is their mother who pushes them forward. But to be near to Christ—either in this life or the next—a man has to be Christlike and, on their current showing, James and John had still a long way to go.

But if these two revealed their ignorance, they also displayed an unwarranted self-confidence. 'We are able' (v. 22) they said when challenged by Jesus, forgetting that leadership in the Kingdom involves lowliness. In the economy of the Spirit the higher a man's place, the humbler his duties, so that it is the slave (v. 27) who stands—so to speak—at the top of the tree.

This basic truth is underlined by the example of Jesus Himself. He who 'thought it not robbery to be equal with God' gave His life 'a ransom for many'. The Cross was not an unfortunate mischance. Jesus did not die because of some human blunder. 'No one has robbed Me of My life', He said. 'I am laying it down of My own free will' (John 10:18, N.E.B.). As Max Warren wrote: 'The Cross is not only the central theme of evangelism; it has to be the central experience of the evangelist.'

MATTHEW 20: 29–34

'Jesus stood quite still and called out to them, "What do you want Me to do for you?"' (v. 32, J. B. Phillips).

CAN WE FACE THIS QUESTION? Perhaps more than any other Gospel-writer the author of the first Gospel was keenly interested in the structure of his book. It is no coincidence that the healing of these two blind men immediately follows the request of two disciples who were blind to the nature of Christ's kingship, and therefore to the sacrifices involved in sharing His glory. To both the mother of James and John and to the blind men Jesus puts almost identical questions: 'What is it you wish?' (v. 21), 'What do you want Me to do for you?' (v. 32, N.E.B.).

What do we really want? What do we hope to receive from our allegiance to this King? Is mediocre conformity and respectability the height of our ambition? Or have we allowed Christ to implant the longing for sanctity, or wholeness, in our hearts? Few questions are more important, for the latter is never achieved without pain.

A character in Morris West's *The Shoes of the Fisherman* says, 'It costs so much to be a full human being that there are very few who have the enlightenment, or the courage, to pay the price ... One has to abandon altogether the search for security, and reach out to the risk of living with both arms. One has to embrace the world like a lover, and yet demand no easy return of love. One has to accept pain as a condition of existence. One has to court doubt and darkness as the cost of knowing. One needs a will stubborn in conflict, but apt always to the total acceptance of every consequence of living and dying.'

MATTHEW 21: 1–11

'Go into the village in front of you and you will at once find there an ass tethered, and a colt with her. Untie them and bring them to Me' (v. 2, J. B. Phillips).

HE CHOOSES US. We move on in the sequence of our readings to the momentous event the Church celebrates every Palm Sunday: the entry of Christ the King into the city where He would be crucified. The choice of an ass was highly significant, for this lowly animal was yet considered a beast of kings, though used by kings on missions of peace and goodwill. Also, the ass was essential to Jesus' claim that He was fulfilling the ancient prophecy of Zechariah (9: 9).

For D. T. Niles the ass suggests 'the previousness of the Master'. He also lays hold of us and seeks to use us in His plan. The process can never be reversed. 'The Christian life begins,' he writes, 'when one is found by God in Jesus Christ. It is the mercy and unexpectedness of this finding which the ass symbolizes. God found us, even though we were ordinary, very ordinary.'

Ruth Siegfried, Salvationist missionary to the Congo, was the child of a Lutheran pastor in Alsace. As a girl she attended a missionary meeting and when the collection was about to be taken she took a piece of paper, scribbling on it the words, 'I give myself.' Before we ever come to that place of self-offering, however, we must feel ourselves laid hold of by Christ.

MATTHEW 21: 12–17

'But when (they) saw His wonderful deeds and saw the children who shouted . . . "Hosanna", they were indignant' (v. 15, Moffatt).

THE OFFENCE OF ENTHUSIASM. The prophet Malachi had declared: 'And the Lord . . . shall suddenly come to His Temple . . . But who shall abide the day of His coming? . . . for He is like a refiner's fire . . .' (3: 1, 2). Did the priesthood recall such words as these on the day Jesus cleansed the Temple?

William Temple called this 'a tremendous scene', and continued, 'The Lord dominates the multitude by the righteousness of His energy and the energy of His righteousness.' The crowd itself was probably on His side, but His act was an open challenge to the priests who had a financial interest in the selling of animals and birds for the sacrifices. They would not hesitate to strike back. This act must be seen as part of our Lord's strategy to compel the nation to decide for or against Him.

What follows is both beautiful and significant. Verse 14 tells of men being healed; verses 15 and 16 speak of the joyful praises of happy children—and also the indignation of the Jewish leaders. In their eyes this was nothing other than a disturbance likely to lead to a breach of the peace. But what v. 16 also implies is that 'flesh and blood had not told the children what they should say but the Father in heaven'.

MATTHEW 21: 18–22

'All that ever you ask in prayer you shall have, if you believe' (v. 22, Moffatt).

CALL FOR FAITH. An account of this is found in Mark 11:13, 14 but, as Commissioner Samuel Brengle said when commenting on the story of Jonah—'Forget the whale and see God at work', so here we can forget the fate of the fig tree and note our Lord's call for faith.

If the fig tree represented the Jewish people, having the promise of fruit but in actuality bearing none, then this was but the sad yet sober truth. It may be urged that the Gentile world was even more barren, but they had not been given—nor did they claim as did the Jews—a special place in the plan and purpose of God. But of all of us it is true that to whom much is given, from him will much be required.

By contrast, the man of faith will find his life bearing such fruit as will glorify the Father. Eastern imagery is not meant to be taken literally. What v. 21 is saying is that with faith the seemingly impossible becomes gloriously possible. The promise in v. 22 is virtually repeated in John 15: 7.

MATTHEW 21: 23–32

'I tell you solemnly, tax collectors and prostitutes are making their way into the kingdom of God before you' (v. 31, Jerusalem Bible).

SAYING 'YES' AND DOING IT. As the Jewish authorities would not enter into any discussion on so sensitive a point as the authority of John because of the dilemma in which it would place them, Jesus refused to answer their question about His authority but went on to deal with a very practical matter—the nature of true obedience.

While neither of the two young men in the parable was a model son, the one who said, 'I will not go,' and went, obviously brought the greater satisfaction to the father. One paid only lip-service: his profession was not matched by his performance. The other acted better than his words suggested he would.

Comparing the two classes of people the sons represented is a humbling experience for the religious man, as Jesus meant it to be. He wants us to see that the reality of Christian experience cannot be gauged by what a man says, but by what he does, for this proves what he is. To make loud protestations of love to God, and to avow one's intention to serve and obey, mean nothing at all unless action accompanies words.

On the other hand, it must frankly be acknowledged that countless noble deeds are performed by people who make no profession of the Christian faith, and by some who openly reject it. They are like the man who said 'No!' with his lips and 'Yes' with his life. We Christians may be puzzled by this, but must thank God for every act of love as we allow the selfless deeds of non-Christians to challenge us and spur us on to better service. These, too, are evidences of the work of the Holy Spirit for, as has been observed more than once in this study of the parables, God does not work only through His Church. Neither son portrays the ideal Christian. It is always better both to say 'Yes' and to do it.

MATTHEW 21: 33–46

' "He will ... let out the vineyard to other tenants who will give him the fruits in their seasons" ' (v. 41, R.S.V.).

ABUSING OUR PRIVILEGES. As a rule the details of a parable should not be stressed, for usually only one point is intended. This parable is different. The details do have their meaning. The owner of the vineyard is God, the husbandman the Israelite nation, the servants the Old Testament prophets and the son Jesus Himself. Having been entrusted with precious truth and been named the Chosen People, the Israelites had proved unfaithful. They had killed those whom God had sent to guide them, and they had it in mind to destroy even His Son. It was a bold indictment of the nation, and especially of its leaders that, as G. E. P. Cox has said, 'their concern to retain control of the Lord's vineyard at all costs, even by the "elimination" of the Messiah, was a usurpation which would seal not His doom but their own. They and their privileges would be swept away in favour of more faithful men whom they despised.'

The abuse and usurpation of privileges and gifts are faults of which we all may be guilty. We forget that what we possess—our intellect, health, goods—are gifts. We may have developed them, but they originate in God Himself. Failure to acknowledge their source so easily leads to self-congratulation and smug satisfaction with what we imagine we have achieved. We are stewards, and are therefore accountable to God for all we have, and we deceive ourselves if we think this is not so.

It is a recurring theme of the Bible that privilege imposes responsibility. It applied to the Israelite nation. No less truly it applies to us.

MATTHEW 22: 1–10

'The invited guests paid no attention and went about their business' (v. 5, Good News for Modern Man).

WHY MEN REJECT GOD. It would appear that at least two

parables, or parts of them have become linked together in verses 1 to 14 of this chapter. We shall look at the second of these (verses 11 to 14) below. In the first, the Parable of the Marriage of the King's Son, the behaviour of the 'others' (v. 6) is difficult to understand. Who were they and what reason had they for killing the message bearers? The military expedition of punishment—while the dinner waited on the table!—also defies satisfactory explanation. But the main point of the parable is not in doubt: the strange reluctance of men to accept God's grace.

It is difficult enough to believe how people could react in so outrageous a way to an invitation to a wedding, but how much more incomprehensible is men's refusal of God's invitation to life and hope and joy. The question of why men turn their backs on God could occupy us for a long time, for there are undoubtedly many aspects of the problem. But there we will confine ourselves to one challenging thought. It is this: for many people the Christianity portrayed by the Church is quite unrelated to life and is therefore rejected.

In his book *Come out the Wilderness*, Bruce Kenrick wrote of a brave and imaginative experiment in Christianity in East Harlem, New York. He observed that 'most of East Harlem's residents held that if God wasn't interested in their world, in their welfare allowances in their need for good police, if God wasn't interested in such earthly issues, then they just weren't interested in God—He was irrelevant.' But God is relevant; He is concerned about the problems of human life. And it is the personal responsibility of all believers to show this by their own concern. Living the gospel is always more meaningful than merely talking about it.

MATTHEW 22: 11-14

' "Friend," he said to him, "why have you come like this, without wedding clothes?" ' (v. 12, Barclay).

MAKING AN EFFORT. Some scholars have suggested that this is part of a different parable from the one considered above. A guest could hardly be blamed for being incorrectly dressed for a wedding when he had been hurriedly swept in off the street! Whereas the first parable points to men's reluctance to receive God's gracious invitation to life, the second shows how foolish and self-defeating it is to fail to do so. The responsibility to respond to truth is our own. We may refuse or we may accept the truth, for free choice is God's awesome gift to us all.

It is true that many factors shape our lives and the decisions we make—the home into which we were born, the kind of parents we had and so on. But in the context of all this we have a measure of freedom and our choices have eternal significance.

In a sermon on the New Birth, Hugh Montefiore spells out the striking parallels between physical birth and spiritual re-birth and points out the necessity in both for making effort. 'The day we were born,' he says, 'was the day when we had to start to make an effort', observing that if we had not done so we should not have survived. 'It is equally true,' he continues, 'that we should perish in the spiritual life unless we make an effort.' This is the point of the parable. The wedding guest was expelled from the feast because he had failed to make suitable preparation for it. We may ask ourselves: What conscious response are we making to God's gracious approach to us?

MATTHEW 22: 15–22

'This reply staggered them, and they ... let Him alone' (v. 22, J. B. Phillips).

THE QUESTION OF TRIBUTE. The transparent flattery of the Pharisees and Herodians did not deceive Jesus. Had He given a straightforward answer of 'Yes' He would, His questioners felt, lose the sympathy and support of the crowd. If He had answered 'No', they would have a clear case of sedition to bring against Him before the Roman authority. Every patriotic Jew abominated the payment of tribute, the symbol of their subservience to the might of Rome.

Jesus' clever answer must not be taken as meaning that the debt to Caesar was on the same level as a man's obligation to God. A. M. Hunter writes: 'So long as God's rights were safeguarded there was no need to question the rights of Caesar. Civil obedience, attested by the payment of the tax, no more contradicted than it abolished the obedience due to God.'

Caesar required material tribute, and God requires spiritual. Said Erasmus: 'Give back to God that which has the image and superscription of God—the soul.' Later, the situation arose when another Caesar tried to demand what is due only to God, and the Christians clearly were right in refusing such obedience. They faced torture and death rather than be disloyal to their Lord.

'God is not God of the dead but of living men!' (v. 32 J. B. Phillips).

RESTRICTIVE OUTLOOK. The Sadducees regarded the first five books of the Old Testament, the Pentateuch, as the most important part of Scripture; and, as Josephus observed, they believed 'that souls die with the bodies'. Their story of the resurrected woman faced at once with seven living husbands was enough to enliven any debate and even provoke a cheap giggle. Making eternity merely an extension of life as we now experience it frequently has similarly ludicrous results.

Jesus met the Sadducees on their own battle-ground. In their sacred writings God declares Himself 'the God of Abraham, the God of Isaac, and the God of Jacob'. One commentator suggests the translation 'the God to whom Abraham belongs'.

Jesus attacked the Sadducees' limited view of reality. Today, a similarly restrictive outlook is sometimes justified in the name of science—'the new mythology'. Often it is not so much the true scientist, who is all too aware of man's ignorance, as the man with a smattering of scientific knowledge, who claims all mystery is dispelled and spiritual values invalidated.

A. N. Whitehead once remarked that a man may know all about the laws of light and yet, perhaps just because he has learned so much about them, 'miss the radiance of the sunset and the glory of the morning sky'. The spirit of our times constantly tempts us to reduce life's meaning to what can be measured, but 'there are more things in heaven and earth than are dreamt of' in the philosophy of the materialist.

MATTHEW 22: 34-46

'Everything ... hangs on these two commandments' (v. 40, N.E.B.).

'THE GREAT COMMANDMENT.' The Jews certainly needed a system of priorities in regard to the requirements of the Law, for the rabbis sought to impose no less than 613 commandments. Our Lord's two quotations are from Deuteronomy 6: 4, 5 and Leviticus 19: 18. We here see Him distilling all that was essential from the revelation of former days.

We cannot love God with only a part of ourselves, but must be unanimous within—heart, soul, mind and strength must all be fully involved and there is no antithesis between the two commandments. For the believer the love and service of God are the springs from which issue the call to the love and service of men.

And the Christian is not at liberty to withdraw his service of love from anyone on the grounds of race, class, colour or creed. For most Jews the word 'neighbour' would be interpreted as meaning his fellow-Jews, but Jesus made it clear by His parable of the Good Samaritan that it meant anyone in need of loving help, and anyone who responded to the call of human need.

MATTHEW 23: 1–12

'The Scribes and Pharisees speak with the authority of Moses. . . . But you must not imitate their lives! For they preach but do not practise' (vv. 1–3, J. B. Phillips).

SELF-CENTRED RELIGION. 'To call Jesus "Lord" is orthodoxy,' says Leslie Weatherhead, 'and to call Him "Lord, Lord" is piety, but to call Jesus "Lord, Lord" and do not the things that He says is blasphemy!' The Founder of The Salvation Army had such hypocrisy in mind when he wrote: 'There is nothing, I fear, easier of acquisition than the aspirations and the language of devotion while living a life the opposite of all they imply.' This was the sin of the Scribes and Pharisees.

They did the right things for the wrong reason. What they did was often acceptable; why they did it was usually despicable. They said their prayers to attract attention to their piety. Phylacteries were small leather boxes containing parchments of Scripture. They were worn one on the wrist and another on the forehead; and the Pharisees enlarged them to parade their devotion. Jesus condemned such ostentation in the plainest terms.

He judged a deed by its intention. The Pharisees, making religion a matter of outward observance, were wholly concerned with their manner of life; Jesus, stressing the inwardness of religion, was concerned first with motive of life. In consequence, He recognized the Pharisees' religiosity as a sanctimonious expression of their own unyielding self-centredness. But can our motives always bear His scrutiny?

**'But woe unto you, Scribes and Pharisees, hypocrites!'
(v. 13).**

THE MEANING OF CHRIST'S ANGER. Someone has said that the original angry young man was Martin Luther, who wrote in his *Table Talk*: 'I never work better than when I am inspired by anger; when I am angry, I can pray, preach, and write well, for then my whole temperament is quickened, my understanding sharpened and all mundane vexations and temptations depart.' (It need hardly be said that the great reformer knew the difference between righteous indignation and bad temper.) But we can surely say with all reverence that the original angry young man was Luther's Master, Jesus Himself.

His anger was always the expression of loving concern. Jesus spoke out so fiercely because He felt so desperate about rescuing these men enslaved by their own bigotry and self-righteousness. 'The violence of the language of Jesus', says Bishop Stephen Neill, 'is a measure of the unwillingness of those who have become enmeshed in a system to emerge from it and once again to look at the world as it is. He is giving them their last chance, a chance which for the most part they will not take.'

The word translated woe includes in its meaning both wrath and sorrow. And this is the clue to the meaning of Christ's anger. If He spoke sternly it was because He cared so deeply. Looked at in this light, our placidity could be our shame, revealing not God's peace guarding our hearts, but contentment camouflaging our complacency.

MATTHEW 23: 16-22

'Blind fools, which is greater, the gift, or the altar that consecrates the gift?' (v. 19, Knox).

CAN OUR WORD BE TRUSTED? Another reason for Jesus' anger was the basic deceitfulness of these pious pretenders. An oath was utterly binding, they believed, if it incorporated the name of God, for this made Him a partner of the promise, and to break it was to insult Him.

So these master-minds of evasion worked out a technique of respectable release from their obligation. To swear by the Temple, they said, was nothing, but to swear by the gold of the Temple was everything; to vow by the altar was not binding, but to vow by the gift on the altar was for ever binding. (Jesus was possibly criticizing their attitude rather than saying that this was what they actually did.) One conclusion emerges for our unhurried consideration.

It is possible to be secretly disloyal to a promise and yet give the opposite impression. Our promises are sometimes spoken so cheaply; but having committed ourselves, we then search for ways of saving face without keeping our word. We justify, excuse and explain to hide from ourselves and others that our promises are worthless.

A Christian's word should be his bond. Though the sky fall, he should mean what he says and be loyal to it. The Pharisees, forgetting that God was aware of their every word and secret intention, self-righteously justified their broken promises and unfulfilled obligations. But are we entirely free of this tendency about which Christ was so angry?

MATTHEW 23: 23, 24

'Woe unto you, you impious Scribes and Pharisees. ... Blind guides that you are' (vv. 23, 24, Moffatt).

IRRELIGIOUS RELIGION. Main crops were of course tithed, a tenth being laid aside as an offering to God. But mint, dill and cummin were herbs of the kitchen garden, and to tithe them was to deal in terribly small quantities. Yet the Pharisees painstakingly tithed every single plant, and conveniently overlooked more important matters. Jesus summed them up as being like men who, anxious to keep their food clean, strained out a gnat, but cheerfully swallowed a camel. This outlook by no means belongs only to the past.

The Pharisees mistook religious practices for real devotion. Have we not known people who kept all the rules, whose habits were faultless, and yet whose 'sanctity' was cold and unattractive? They lacked a sense of the significant, giving priority to trivialities, putting procedure before people, and conformity before compassion. Their religion was all law and no grace.

The Pharisees illustrate how easy it is to perform religious activities and yet be irreligious through a twisted sense of values. The Christian is not better when he is pious at his place of worship, but moody at home; conscientiously supports the Lord's work, but gives less than his best at work; shuns every appearance of evil, but never goes the 'second mile'; thinks more of his reputation than his righteousness; considers himself good merely because he is not bad. Let us remember that Jesus was angry because reputedly religious men made the wrong emphasis!

'What miserable frauds you are, you Scribes and Pharisees' (v. 29, J. B. Phillips).

STUDIED PRETENCE. It was Lord Cardigan who took his yacht to the Crimean War, though he knew absolutely nothing about yachting. When his skipper asked him, 'Will you take the helm, my lord?' he replied, 'No, thank you. I never take anything between meals.' Yet Lord Cardigan owned the yacht and looked like a sailor! This false impression, however, was not intended.

Jesus 'wiped the floor' with the Pharisees because of their studied pretence. They deliberately gave the impression of being devoutly religious, but their hearts, known to the insight of Jesus, denied this appearance of righteousness. His blistering denunciation is the measure of His hatred of humbug. Now before we feel superior in our freedom from this hypocrisy, let us ask ourselves a couple of questions. Are our actions never governed by what people will think of us? Is there never any inconsistency between what we say and what we secretly think?

The Pharisees had greater regard for men's praise than for God's approval. They wanted more to be thought righteous than to be righteous; hence their preoccupation with the impressions they were creating. We can do no better today than to ask God to deliver us, or to keep us, from this 'respectable' yet terrible failing.

> Be what thou seemest, live thy creed,
> Hold up to earth the torch divine.
> Be what thou prayest to be made;
> Let the great Master's steps be thine.

'Ye serpents, ye offspring of vipers, how shall ye escape the judgment of Hell?' (v. 33, R.V.).

RELIGIOUS SELF-DECEIT. There is a drawing of William Blake's in which a little man, standing at the foot of a ladder that reaches to the moon, cries, 'I want, I want.' The artist intended the drawing as a comment upon human nature. No matter how many wants are supplied, man still cries 'I want.'

This 'I want' complex expresses itself in all manner of ways. It caused the prophets of God to be put to death by supposedly religious men; it caused the descendants of these misguided fanatics to build tombs to the revered memory of the martyrs and yet at the same time to persecute the prophets of their own generations. Why? Because the 'I want' outlook is made no less self-centred and bigoted and evil by being dressed up in religious garments.

Jesus was angry with the reputedly devout men of His day because they refused to see that their religious zeal, like their religious history, was an expression of pious selfishness, the worst of all sins. 'The zeal of many a reformer,' wrote Nels Ferré in *Strengthening the Spiritual Life*, 'is disguised atheism.' Such zealots allow their particular activity to take the place of God in their thoughts and affections; and their religious fanaticism increasingly becomes unrealized self-assertiveness. No wonder Jesus did not mince His words, for how else could such self-deceivers be delivered from the blindness of their 'religion'.

MATTHEW 23: 37–39

'How often have I longed to gather your children, as a hen gathers her brood under her wings; but you would not let Me' (v. 37, N.E.B.).

THE CURE OF UNREALITY. On several occasions we have noted this gospel-writer's orderly arrangement of material. The first block of teaching, the 'sermon on the mount', commences with the beatitudes; by contrast, this last section opens with seven 'woes' pronounced upon the scribes and Pharisees. These have not been treated in detail in these readings which have focused upon that external fastidiousness and passion for inessentials by which men attempt to compensate for inner unreality.

The 'woes' contain no element of vindictiveness, and lead up to a moving lament. Indeed, the nation's only hope of cleansing from unreality would have been in responding to the love throbbing through this appeal. Love-inspired religion alone is free from exhibitionism, unreality and compensatory harshness. We cannot produce this love; it is aroused when we recognize we are loved.

God's love is usually portrayed in terms of His Fatherhood. Here Jesus deliberately chooses the maternal protectiveness of the hen as a model of His care. Parental love in its fullness must be seen in terms of both fatherhood and motherhood; therefore both are essential to a complete portrait of the divine compassion. E. N. Ducker has commented: 'A fundamental need of man is to feel secure, and the only abiding security is that of the "Everlasting Arms" and the divine promise to be with us always ... It is through a sense of relatedness at this deepest level that we shall draw closest to the perfect wholeness.'

MATTHEW 24: 1–14

'Take care that you do not allow anyone to deceive you' (v. 4, Knox).

ENDURING TO THE END. Chapters 24 and 25 contain Jesus' teaching about the future. As in the Sermon on the Mount Matthew brought together our Lord's moral message, so here he assembles all the various strands of His eschatological message. This sometimes makes interpretation difficult, for we may not always be sure whether Jesus was referring to what would happen immediately following His death, the overthrow of the nation and destruction of Jerusalem that took place forty years later, or the ultimate end of all things.

Undoubtedly the Early Church expected our Lord to return to earth almost immediately, which is rather surprising seeing He uttered a solemn warning against false alarms. (Verses 4 to 6, concluding with the words, 'but the end is not yet'.) He also declared that He did not Himself know when the end would be (v. 36), but taught that the gospel must be preached to all nations (v. 14) which seems to push the final consummation well into the future. Yet in every generation of Christians since the first there have been sincere people anxious to fix the date and settle all the details concerning the Second Coming.

Catherine Booth had little patience with those whose religion was theoretic and impractical. She wrote to T. A. Denny:

'And now there are thousands talking about His 'second coming' who will neither see nor receive Him in the person of His humble and persecuted followers. Christ manifested in flesh, vulgar flesh, they cannot receive. No, they are looking for Him in the clouds!

Oh, for grace always to see Him where He is to be seen, for, verily, flesh and blood doth not reveal this unto us! Well, bless the Lord, I keep seeing Him risen again in the forms of drunkards and ruffians of all descriptions.'

The note of urgency in the proclamation of the truth should not be dependent upon the end being imminent. The only certainty for each of us is death; we are living all the time in our own 'last days'. We have the obligation by word and by life to speed the gospel of light, for wherever we live we are in contact with 'pockets', if not 'realms', of darkness. 'Life is real, life is earnest'— and only those who endure are finally saved.

MATTHEW 24: 15-28

'Signs and wonders to mislead ... even God's own people. Listen, I am warning you' (v. 24, J. B. Phillips).

PASSING TRIALS AND THE LAST. Verses 15 to 22 refer to the horrors of the Jewish War and the siege of Jerusalem of A.D. 66–70. Verses 23 to 26 refer to those various threats to the faith which are a constant part of Christian history. Verses 27 and 28 seem to refer to the final consummation.

'The abomination of desolation' refers to Daniel 9: 27, 11: 31 and 12: 11, where the reference is to the desecration of the Jerusalem Temple by Antiochus Epiphanes in B.C. 168. Actually, in A.D. 40, the mad Emperor Caligula tried, unsuccessfully, to repeat this sacrilege, and very soon Christian believers were confronted with the challenge of worshipping the Roman Emperor or taking the consequences.

The main lesson of the passage, however, is that we must never identify one period of trial, however grave, with the final crisis and the end of the world. This has always been a temptation for Christian people, and every period of special suffering and trial has been marked by a recurrence of 'eschatological expectation'.

The final climax of history, the one that will open out into eternity, must be quite impossible for us to imagine. When it comes, however, it will be quite unmistakable, and recognizable over all the earth. Meanwhile, we must daily live to the glory of God.

MATTHEW 24: 29-41

'No one knows, however, when that day and hour will come ... the Father alone knows' (v. 36, Good News for Modern Man).

THE ULTIMATE DAY. Clearly this is a difficult passage of Scripture. It is necessary to make verse 34 apply to our Lord's predictions concerning Jerusalem, for these words cannot be associated with the Second Coming. The Kingdom of God was initiated by the Cross and Resurrection; the Church of Christ was created by the Holy Spirit on the day of Pentecost; and before the generation that knew Jesus Christ in the flesh had passed away, Jerusalem was destroyed and the Jewish nation crumbled.

But much in today's reading undoubtedly refers to the end of the world, an event the date of which is known only to God the Father. Reference is made to the days preceding the flood (vv. 37–39).

There is nothing wrong 'in eating and drinking, marrying and giving in marriage'; those are common activities of life. But there is everything wrong in being so absorbed in the things of everyday life that God and His claims are left out.

This may be God's word to us today. Are we so preoccupied with the material—which is the temporal—that the spiritual— which is the eternal—is undervalued? How foolish it is in life to concentrate on those things we must leave behind, when we can begin to live by Kingdom values and thereby 'lay up treasure in Heaven'!

MATTHEW 24: 42–51

'What sort of servant, then, is faithful and wise enough for the master to place him over his household to give them their food at the proper time?' (v. 45, Jerusalem Bible).

CHRISTIAN RESPONSIBILITY. We have noted that Christ's parables, in common with all artistic creations, have additional meanings to those first intended; yet we must always begin by inquiring what they meant when originally spoken. The author of this Gospel, writing at a time when some believers were asking why Christ had not already returned, has grouped together several parables which answered their questions. The servant left in charge of his master's affairs must not spend each day scanning the road; he must faithfully get on with his duties.

For us today, this group of parables conveys other messages as well. So with the parable of 'The Trusty Servant': it refers not only to temptations arising from the master's delayed return; it stirs the conscience of any bearer of responsibility 'not hardened against self-examination'.

Christian responsibility includes responsibility for what we make of ourselves as well as how we act towards our family, community and, as far as possible, the wider family of mankind. Some claim that modern psychology has diminished responsibility now that we recognize how often people are impelled by unconscious drives. Yet this same discovery increases responsibility in another direction. It underlines the need seriously to undertake the life-long task of self-understanding, for this brings increased freedom to fulfil well all our other responsibilities. This does not call for continual introspection, but for honest and regular self-examination carried through with the assurance of God's unfailing love.

MATTHEW 25: 1-1

'At midnight a cry was heard, "Here is the bridegroom! Come out to meet him" ' (v. 6, N.E.B.).

WHAT CANNOT BE BORROWED. Today's parable is often considered to relate only to the Second Coming of Christ, but it is by no means certain that this is the only meaning of the story. In its immediate application it highlighted the unpreparedness of the Jews who, though the Chosen People, were unready to receive Christ when He came. Wrote John, 'He entered His own realm, and His own would not receive Him' (John 1: 11, N.E.B.). But the parable also has a wider application. It underlines the necessity for the individual to be spiritually prepared for life as it unfolds.

The point is that there are some things, particularly in the realm of character, that cannot be borrowed at 'the last moment'. Hugh Martin makes this perceptive comment: 'You cannot borrow another's Christian character; you must grow your own. You cannot improvise a strong will. It is true in the physical realm. If a misused and unhealthy body has to meet a sudden assault of disease it may be too late then to work to create a sound constitution. The penalty for past thoughtlessness may be fatal, however eager friends and doctors may be to help. A serene faith in immortality cannot be suddenly acquired when death visits your home. It has its roots in an established and tested faith in the love of God. The sudden midnight cry reveals the personality that the past years have been building.'

MATTHEW 25: 14-30

'He gave one five thousand pounds, another two thousand and another one thousand—according to their respective abilities' (v. 15, J. B. Phillips).

FACING FACTS ABOUT OURSELVES. It is the responsibility of every Christian to learn to accept other people as they are, with their limitations and foibles. It is no less important that a man learn to accept himself. Of course, self-acceptance may be nothing more than laziness; unwillingness to make an effort at effecting a remedy in circumstance, character and conduct. When improvements can be made it is plainly our duty to make them. But where there are personal limitations about which nothing can be done, the fact should be honestly faced. When we realize that our youthful dreams are not to materialize, it is of little use our sitting down to lament the way life has treated us. We have to accept the situation as it is and do with it what we may.

Too often people who feel they have 'missed out' in some way fail to take advantage of what they have, which may be considerably more than, in their self-pity, they have realized. The one-talent man in Jesus' parable is true to life. He mistrusted himself, developed an inferiority complex and did nothing at all with what he possessed. This is the trap in which one-talent people are often caught.

Writes William Barclay: 'God never demands from a man abilities which he has not got: but God does demand from a man that he should use to the full the abilities he does possess. Men are not equal in talent; but men can be equal in effort.' For our encouragement (are not most of us just ordinary folk?) Jesus taught that we shall not be blamed for having only one talent, but we shall be judged by how we use it.

MATTHEW 25: 31-40

'Anything you did for one of my brothers, here, however humble, you did for Me' (v. 40, N.E.B.).

CHRIST'S VERDICT. This drama has political as well as personal implications. It is 'the nations' which appear before the Son of Man and many scholars regard this parable as Christ's 'final verdict on international history'. One interpretation is that the needy, whom the king calls 'my brothers', are the Jews. Gentile nations will be judged by their treatment of the wandering

Jew. Certainly Jesus realized the terrible fate awaiting His nation (Luke 23: 28ff).

A wider interpretation is possible, however, for the Old Testament teaches that God makes the cause of the afflicted His own (Isa. 63: 9; Psalm 74: 22; Prov. 19: 17). When nations, or for that matter the Church, neglect the needy they come under His judgment. Barbara Ward writes, 'In Christianity the man who loves his neighbour is quite simply the man who feeds him, shelters him, clothes him and heals him. It is all very direct and physical and lacking in "spiritual" overtones. Yet the food given to the least of the little ones is given to God Himself. One can therefore understand why Marx in the England of the 1840s—where children still laboured sixteen hours a day and died at their looms—failed to see much connexion between contemporary religion and social justice and constructed instead his own secular version of Christianity's Messianic dream.' When Christians are untrue to their calling, the initiative passes into other hands.

We have little power to influence the policies of nations, but Christian integrity demands that we use our vote, not to safeguard our own interests, but in the interests of mankind. We should also compare our spending on luxuries with the extent of our practical concern for the hungry millions. As Nicolas Berdyaev has well said, 'Bread for myself is a material problem; bread for other people is a spiritual problem'.

MATTHEW 25: 41–46

'Believe Me, when you refused it to one of the least of My brethren here, you refused it to Me' (v. 45, Knox).

JUDGMENT NOW. We have seen that this parable portrays God's verdict on the nations. Consequently a Christian's political action, whether as a voter or a politician, must recognize this standard of judgment. But we cannot escape the more personal challenge of the story. Christ Himself confronts us in our fellows. Two important truths follow from this.

We come closer to Christ as we get closer to people—especially those in need. Describing Dick Sheppard's early development his biographer inquires where and how Dick acquired his deep personal love for Christ. He never had a conversion experience which he could pin-point in time. But, writes R. Ellis Roberts, 'as he read the Gospels and as he worked among the poor in the East End, he was seized with an ardent love for them, a passionate desire to help them, and he recognized that this desire in him was reflected from his own conviction of the love of Jesus for them and for him. Quite simply he found Christ in the poor and dispossessed.'

Judgment is a continuous process. Read this parable alongside the story of the Good Samaritan. Obviously the separation which the Son of Man makes explicit at the last judgment actually occurs much earlier. The Priest, the Levite and the Samaritan passed judgment upon themselves by their response to the roadside victim. Our response to others reveals our characters, and each response we make either increases or diminishes our sensitivity to human need. This is judgment indeed.

MATTHEW 26: 1–13

'Jesus knew what they were saying and spoke to them: "Why must you make this woman feel uncomfortable? She has done a beautiful thing for Me"' (v. 10, J. B. Phillips).

PERSONAL CONVICTION. This chapter begins the last section of the Gospel, and in a book containing a great deal of teaching there are only fourteen occasions in these chapters in which Jesus speaks, usually quite briefly. Action increasingly takes the place of speaking as the Teacher ratifies His own teaching and reveals Himself as more than a teacher.

Anointing was performed for the dead; anointing on the head was a sign of kingship. Did a woman's intuition see in the eyes of Christ the sovereignty and the costliness of self-giving love? If so, she shared with Him a secret hidden from the rest of the company.

Religious communication is usually at this personal level. Its truth is validated in community but conviction is strongest when its reception is most personal. Viktor Frankl, a psychiatrist, writes of a desolate moment which became for him the occasion of personal conviction and truth. With fellow-prisoners he was digging a trench, inwardly struggling to find a reason for his suffering. 'In a last violent protest against the hopelessness of imminent death, I sensed my spirit piercing through the enveloping gloom. I felt it transcend that hopeless, meaningless world, and from somewhere I heard a victorious "Yes" in answer to my question of the existence of an ultimate purpose. At that moment a light was lit in a distant farmhouse, which stood on the horizon as if painted there, in the

midst of the miserable grey of a dawning morning in Bavaria . . .
and the light shineth in the darkness.'

'The Master says: "My time is near. It is at your house
that I am keeping the Passover with My disciples" ' (v. 18,
Jerusalem Bible).

MAN'S BASENESS AND GOD'S PLAN. Perhaps the most
startling, yet the most significant juxtaposition in this passage is
the scheming treachery of Judas and the calm announcement of
the Master, 'My appointed time is near' (v. 18, N.E.B.). How can
man's baseness provide material for the divine purpose? The
Passion of Christ, by proving this can be so, becomes the supreme
illustration of how evil is transcended and even used for good.

The betrayal of Jesus by Judas, 'one of the twelve', was and
always will be a mystery. The gospel-writer saw avarice as his
downfall. Recent commentators tend to look for a more complex
motive, and his suicide would tend to support them.

The miracle is that the treachery of Judas signals for Jesus the
approach of His 'appointed time', that it is woven into the plan of
redemption, that in consequence we need never cease to hope that
evil may be turned to good.

One way this occurs was described by Albert Schweitzer when
he described the fellowship of those who bear the Mark of Pain.
'He who has been delivered from pain must not think he is now
free again, and at liberty to take up life just as it was before, entirely forgetful of the past. He is now a "man whose eyes are
open" with regard to pain and anguish, and he must help to
overcome those two enemies (so far as human power can control
them) and to bring to others the deliverance which he has himself
enjoyed.'

'Drink of it, all of you; this means My blood, the new
covenant-blood, shed for many, to win the remission of
their sins' (v. 28, Moffatt).

HIS SACRIFICE—OUR SHARING. From this event upon
which Christian devotion has focused for centuries we have space
to emphasize just two themes. Jesus' identification of the bread
and the wine of the Passover meal with His body and shed blood

D

clearly shows how He viewed His imminent death: it was to be a sacrifice by which God and man would be joined in a new relationship. 'For many' is a Semitic way of saying 'for everybody'.

Even under the old covenant the outpoured blood of the sacrifice was not offered in place of any offering the worshipper could make, but as representing the outpoured life which the worshipper desired to present to God. So the bread and the wine was given to His disciples. Christ offered a perfect obedience to God, even to death. He called His disciples, as He calls us, progressively to receive His life and so identify ourselves with His offering.

This sharing and identification is made by some Christians in the service of holy communion. Salvationists, together with the Society of Friends, witness that this reality does not depend upon visible symbols. So the Quaker Isaac Penington wrote from Aylesbury Gaol in 1667, 'O abide in the simplicity that is in Christ, in the naked truth that ye have felt there, and there ye will be able to know and distinguish your food, which hath several names in Scripture, but is all one and the same thing—the bread, the milk, the water, the wine, the flesh and blood of Him that came down from heaven.'

MATTHEW 26: 30–35

'Peter said, "Even if I must die with You, I will never disown You" ' (v. 35, N.E.B.).

VULNERABLE IN SELF-IGNORANCE. Warning His disciples of the coming crisis, Jesus speaks of both disaster and then hope. 'I will go before you' may mean 'I will lead you on, like a shepherd'. So the stricken Shepherd is to continue His shepherding; the flock will not be ultimately abandoned.

Peter's false confidence was the measure of his self-ignorance, and equally the measure of his vulnerability. Those aspects of our personalities which we refuse to recognize always pose the greatest threat to our integrity. These notes frequently comment on the need for self-knowledge. Religious people particularly are tempted to ignore this task, for it requires us to recognize some far from comforting facts about ourselves. But if we ignore what has been called the 'shadow' side of our character it will play some unpleasant tricks. As one commentator remarks, Peter was 'foremost in speech, he is also to be foremost in failure'.

The need to know ourselves, while stressed by modern psychology, was equally a theme for the older spiritual guides. The eighteenth-century Jesuit, John Nicholas Grou, claimed that conversion was usually followed by a period of pure peace and joy. But as soon as God is certain of a man, 'immediately He begins to enlighten him as to his defects; He raises by degrees the veil which concealed them from him, and He inspires him with a firm will to overcome them ... God shows him all this gradually; for if He were to show it to him all at once he could not bear it, and would fall into despair ... If a man is courageous and faithful, what does he do then? He humbles himself, without despairing; he places all his confidence in God.'

MATTHEW 26: 36–46

'Anguish and dismay came over Him, and He said to them, "My heart is ready to break with grief. Stop here, and stay awake with Me" ' (vv. 37 and 38, N.E.B.).

ENGULFING LOVE. Writing to his family, after his sister had been stricken with a serious and ultimately fatal illness, Teilhard de Chardin said, 'You must find strength in the thought that suffering accepted in the right spirit has the most valuable, the most lasting and the happiest results ... It's hard: but God knows how hard.' The truth contained in those last five words, portrayed for the Christian in the story of Christ's Passion, has comforted believers for nearly two thousand years.

The Gospel records suggest that the spiritual agony of Gethsemane equalled the physical suffering of Calvary. 'My soul is very sorrowful, even to death', implies an abyss of anguish we can barely glimpse. Yet what strength is brought to us when we face even lesser calvaries by the fact that Christ refused the way of escape.

'Too often in the past', writes Harry Williams, 'God and religion have been presented as pain-killers, as though God were a magician who will melt our troubles away like snow in the sun, giving us a divine relief from the hard facts of the real world. But God is not a funk-hole, however much Christians may have tried to use Him as one. And this is what Jesus understood when to His natural request for relief He added, "If it be possible".'

Jesus took with Him to the scene of His agony the same three disciples who saw Him transfigured. He wanted them to know that suffering and glory can be one.

'At this point all the disciples deserted Him and made their escape' (v. 56, J. B. Phillips).

THE LONELY CHRIST. The story of Christ's Passion is harrowing in its record of increasing isolation. In Gethsemane the disciples were near, even though asleep. Yet after a mistaken but brave scuffle in defence of their Master—made, as the fourth Gospel tells us, by Peter—there is a panic desertion. From this point Christ's loneliness becomes ever more acute until from a gaunt Cross there echoes into an empty sky the cry of ultimate desolation.

Karl Rahner has suggested that the Christian confession of God is especially difficult 'at that point where we are supposed to find God in the dark bitterness of the world and in the obscurity of the future, while addressing Him as "Father" with a feeling of security against all insecurity'. Certainly Christ has trodden this almost impossible path before us. Even at the point of arrest He still speaks of God as 'My Father'.

The loneliness of Christ contains no trace of aloofness, indifference or resentment. So happy at a party that He scandalized the Pharisees, so human in His need of friends that He affectionately tells His disciples, 'You are they who continued with Me in My temptations', He now takes a path which will bewilder and offend His dearest friends (v. 31). Why? Because it is a greater, not a lesser, love which dares not tamper with the highest loyalty of all—man's loyalty to God. H. H. Farmer has commented: 'When love is crying out for fellowship it is the hardest thing in the world deliberately to pursue a course which you know will for the time being destroy it. Yet sometimes it is necessary. For a love which is not loyal to the truth, which is not rooted and grounded in the ultimate reality of things, is a perverted and horribly insecure thing.'

'The men who had seized Jesus took Him off to Caiaphas the High Priest in whose house the scribes and elders were assembled' (v. 57, J. B. Phillips).

THE POISON OF CYNICISM. Of the varied examples of human folly and weakness which contributed to the sufferings of Christ, Caiaphas was the real villain of the piece. Others were tripped up or trapped by their fear, ignorance and prejudice. This man pursued Jesus with implacable hatred and relentless cunning. A member of the religious aristocracy, he was incensed by what he considered the pretentiousness of a village carpenter who attacked the temple profiteering which made him rich.

The crowning vice of Caiaphas was his cynicism. The depths of illegality and cunning to which the High Priest, God's representative to His people, could stoop were possible only to one from whom all idealism had flown.

What makes a man cynical? We need to ask this, for we live in a culture which has deep seams of pessimism running through it. Brecht's lines are typical:

> Praised be the chill, the darkness and the doom.
> Look up and see!
> You do not count,
> and you can die without worrying.

Pessimism is not necessarily cynical but it easily becomes so. The cynic is often a man who has made the wrong reaction to suffering, who has projected his own darkness outwards so that life itself is hateful and all goodness 'too good to be true'. If one of the main themes of the Passion story is that of evil transformed into good, Caiaphas is a warning that goodness may be poisoned by evil.

MATTHEW 26: 69–75

'A maidservant came up to him and said, "Weren't you with Jesus, the Man from Galilee?" But he denied it before them all' (vv. 69 and 70, J. B. Phillips).

GRACE ABOUNDING. Cyril Smith, the famous concert pianist, describes a visit to Liverpool to make a recording of Dohnanyi's *Variations on a Nursery Theme*. The recording company had gone to great expense in hiring Sir Malcolm Sargent, an orchestra and suitable hall. Cyril Smith's own part at the beginning of the piece was almost ridiculously easy. After four minutes of heavy, ponderous orchestral music the pianist comes in to play a one-finger air. His humiliation could hardly have been greater when, after playing three simple notes, he made a ghastly error.

How typical of life that the simplest tests are often the ones we fail! We have already seen that Peter possessed a tragic blind spot regarding his own nature. In his favour we recall his defence of his Master in the garden, and his position in the place of greatest danger. He alone seems to have penetrated right into the enemies' camp. He acted with great courage, until a servant girl jeered.

The writer of the first Gospel significantly adds to Mark's account that Peter denied his Lord 'before them all'. So careful a writer could not have forgotten that some sixteen chapters earlier he had recorded the words 'Whoever denies Me before men, I also will deny in heaven' (10: 33). The implication is clear: 'Even the words of Jesus must not be used to limit God's grace' (J. C. Fenton). Peter's penitence opened the way to pardon, as penitence always does.

MATTHEW 27: 3–10

' "I have sinned," he said, "I have betrayed innocent blood" ' (v. 4, Jerusalem Bible).

REPENTANCE AND REMORSE. The failure of both Peter and Judas was alike deplorable, but we are surely right in seeing in the betrayal by the latter a dimension of transgression quite foreign to the denials of the former. For one thing, Peter's denials were occasioned by his circumstances, being a kind of defence reaction. Judas, on the other hand, took the initiative himself, made his bargain with the chief priests, disclosed our Lord's whereabouts and even led His enemies to the spot.

Here are these two men, each of whom had sinned grievously and was swept by a storm of grief. It has been well said that in the case of Peter, grief took the form of genuine repentance. In the case of Judas, after one abortive attempt to ease his conscience by returning the money (v. 5) his grief led him to suicide. The first, certainly at any rate from the moment that the Lord 'turned and looked upon' him (Luke 22: 61), knew his Master well enough to be assured of forgiveness. The second, though he had companied long with Him, saw no hope of forgiveness and took his life into his own hands instead of committing it to Jesus, even at the end.

MATTHEW 27: 1, 2, 11–18

'The Governor asked Him, "Are You the King of the Jews?" "The words are yours", said Jesus' (vv. 11 and 12, N.E.B.).

YES AND NO. One common failing is not to recognize the

limitations of language. The word 'let', for instance, has reversed its meaning since Shakespeare's day. When Hamlet, chasing his father's ghost, says 'I'll slay the man that lets me!' he means he will kill whoever tries to stop him. Even more confusing is the situation when the same word has contrary meanings at the same time.

When Pilate asked Jesus, 'Are You the King of the Jews?' the question was almost impossible to answer. The word king meant two quite different things to Pilate and Jesus. To one it spoke of a worldly throne, honours and the use of force; to the other it indicated a Cross, ignominy and the conquest of men's hearts by love.

Even today, we need to question our use of this title. Colin Alves describes a visit of the British monarch to his town at a time when he was entertaining Swedish guests. 'They were astonished to learn that this was the first occasion on which any member of our family had ever had an opportunity even to see the Queen in person. For them, living in Stockholm, the situation was that they might find themselves one day talking to their King in a shop, or on the street, possibly without recognizing him.'

When we speak of the kingship of Christ, even that which He will exercise when 'every knee shall bow', we must be careful to discard every association incompatible with the Cross.

MATTHEW 27: 19–26

'Now as he was seated in the chair of judgment, his wife sent him a message, "Have nothing to do with that Man; I have been upset all day by a dream I had about Him" ' (v. 19, Jerusalem Bible).

A MAN AND HIS WIFE. Two minor incidents, both of them recorded only in this Gospel, now occupy our attention the warning dream of Pilate's wife and the Governor's pathetic attempt to exonerate himself from blame for the death of Jesus by publicly washing his hands.

A century ago some sophisticated people raised their eyebrows at Bible stories in which guidance came via dreams and John Sanford even now calls dreams 'God's Forgotten Language' in a book by that name. We now know that dreams are not the nonsense they appear; they frequently contain truths we have 'forgotten' or banished from consciousness. One psychotherapist, while recognizing that dream analysis is specialists' work, suggests we should 'befriend' our remembered dreams, turning them over in our minds for a while, recalling their mood, remembering they are an aspect of our personalities calling for attention. Pilate's wife, perhaps consciously most unwilling to question her husband's judgment, yet saw in her dream his danger of making a terrible compromise.

Pilate's attempt to evade responsibility for the death sentence he alone could impose was crude and ineffectual. Contrast with him the character of Franz Jäggerstatter, the Austrian peasant who was martyred for refusing to fight in Hitler's war. Even when the prison chaplain tried to dissuade Franz from his course of action, saying the Church would need men like him after the war, his reply was, 'I cannot turn the responsibility for my actions over to the Führer'.

MATTHEW 27: 27–32

'Then the governor's soldiers took Jesus into the governor's palace and collected the whole guard around Him' (v. 27, J. B. Phillips).

INTO THE HANDS OF MEN. On Roman coins of the first century the emperor is shown wearing a crown of radiant spikes and holding a staff or sceptre in his right hand. It was this the soldiers sought to parody as they took their fill of crude fun at the expense of their Prisoner. Not only was this mockery an ironic reflection of a Kingship they never glimpsed; it symbolized the truth that, in one sense, God does hand Himself over into the hands of men.

Dorothee Sölle, a lecturer in the university of Cologne, claims that the atheism of modern times has drawn its strength, not from the wells of scientific rationalism, but from the pain and suffering endured by the innocent. 'In all religions, a question mark has been set against the omnipotent and serene gods by the sufferings of men. But only in Christ does the concept of a suffering God appear.'

In Stanley Spencer's painting, *Christ Carrying the Cross*, now in the Tate Gallery, London, most of the onlookers are people who lived with the artist in the village of Cookham. The procession itself is placed in the village, not Jerusalem. 'The King of the World passes on His way to death,' comments Maurice Collis, the artist's biographer. 'What an event that He should pass through Cookham!'

The Christian believes in no spectator god, but a God who willingly places Himself in our hands today, and who passes along our road bearing His Cross.

MATTHEW 27: 33–54

'**The chief priests with the lawyers and elders mocked at Him: "He saved others," they said, "but He cannot save Himself . . . Let Him come down now from the cross, and then we will believe Him"** ' (vv. 41 and 42, N.E.B.).

NOT SPARING HIMSELF. Jesus' cry of lonely desolation seemed to some onlookers addressed to Elijah. Strangely enough, this prophet too had the struggle of a life-time on a hilltop. Elijah had taunted the false prophets with the silence and inaction of their god, the implication being that he was no god (1 Kings 18: 27). 'The crowd on the hill of Calvary also taunts Christ and the same implication is there, only the roles are reversed. Now it appears that it is the solitary prophet whose god is failing, and the crowd see themselves as on the side of Elijah' (Malcolm France).

God's refusal to rescue His Son, the Christian believes, was not due to impotence. 'God was in Christ, reconciling the world to Himself' (2 Cor. 5: 19). Here we see God taking upon Himself, not for a few brief agonizing hours, but for all time, the sins and sorrows of humanity. Sydney Carter, in his song *Friday Morning*, imagines one of the two thieves addressing Jesus:

> Now Barabbas was a killer
> And they let Barabbas go.
> But you are being crucified
> For nothing, here below.
> But God is up in heaven
> And he doesn't do a thing:
> With a million angels watching,
> And they never move a wing.
> It's God they ought to crucify
> Instead of you and me,
> I said to the carpenter
> A-hanging on the tree.

If Jesus had been spared the ultimate desolation God would have spared Himself. We could not then believe in a God who goes to all lengths, taking on Himself the responsibility for His own erring creation. As it is, we call even this Friday good. As William Booth remarked: 'They would have believed if He had come down. We believe because He stayed up.'

MATTHEW 27: 55-66

'They went and made the grave secure, putting a seal on the stone and leaving the soldiers on guard' (v. 66, J. B. Phillips).

UNCONSCIOUS TRIBUTE. In this pause between Good Friday and Easter we may usefully remind ourselves of a truth brought out in an interview between Kenneth Harris and Dr. Geoffrey Fisher, then Archbishop of Canterbury. Harris had asked whether the church's teaching about the Crucifixion and Resurrection was an obstacle to some people. Dr. Fisher replied, 'Oddly enough, all the Church teaches formally about the Crucifixion and Resurrection is that they happened, and that they happened "for us men".' Although volumes have been written, and millions of words spoken, about these two tremendous events the Church has been wisely guided never to limit their meaning. In different ages of history, and at different periods in our own lives, they fully meet human need. We can never exhaust their significance, and for this we are profoundly grateful.

The meticulous precautions of the sealed tomb and the guard seem at once ludicrous and significant. Surely the religious leaders were not seriously disturbed by what this group of Jesus' disciples, who disappeared so conveniently on the night of their Master's arrest, could accomplish. Was their action rather an unconscious tribute to the impression Christ had made of possessing life indestructible? This abundant life is what the world looks to the Church to exhibit, and our only chance of meeting this expectation is by our communion with the Risen Christ.

MATTHEW 28: 1-10

'Quite suddenly, Jesus stood before them in their path, and said, "Peace be with you!"' (v. 9, J. B. Phillips).

AN ABIDING PRESENCE. The Resurrection of Christ is no mere appendage to the main body of Christian faith, any more than it was just a 'turning of the tables' on those who put Jesus to death. Resurrection was expected only at the end of time. 'The truth that left human minds dazed and human spirits reeling is precisely and exactly this: that the Last Day at the end of history had taken shape on the third day in the midst of history' (Neville Clark). In other words, a new age had begun and we now live in that new age. Death, history, and the future could never again be regarded in the same way by believers in Christ. This shattering conquest of evil holds the promise of ultimate and final victory.

At the beginning, as now, the Resurrection came with particular comfort and meaning to different individuals. Mary of Magdala, for instance, may have been the kind of person who clings compulsively to others because in herself she lacked any sense of personal reality. Andrew Todd suggested that she found in Jesus what all such sufferers are seeking, a Person truly loving and utterly reliable. The Resurrection would at first seem to her simply to reverse the catastrophe of Good Friday. She clings ecstatically to Risen Jesus (v. 9; John 20: 17). But Christ sends her away on a mission, and in the coming days she is to learn that the Resurrection means an abiding spiritual Presence of which nothing can ever again rob her.

MATTHEW 28: 11-15

'The chief priests offered the soldiers a substantial bribe and told them to say, "His disciples came by night and stole the body while we were asleep"' (vv. 12 and 13, N.E.B.).

FIRST OF MANY. About any event which men have continued denying for nineteen centuries we should doubt their denials! Most attempted 'explanations' of the Resurrection by unbelievers strain credulity more than the Christian belief that Christ was raised by God from the dead. So with this first attempt to 'hush up' the gospel: that men would be prepared to die, as the disciples were, just for a hoax is simply too much to believe. Yet to prove how unlikely are the alternatives is not the same as producing faith.

Sometimes, before faith can become real, a whole false view of the universe must be shattered. Writing for his agnostic friends, Nathaniel Micklem, one time Principal of Mansfield College, Oxford, tells the story of the person who being suddenly confronted by a giraffe declared categorically that no such beast existed. Many today hold a narrow materialist view of the universe which makes belief in the Resurrection impossible; yet their view, if logically carried through, also excludes the reality of many spiritual values they refuse to abandon. 'It might be true that Jesus is alive and His presence is felt by men today,' continues Dr. Micklem, 'and the agnostic might find it to be true if with an open mind and a willingness to be persuaded he attended High Mass or went into the slums with The Salvation Army. Much irreligion (but not all) is due to sheer laziness and unwillingness to be persuaded.'

MATTHEW 28: 16–20

'Behold I am with you all through the days that are coming, until the consummation of the world' (v. 20, Knox).

GOD WITH US. The thought has been put forward that the writer of the first Gospel intended the last four chapters of his book to balance the first four. J. C. Fenton has suggested that 'the trials by the Jews pair off with the temptations by the devil; the death pairs with the baptism; with His going from Jerusalem to Galilee after the Resurrection, compare His withdrawal into Galilee in Chapter 2; and His last word in the Gospel, I am with you always, is a fulfilment of the prophecy in Chapter 1, Emmanuel (which means, God with us).' Whatever we think of this proposal, has any book a more glorious conclusion than the promise on which this Gospel ends?

'All through the days that are coming' (Knox) is much more reassuring than the straightforward 'always' of some versions. The meaning is no different but the former seems to take fuller account of the chequered course both of history and of our personal lives. It includes what some have called 'the ages of faith' as well as eras of doubt and denial. It embraces sunny days when life smiles upon us and the future is full of promise, and also those periods of gloom when our spirits are laid low by mysterious inner compulsions we cannot understand. Not until we have learned to affirm (not necessarily to feel) His presence all the days have we become mature Christians.

THE GOSPEL ACCORDING TO MARK

Strong Son Of God

INTRODUCTION

It is generally agreed that this gospel was the first to be written
—about A.D. 65, soon after the Great Fire of Rome—and that it is
based upon the memories of the Apostle Peter.

Irenaeus, who lived in the second century, says: 'Mark, the
disciple and interpreter of Peter, himself also handed down to us
in writing the things which Peter proclaimed.' Papias, whose
writings are known to us through the fourth century historian,
Eusebius, and are probably of an earlier date than those of
Irenaeus, says: 'Mark, having become the interpreter of Peter,
wrote down accurately everything that he remembered ... for
he made it his one care not to omit anything that he heard or to
set down any false statement therein.'

Here, then, is virtually an eye-witness account of the life of
Jesus, written with the non-Jewish world in mind, for there are
few references to the Old Testament and Jewish customs are carefully explained. There emerges the haunting figure of One who is
Son of man but also strong Son of God.

'John the Baptizer appeared in the wilderness pro-claiming for the forgiveness of sins, a baptism of re-pentance' (v. 4, Rieu).

REPENTANCE. Alan Walker, well-known Methodist leader in Australia, tells the story of a man whose wife was unfaithful; yet whenever she returned he always lovingly received her back. On one occasion the man took to Mr. Walker the news that she had gone again, and in subsequent conversation made a significant comment: 'I noticed when she came back last time, she claimed she was sorry. But she wasn't repentant.'

John the Baptist came preaching repentance (v. 4), which is far more than sorrow for sin. We are right to sing, 'With a sorrow for sin must repentance begin', so long as we realize that sorrow is only the beginning of repentance. 'We have not got to feel sorry for our sins,' writes Cuthbert Butler, 'but to be sorry; and the being sorry is ... of the soul's highest powers, the intellect and will.' Put otherwise, repentance means a radical change of mind, of outlook and attitude. This surely is also a happy experience, being the gateway into a new relationship with God and our sinful past. But it can only begin when a man ceases to be concerned about himself in his interest in others and in the consequences to them of what he has done. That is noble and creative sorrow, not another expression of self-centredness.

'It was in those days that Jesus arrived from the Galilean village of Nazareth and was baptised by John in the Jordan' (v. 9, J. B. Phillips).

THE MEANING OF CHRIST'S BAPTISM. John came preaching a baptism of repentance. Then why was Jesus, who had no sins of which to repent, baptized? The answer should drive us to our knees in worship: Jesus, sinless Son of God, was taking His place alongside sinful men, not as one of them, but as One for them.

Love always wholly identifies itself with the beloved. 'Some white people,' said the great African educationalist, James Aggrey, 'ought to be transformed into negroes, just for a few days, so as to feel and suffer as we suffer.' But he also made this comment: 'If I were to go to Heaven and God said, "Aggrey, I am going to send you back, would you like to go as a white man?" I should reply, "No, I have a work to do as a black man that no white man can do. Please send me back as black as you can make me." '

Stripped of all privilege, the Son of God became the Son of Man, that the sons of men might become the sons of God. His identification was, as the beloved Russell Maltby used to say, 'for better for worse, for richer for poorer, in sickness and in health, to love and to cherish'. The baptism of Christ is another evidence that nothing can separate us from the love of God, as far as He is concerned; for He has given Himself completely.

MARK 1: 14–20

'Come ye after Me, and I will make you to become fishers of men' (v. 17).

FOLLOWING AND BELIEVING. Notice that Jesus also came preaching repent (v. 15)—change your mind and believe the gospel. But He did not immediately ask the four fishermen to believe; He first asked them to follow—'Come ye after Me' (v. 17). The reason is not hard to see:

Belief 'in' a person depends upon personal knowledge. We do not commit anything precious into the keeping of a stranger. On the contrary, the more precious it is, the more we have to be convinced that the chosen custodian is absolutely trustworthy. So Jesus invited the two pairs of brothers not to believe a credal statement about Him, but to accept His way of life, to follow Him.

We must beware lest, particularly in dealing with young people, we put the proverbial 'cart before the horse'. The first disciples (learners) followed Christ before they believed that He was the Son of God; their conviction about His true identity was more a dawning awareness than an instantaneous realization; and it came as they followed.

There is no need to postpone Christian discipleship until Christian doctrine can be wholly accepted. Said a young man converted during a convention led by Alan Walker: 'Brought up in a very narrow home, I had the impression that to be a Christian meant accepting a series of doctrines and taking without question a set of intellectual propositions. Later I felt that I could no longer hold them, and gave the Christian faith away. For years I've been living the life of an escapist, playing endless tennis and listening to gramophone records ... One day it all became clear. I suddenly saw that to be a Christian was not to be loyal to a series of intellectual beliefs, but to be loyal to a person named Jesus Christ. It is this allegiance I now accept.'

MARK 1: 21–28

'They were amazed at His teaching, for He sat there teaching them like one who had authority, not like the Scribes' (v. 22, Knox).

THE SOURCE OF AUTHORITY. There is an immense difference between speaking with authority and speaking from authorities. The Scribes taught from second-hand knowledge, for their authority stemmed solely from their ability to quote from authorities. Jesus, on the other hand, though He knew the works of these authorities, spoke with an authority that was new and unmistakable.

Spiritual authority always expresses intimate fellowship with God. William Temple was once asked, 'What religious leader has most effectively appealed to the student-classes in recent years?' He replied instantly, 'Without any exception of any sort, unquestionably Maltby.' Dr. Russell Maltby unconsciously revealed the source of this influence when addressing a critical but suddenly hushed crowd of Oxford undergraduates: 'If you were to ask me', he said, 'why I am a Christian, I could give you no better answer than in the simple words of the children's hymn:

> Wonderful things in the Bible I see;
> This is the dearest that Jesus loves me.'

Spiritual authority, which spurns equally both proud ignorance and proud scholarship, does not have to raise its voice or become dogmatic; its power and winsomeness are in its certitude. Jesus taught with authority (v. 22) and commanded with authority (v. 27) because He safeguarded His fellowship with God.

'Then, in the early morning, while it was still dark, Jesus got up, left the house and went off to a deserted place, and there He prayed' (v. 35, J. B. Phillips).

THE BALANCED LIFE. After a strenuous day of teaching and healing, Jesus recuperated not by 'lying in' on the following morning, but by 'rising up a great while before day' to pray (v. 35). He knew, and we must learn, that virtue expended in service is primarily replenished by waiting upon God, though physical relaxation obviously has its place. The ideal is a balanced life— prayer and perspiration; silence and service; worship and work. Writing of what she called the 'balanced expression of one spirit of life', Evelyn Underhill urged that prayer and deeds of service 'ought to be trained together and never dissociated'.

Our danger is that we tend to emphasize one—there is no need to say which one!—to the fatal detriment of the other. Wrote Olive Wyon: 'If we are rushed and hectic and snappy, or indolent and careless in our ordinary work, our prayer will suffer accordingly. . . . If we have allowed certain elements in our lives to get out of proportion . . . if we are having too much sleep or too little, if we are underfed or overfed—all these apparently irrelevant things will affect our prayer life. It is impossible to isolate the practice of prayer from the rest of life.' This should help us to understand our distaste for secret prayer, without which life becomes unbalanced, and therefore our service increasingly burdensome.

' "If You only choose, You can cleanse me"; so He stretched His hand out in pity and touched him saying, "I do choose, be cleansed" ' (vv. 40–41, Moffatt).

WILLING AND ABLE. In his spiritual autobiography entitled *Elected Silence*, Thomas Merton tells of standing as a child by the hospital bed of his father, known to be suffering from a fatal disease, and experiencing the agony of loving helplessness. He was desperately willing but completely unable to help. The leper, however, was sure that Jesus was able; but was He willing?—'If Thou wilt, Thou canst,' he said.

The spiritual history of man reveals that, though he may not have doubted God's power, he has often doubted the benevolence of that power. It is told of F. W. Myers that he and a friend were gazing at the Sphinx in Egypt when the friend asked him, 'If you were able to ask the Sphinx one question with the assurance that you would get a definite answer, what question would you ask?' After a moment or two Myers replied, 'I would say, "Tell me, is the universe friendly?"' Here is the answer—given once and for all—Jesus touched the leper and said, 'I will; be thou clean.'

God is both able and anxious to meet our need. In cold print, this precious truth possibly seems devoid of particular significance, yet here surely is the very heart of the revelation that Jesus brought about God.

> Think not thou canst sigh a sigh
> And thy Maker is not by:
> Think not thou canst weep a tear
> And thy Maker is not near.

MARK 2: 1–12

'The man sprang to his feet, picked up his bed and walked off in full view of them all. Everyone was amazed, praised God and said, "We have never seen anything like this before"' (v. 12, J. B. Phillips).

TRANSFORMING ADVERSITY. The characters in this well-known story still have much to teach us. We could, for instance, linger over the loyalty and persistence of the four friends, or the reaction of the Scribes, whose bigotry and prejudice made faith in Christ impossible, or the immediate obedience of the sick man. But we only have space to seek the meaning for ourselves of six words spoken by Jesus: 'Take up thy bed, and walk.'

We need not be conquered by infirmity. Our 'bed' probably bespeaks more spiritual than physical disability—hasty temper, envy, indulgence, laziness, undisciplined talking (gossip), moods —but whatever its nature it need not for ever make failure— 'crippled' living—inevitable. 'Not by quitting our appointed battle of life', says Cuthbert Butler, 'but by overcoming in it do we prove our love and service of God.' And this conquest makes possible an even more wonderful development.

The sign of our previous weakness becomes symbolic of our strength. The healed man's bed, once needed to carry him, is now carried by him; what once represented incapacity now represents the very opposite. So Helen Keller's physical limitations became her glory, and President Roosevelt's affliction from poliomyelitis became evidence of self-conquest; they, and many others, resolutely 'taking up' their adversity, completely transformed its once ominous meaning.

MARK 2: 13–17

'It came about that Jesus sat down to a meal in this man's house and a number of tax-collectors and outcasts joined Him and His disciples at the table' (v. 15, Rieu).

'UNRELIGIOUS' EVANGELISM. Levi's first instinct after following Jesus was to introduce his old associates to his new Master, not with stiff formality, but by inviting them to supper. When Dick Sheppard was visiting some troops, the chaplain pointed out one soldier and said, 'I can't get near him at all. Religion doesn't interest him and I can make no impression.' Later Mr. Sheppard and the soldier were seen in animated conversation, and the chaplain asked the secret. 'I should be glad,' he said, rather pompously, 'if you would explain what religious approach you made to a person who seems entirely indifferent to religion.' 'Religion!' said Dick Sheppard, his eyes twinkling, 'I didn't talk religion. I told him two funny stories and then asked after his mother.'

The ex-tax-collector of today's reading also recognized the futility, on this occasion, of a direct evangelical approach. He saw that the psychological moment to introduce Christ needed adequate preparation, not least of a social character. We are not always so wise, perhaps because it is far easier to 'talk religion' to the disinterested than to open our homes as an aid to their becoming interested.

MARK 2: 18–22

'Do friends of the bridegroom refuse to eat at the wedding feast?' (v. 19, The Living Bible).

DISTINCTIVE MARK OF CHRISTIANS. When people married in Palestine, they did not go away on honeymoon, but stayed at home and, for a week, kept open house. They dressed in their best and even wore crowns; for a week they were king and queen, and their every wish was law. The guests were called children of the bridechamber. Jesus used this picture of laughter and gaiety to illustrate the essential nature of Christian discipleship.

The Pharisees, like some misguided believers today, were suspicious of joy and merry-making. Their piety was expressed in ostentatious fasting, which stemmed from the still popular notion that religion is irksome and only sincere when causing discomfort.

Jesus taught that Christian discipleship is like the joy of a wedding feast. 'There is much to be said for the view', observed Nathaniel Micklem, 'that happiness is the distinctive mark of Christians.' What cannot be denied is that, in the New Testament, joy is a primary Christian characteristic.

This does not mean that Christian living is free of sorrow. 'The opposite of joy is not sorrow, but sin,' said Temple Gairdner, quoting a truth learned at the death-bed of his dearest friend. 'Pure joy and pure sorrow can live together.' The concluding words of Jesus in today's reading point to this same insight; for nothing can destroy the joy of God's presence.

MARK 2: 23–28
'The Son of Man is Lord also of the Sabbath' (v. 28).

LAW AND LOVE. The shewbread, twelve wheaten loaves baked of flour sieved eleven times, and symbolic of God's presence, could be eaten by none but the priests (Lev. 24: 5–9). Yet David and his men had satisfied their hunger with it, without apparent stricture. In using this incident to refute the charge against His disciples of Sabbath breaking, Jesus underlined a failing against which Bible students must always guard. He said to the Pharisees, 'Have ye never read what David did?' and they answered, 'Yes.'

They knew the Bible story, but did not understand its essential meaning. Bigotry made the safeguarding of their traditions more important than the recognition of new truth; indeed, the one precluded any possibility of the other. We must read God's word with open minds and open hearts, seeking the insight of love, not the confirmation of our own ideas.

In uttering His great principle—'The Sabbath was made for man, and not man for the Sabbath'—Jesus was again emphasizing that people are more important than things. He did not deny the value of the Sabbath, but brought its spirit and purpose to the forefront: rest was not necessarily inactivity; it could be maintained in the heat of demanding service. Of this we can be sure—fastidiously to observe the prohibitions associated with the Lord's Day is no guarantee that it is actually being kept.

' "Is it right to do good on the Sabbath day or to do harm? Is it right to save life or to kill?" There was a dead silence' (v. 4, J. B. Phillips).

REDEEMING THE TIME. Here again is the emphasis that people are more important than laws, even those maintained in the name of religion. 'Jesus openly broke the Sabbath, for healing was work, and work was prohibited. True, healing was permitted in extreme cases, but this man with the withered hand was obviously in no danger. His healing could wait!' So argued the Pharisees, more concerned about their traditions than human suffering and infirmity. But Jesus could not wait. He must do all the good He could while He could; He must redeem the present moment for service. This urgency characterized His life, despite His unhurried pace.

Few sins do more harm to the Kingdom of God than procrastination. 'The devil knows,' exclaimed William Booth, 'he understands how to waste time and stop progress.' All of us are guilty of missed opportunities through waiting for a more 'convenient' moment; and possibly guilty, as were these Pharisees, of allowing our loyalty to unbending tradition to hinder our loyalty to God.

It is never wrong to do good, to relieve suffering, whatever its form; and to live in this spirit is both to redeem the time and to make every day the Lord's Day.

MARK 3: 7-12

'The unclean spirits, too, whenever they saw Him, used to fall at His feet ... and He would give them a strict charge not to make Him known' (vv. 11-12, Knox).

POPULARITY. 'I know both how to be abased', claimed Paul, 'and I know how to abound.' Most of us know how to be abased, for adversity usually drives us to our knees, with a new awareness of our dependence upon God. But humbly to abound is much more difficult. Material success tends to encourage spiritual apathy and, of course, pride, the deadliest sin of all. To be a good loser is often less demanding than to be a good winner.

With this in mind, look at Christ's example in the light of this reading. He was confronted by a temptation that few individuals entirely master—popularity. The widely scattered areas from which people came to hear Him indicate the extent to which His reputation had spread. From the obscurity of Nazareth He faced the subtle dangers of popular approval; even the kingdom of darkness acknowledged His true identity, 'unclean spirits' saying, 'Thou art the Son of God' (v. 11). Yet we know how completely He remained true to Himself and His cause.

We should remember this when tempted to lower our standards for the sake of remaining 'in the swim'. None of us likes being the 'odd one out', whether through refusing to share gossip, buy a raffle ticket, overlook a dishonourable 'done thing' in business, keep quiet in the hearing of a smutty story, or protest against other enticements to compromise. But such principle before popularity is essential to Christian character.

As the Bishop of Southwell said in *Christianity and Psychology*: 'A life can reach its highest level only by stern and continued loyalty, exercised in our hourly, trivial choices, to the highest that we know.'

MARK 3: 13–19

'He appointed twelve to be His companions, and to go out preaching at His command' (v. 14, Knox).

WORKING IN HARMONY. The fact that quisling Matthew and fiery nationalist Simon the Canaanite could be bound together by their common loyalty to Christ indicates both the greatness of their Master and the secret of Christian fellowship at depth. Few things make a mockery of Christianity more than disunity among believers. Yet how often strained relationships characterize our so-called fellowship! The answer to such animosity, or polite painful tolerance, is a new personal devotion to Christ.

When Pliny, the governor of Bithynia, was writing to the Roman emperor Trajan about trying to stamp out Christianity in his province, and persuade Christians to worship Caesar and curse Christ, he said in bewilderment: 'Real Christians can never be forced to do so.' And such devotion to their Lord inevitably expressed itself in loyalty to each other, for they looked upon themselves as a community of forgiven sinners and therefore as of the communion of saints.

Christ calls His disciples 'that they should be with Him' (v. 14); and having imbibed His spirit, they are sent out to work for Him, and with each other, on a threefold mission: to witness, to heal, and to deliver from evil, activities that should distinguish every individual Christian and the fellowship to which he belongs. 'I am the sort of horse that cannot be harnessed in a team,' confessed Albert Einstein. If this is true of us, to whatever limited extent, we are falling down seriously in our devotion to Christ, which is the indispensable element in harmonious relationships and co-ordinated service.

MARK 3: 20-30

'Whoever blasphemes against the Holy Spirit, he never is forgiven, he is guilty of an eternal sin' (v. 29, Moffatt).

THE UNFORGIVABLE SIN. Innumerable people have pathetically imagined themselves to be guilty of the sin against the Holy Spirit, and often no amount of assurance to the contrary has released them from their fear. What exactly is this unforgivable sin?

It is not any particular act of wrongdoing. Jesus constantly taught, and generations of Christians have proved, that if we confess our sins God is faithful and just to forgive, and to cleanse us from all unrighteousness. Not only does He forgive, but He 'breaks the power of cancelled sin'. Genuine repentance always results in God granting forgiveness and restoring the broken relationship between Himself and the forgiven.

The unforgivable sin is a condition of soul. The Scribes looked at the Son of God and called Him Beelzebub, the prince of the devils. By repeatedly rejecting the light, and so shutting their minds ever tighter to new truth, their evaluations became inverted. Though unaware of it themselves, they were actually thinking of good as evil, of truth as falsehood, of moral white as black. This being so, there could be no hope of repentance, for their hardened condition (fixation) of soul made impossible even the awareness of their need for repentance; and without repentance there can be no forgiveness.

MARK 3: 31-35

'Wherever there is one who has been obedient to God, there is My brother—My sister—and My mother' (v. 35, Weymouth).

CHRIST'S TRUE KITH AND KIN. It is not hard to see that some things bind people together, and generate personal loyalty, even more than the ties of flesh and blood. Comparative strangers, for example, have found true brotherhood in costly faithfulness to a common cause. This is clearly implied in today's reading, which suggests two truths for our consideration.

Obedience to God's will makes us Christ's spiritual kith and kin. If this sounds trite, it is probably because we have not faced up to the fierce demands of obedience, nor experienced the intimate fellowship with Christ that such faithfulness alone makes possible. 'The spirit of obedience', says Ronald Knox, 'differs from the habit of obedience in three ways. It makes you ready to do the maximum, not the minimum. It makes you ready to obey without murmuring, when the thing you have been ordered to do goes much against the grain. And it makes you go on obeying orders when to do so is to risk great dangers, perhaps death.'

Obedience to God's will makes us members of a world-wide family. If allegiance to Christ involves hard renunciation, sometimes of precious family ties, it also opens the door to innumerable enriching relationships with fellow believers. Jesus Himself had to overcome the misguided good intentions of His family, and He taught that a man must be ready to appear to hate his loved ones for the sake of the gospel. But within the Kingdom of God, loss is always outbalanced by gain in ways unsuspected by worldly eyes.

MARK 4: 1-9

'Anyone who has ears to hear, let him listen' (v. 9, Moffatt).

LISTENING AND HEARING. Among Jewish teachers, the parable was a common and well-understood method of illustration. No one would be surprised, therefore, that Jesus taught in such a manner; and His parables, similar in form to the parables of the rabbis, arrested the hearer by their vividness or strangeness, and left the mind in sufficient doubt about precise interpretation to tease it into active thought. We shall leave the meaning of today's parable for the moment. For the present we must take to heart a needed warning:

Unresponsive listening results in unrealized spiritual deafness. The saintly Savonarola, who poured out his soul to the people of Florence, had every reason to know this. 'Preach to these men as one may,' he said, 'they have taken the habit of listening well and yet acting ill.' So he warned them that they would become 'like a rook on a steeple that at the first stroke of the church bell takes the alarm and hath fear, but when accustomed to the sound percheth quietly on the bell, however loudly it rings'.

An explanation of this unconscious deafness of soul was suggested by Samuel Chadwick: 'Noble hearing is the habit of noble minds. All nobility has its source in the nobility of the mind; and as is the mind, so is the man. The mean man is mean-minded. The impure man has an impure mind. The worldly are worldly minded, and the spiritual are of a spiritual mind. As a man thinks he is; and as he is, he hears.'

MARK 4: 10–20

'Those who take in the seed in good soil are those who hear the word and welcome it and yield a harvest' (v. 20, Knox).

FOUR TYPES OF MIND. Verses 11–12 could appear to suggest that Jesus taught in parables deliberately to confuse the people outside the Kingdom of God, but this must be rejected as utterly out of character and aim. The only satisfactory interpretation is along the lines indicated above—that people can so habitually hear and see without response that finally they lose the capacity either to understand or perceive. Now look at the meaning of the parable for us.

The stony ground represents the shallow mind. Surface religion —an easy acceptance of Christ without consideration of the cost, and concerned with results that must be as quick as they are gained without suffering—has always done more harm to the Kingdom of God than the united testimony of every atheist.

The thorny ground represents the mind over-busy with trivialities. The best is frequently crowded out by the good! We do not so often kill the 'seed' by deliberate neglect as just smother it by thoughtless preoccupation.

The good ground represents the fruitful mind. See how the good hearer responded! He listened attentively, received the word (kept it in his heart and pondered its meaning) and acted (put the truth he recognized into immediate practice).

MARK 4: 21–25

'For he who has, to him shall more be given; while as for him who has not, from him shall be taken even what he has' (v. 25, Moffatt).

SECRET DISLOYALTY. These vivid word pictures illustrate

the contradiction and consequences of secret discipleship. Victorinus, whose conversion profoundly influenced the great Augustine, for a time was afraid publicly to acknowledge Christ. Told by a friend that he would not be truly a Christian until he had openly made his confession of faith, the well-known professor of rhetoric in Rome reported, in derision, 'Is it not enough to believe in my heart?' But there came the day when this distinguished scholar, justly famous for his learning, boldly identified himself with the despised followers of Christ; and to Augustine there came the thought: 'If Victorinus, then why not me?'

To hide our light 'under a bushel' is an understandable temptation, particularly in unsympathetic company, but our denials by silence have serious repercussions, most of all for ourselves. Christ emphasized the folly of pretence, for secret disloyalty, no matter how cleverly concealed, is finally bound to come out (v. 22). More serious, however, than this exposure of spiritual fraud, revealing cowardice, lack of conviction, or lust for comfort, is the inescapable effect of secret discipleship upon character: 'As for the man who has nothing, even his nothing will be taken away' (v. 25, J. B. Phillips). We cannot stand still either physically, mentally or spiritually. The indulgent athlete ultimately loses even the possibility of fitness; the lazy scholar both the knowledge he already has and the ability to think; and the secret disciple the will and capacity to know God. This is the awful nemesis (judgment) of sin again which we are warned.

MARK 4: 26–29

'The Kingdom of God is like a man scattering seed on the ground and then going to bed each night and getting up every morning, while the seed sprouts and grows up, though he has no idea how it happens' (vv. 26–27, J. B. Phillips).

GOD NEEDS TIME. This parable of the seed growing secretly is peculiar to Mark's gospel; and its teaching is urgently needed in a speed-crazy world. We ourselves are sometimes in too much of a hurry spiritually, expecting God at our bidding to work miracles overnight; and all too often we judge the progress of His Kingdom by what we can see.

The building of the Kingdom of God takes time and develops silently. Realization of this truth would save us much disappointment, in ourselves and others, and keep our hope strong in the face of entrenched unbelief. When the white friars began their missionary activity among the Mohammedans in Central Africa, their leader warned them not to expect a convert for the first hundred years. J. G. Paton, aflame for Christ, arrived from Scotland on the cannibal island of Tanna in the New Hebrides, in 1858. 'My first impressions', he said, 'drove me to the verge of utter dismay.' Within three months his wife and child died; he himself buried them, having dug their graves with his own hands. For years he battled against the islanders' superstition and fierce hostility before the first convert was won. Only his conviction that 'the Kingdom of God cometh not with observation' enabled him to defeat despair.

We must beware lest our natural desire for quick spiritual results, both in ourselves and the world generally, leads us to give up, when we should look up. The kingdom of darkness is not easily overcome, but this parable guarantees its ultimate overthrow.

MARK 4: 30–34

'Whereunto shall we liken the Kingdom of God? ... It is like a grain of mustard seed' (vv. 30–31).

LIVING ORDINARY LIFE WELL. We describe anything particularly small in such terms as 'a drop in the ocean', 'a grain of sand' or 'the eye of a needle'. In the days of Jesus, the proverb 'As small as a grain of mustard seed' was used to describe the infinitely small. In actual fact, the mustard seed was not the smallest of seeds, but it was popularly thought of as such.

The greatest things in life often have the smallest beginnings. In this nuclear age, with its emphasis upon mass production and vast combines, the importance of 'little things' is frequently overlooked. We think big and tend to be impressed only by the spectacular. Yet Jesus likened His Kingdom to a mustard seed, underlining a truth with which we should approach every day and every responsibility.

Great spiritual achievements depend upon faithfulness in small things. 'I long', confessed Helen Keller, 'to accomplish a great and noble task; but it is my chief duty and joy to accomplish humble tasks as though they were great and noble.' There is no greater challenge than to live an ordinary life well; and one sure sign of our inability to do this is our constant longing for change, for an escape from the imagined 'little' things of life.

**'Why are you afraid like this? Have you no faith yet'
(v. 40, Moffatt).**

OVERCOMING FEAR. Here are two pictures, one, alas,
typifying our frequent reaction to danger, and the other of what it
should be.

The disciples were terrified. 'Carest Thou not that we perish?'
they cried indignantly. Many experiences in life would suggest to
the shallow thinker that God is either loving and powerless or
indifferent and powerful; certainly not loving and powerful.

Not long ago an African convert to Christianity was asked what
new truth he had learned about God through becoming a
Christian. His answer was interesting: 'That God exists, that we
knew. That God made the world, that we knew. But that God is
Father, that we did not know at all.' If human fatherhood at its
best thinks first of its children's character, not their comfort, we
should not be surprised if God our Father refuses to listen to our
cries for exemption from the trials of life. But see how we can be
serene in such challenging situations.

Christ was trustful. The storm raged! He was 'asleep on a
pillow'. No wonder He asked His disciples, 'Why are you so
frightened? What has happened to your faith?' (J. B. Phillips),
for He knew that God, all-loving and all-powerful, was utterly
trustworthy. With this conviction central, nothing could disturb
His peace. Wrote Middleton Murray: 'He moved about calmly,
quietly, majestically, undaunted, undismayed, always certain of
Himself and of the triumph of the cause committed to Him. And
that was because of His massive certainty in the victoriousness of
God's love and holiness.' Here alone is the answer to our fears and
worries.

**'As they approached Jesus, they saw the man who had
been devil-possessed sitting there properly clothed and
perfectly sane' (v. 15, J. B. Phillips).**

GOD'S FIRST CONCERN. This story, with its legion of
devils, and its herd of swine destroyed seemingly through the
action of Christ, has its difficulties for twentieth-century minds.
But to dismiss it on that account would be the height of folly. Many
missionaries today testify to the reality of 'demon possession' when
African heathenism is confronted by the message of Christ.

The destruction of the swine may be more puzzling, but its meaning for us shines through, and is urgently needed, in this world of twisted values: the loss of the herd counted as nothing in comparison with the rescue of one single human being.

People matter most. We pay ready lip service to this truism, but does our concern indicate that we really believe it? 'It was William Booth', wrote Harold Begbie, 'who taught the world that the first thing to do in seeking to turn a bad man into a good man is to make him feel that you really care for him, really care whether he sinks or swims.' This could explain why more bad men are not being transformed. They have the impression that we do not deeply care, care to the extent of suffering and sacrificing, without cynicism or contempt, on behalf of ungrateful human nature. Today's reading indicates that God's first concern is for ordinary, sin-bound people; we must make the same emphasis.

MARK 5: 15–20

'Go home to your own people, and report to them all the Lord has done for you' (v. 19, Moffatt).

WITNESS AT HOME. Robert Louis Stevenson, as a boy, stood one night at dusk with his nose pressed against a window-pane looking out into the gathering darkness. He was called for supper, but still he stood, watching, fascinated, an old-fashioned lamp-lighter going from light to light in the street. 'Look, look,' cried the boy, 'there's a man out there punching holes in the darkness.' Jesus called upon the man delivered from 'demon possession' to do this spiritually; and he was to begin his witness in probably the most difficult place of all—at home, among the people who knew him best (v. 19).

Our loyalty to Christ should be most apparent in our own homes. Leslie Weatherhead once said that before would-be missionaries are accepted to win souls overseas, they should be asked, 'How many souls have you won at home?' The opportunities there are endless, to people who care. Lying at home on her death-bed, Catherine Booth longed to influence her doctor, a young agnostic. On one occasion, her spirit low through un-relieved pain, she confessed to him her feeling of being unable to do 'any good'. 'You have done me good,' he replied. 'Your courage and anxiety for my welfare are so beautiful.'

William Booth recorded in his diary: 'She spoke to him beautifully, saying that she would like to hear when she got to the other side that the doctor who had attended her had been brought to Christ through her words. I had a few words with him further about spiritual matters downstairs, and he went away in a very subdued manner. In fact, again and again, tears came to his eyes. We must pray for him.'

Is it surprising that William and Catherine Booth were great public evangelists?

MARK 5: 21–24, 35–43

'Jesus gave them strict instructions not to let anyone know what had happened—and ordered food to be given to the little girl' (v. 43, J. B. Phillips).

PRACTICAL OTHER-WORLDLINESS. Here is a picture of a successful man's world suddenly collapsing about his ears. Jairus, being a ruler of the synagogue, was a respected and prominent member of the community. Then his only child, a twelve-year-old daughter, became seriously ill. Frantic with anxiety, he pocketed his pride and sought the help of One whom he knew was the object of severe disapproval by Jewish religious leaders. The pathos of the incident is not hard to imagine. We could learn a lot from the attitude of Jairus and his family, but concentrate instead upon the central character, Jesus Himself, noting particularly the combination of His other-worldliness and his down-to-earth thoughtfulness.

He restored the girl to health. We could expect this of Him, knowing that His divine nature made possible such manifestations of power. But here was no mystic with His head in the clouds. If He could command death itself to loosen its grip, He could also pay practical attention to detail.

He ordered that the girl be given something to eat. Think of the excitement and 'great astonishment' of the occasion. Yet Jesus quietly remembered the restored girl's need of food. Some people, it has been noted, are so heavenly minded that they are no earthly use. Jesus, however, illustrates that to be spiritually minded is not necessarily to be unmindful of mundane matters. True spirituality makes a person more considerate and sensible about the practical things of life.

MARK 5: 25–34

'Thy faith hath brought thee recovery; go in peace, and be rid of thy affliction' (v. 34, Knox).

COSTLY SELF-GIVING. Luke, the doctor, simply tells us

that this woman, afflicted with an internal haemorrhage for twelve years, could not be cured by the physicians. Mark's gospel, record of the rugged Peter's observations, is less delicate. The woman 'had gone through a great deal at the hands of many doctors' from whom 'she had derived no benefit' (vv. 26–27, J. B. Phillips). The story yields two main lessons.

God loves us individually as though He had no one else to love. To a sick woman—a complete stranger—who had been deserted, and had written to him for comfort, Dick Sheppard replied: 'My deepest conviction is that love is the one thing to cling to in all darkness. I too, in many ways different from yours, have been disappointed and disillusioned a hundred times. But nothing and no one has been able to undermine my very simple faith that God is as Jesus Christ.' Then see the meaning of today's reading—Jesus, hustled by a crowd, gave His undivided attention to one needy woman. We possibly cease to wonder and be excited by this incredible truth about God because cheap familiarity has blunted our perception.

God's service demands costly self-giving. Virtue goes from us whenever we give ourselves to people; and anything less than the giving of ourselves, as distinct from the giving of our service, is camouflaged selfishness, perhaps self-protection. Christ was not play-acting when He agonized in Gethsemane; and really to follow Him is to serve at similar personal cost.

MARK 6: 1–6

'There is no prophet without honour except in his own country, and among his own relatives, and in his own home' (v. 4, Weymouth).

PREJUDICE. Jesus returned to Nazareth, to teach in the synagogue; and the response of His listeners could be a reflection of our own attitude in the house of God:

They were so critical of the Messenger that they could not accept His message. Though astonished at His wisdom and incredulous of His authority, they were also mindful of His past—'Is not this the Carpenter, the Son of Mary?' they asked. And this fact, wrongly interpreted, so prejudiced their minds that the truth could not penetrate. Such bigotry is inexcusable, but no more than the prejudice which rejects the light of truth for no other reason than disapproval of the light-bringer. Far more inspiration would perhaps be ours if we paid less attention to the preacher and more to what he was saying.

This tendency to pre-judge is illustrated in a remarkable exchange on the subject of life after death between two of the most intelligent men of this century—William Temple and Bertrand Russell: 'I remember', wrote the Archbishop, 'once saying to Russell: "I believe in it far more than the evidence warrants." He replied: "And I disbelieve far more." ' The danger is that some people pre-judge without realizing it, and then their zeal is always against something, never for something.

MARK 6: 7-13

Christ 'ordered them to take nothing but a stick for the journey, no bread, no wallet, no coppers in their girdle; they were to wear sandals, but not to put on two shirts' (vv. 8–9, Moffatt).

CONDITIONS OF DISCIPLESHIP. In these days of widespread material prosperity, we need to bear in mind the emphasis of this reading.

The servant of God must 'travel light'. Ownership hampers movement and often leads to wrong evaluations. 'The world is possessed by those who are not possessed by it,' said Dean Inge; and those who give undue priority to possessing things soon lose their spiritual appetite. Our homes, like our daily living, should be marked by an essential simplicity. Money is not sinful, but its power to taint the soul means that only the watchful steward of God can handle it without becoming impoverished in character. Any possession which limits our freedom to serve God is unworthy.

The servant of God must be single-minded. Christ called His followers to an heroic renunciation; every encumbrance to their new way of life was to be thrown aside. And He called them to a clearly defined mission: to preach and to heal, to serve men's souls and their bodies. The social work of The Salvation Army indicates that William Booth recognized this two-fold obligation. But have we recognized it? We can best answer this question by asking another: What am I personally doing to relieve human suffering, loneliness and material need?

MARK 6: 14–29

'Herod stood in awe of John, knowing he was a just and holy man' (v. 20, Moffatt).

HUMAN NATURE. Here are three character studies each of them offering possible insight into our own natures.

There is the courage of John. Herod was a tyrant and a king, but the Baptist was fearless in denouncing, face to face, the despot's unashamed immorality. Not that the prophet necessarily felt no fear! Bishop Hugh Latimer, burned at the stake in the reign of Queen Mary in England, wrote from his imprisonment: 'I am so afraid I could creep into a mouse-hole.' Courage is not the absence of fear, but its conquest.

There is the corruption of Herodias. This word corruption is not too strong, for Herodias was prepared even to lead her own child into wrongdoing for the achievement of her own evil ends. Could anything be more despicable? Yet let us not be too hasty in our self-righteous judgments, for we similarly sin whenever our example, perhaps most by what we fail to do and be, leads another astray.

There is the cowardice of Herod. He was a coward, afraid of John and Herodias and his own pride. We all tend to silence criticism by abusing our critics. Herod fooled himself to the extent of believing that he was reluctantly agreeing to a crime in the name of his personal integrity. The real truth was that he found it easier to do further evil than to admit his initial wrong.

MARK 6: 30–44

'Now come along to some quiet place by yourselves, and rest for a little while' (v. 31, J. B. Phillips).

A SECRET OF SERENITY. The apostles returned from their campaign, and Jesus saw that they all needed a bit of peace and quiet. But hardly had they arrived at their retreat before a crowd sought them out; and Christ actually welcomed them.

He was never too preoccupied with His own spiritual needs to ignore the material needs of others or resent His privacy being disturbed. This is something we must all learn. Some men are so busy working for their families that they neglect their wives and children; some wives are so harassed by unending domestic chores that they make life unbearable for their loved ones whose well-being is the only reason for the work; and some Christians are so busy serving humanity that they lose sight of the heart needs of individual men and women.

Jesus allowed nothing, not even His natural desire for leisurely quietness, to stand between Himself and needy people. He, of course, safeguarded time for habitual prayer, but if ever the unexpected disrupted His programme He remained serene because He had His priorities right. Alas, the history of Christianity reveals that even 'saints' have lost their temper through their private devotions being disturbed!

MARK 6: 45-52

'Take courage, He said, it is Myself; do not be afraid. So He came to them on board the boat, and thereupon the wind dropped' (vv. 50, 51, Knox).

CHRIST AND OUR ADVERSITY. Here we have the complementary truth to the previous comment. If Jesus allowed nothing, not even His natural wish for periods of undisturbed waiting upon God, to stand between Himself and human need, He was careful to maintain His habit of prayer: the people's needs unhurriedly met, He sent them away and 'departed into a mountain to pray'. Our tendency is to make our over-busy-ness in service an excuse for our inconsistency in secret prayer; the result is weariness in well-doing or cynicism, or both.

The story of the disciples toiling against a 'contrary' wind, typifying a common experience for many people today, and of Jesus coming to them with the assurance, 'Be of good cheer: it is I; be not afraid', illustrates that Christ unfailingly comes to us in our need, whatever its nature. 'There is no "getting over" sorrow,' said F. W. Robertson. 'I hate the idea. But there is a "getting into" sorrow, and finding right in the heart of it the dearest of all human beings—the Man of Sorrows.' There is the same insight in the lines:

> Let us learn like a bird for a moment to take
> Sweet rest on a branch that is ready to break;
> She feels the branch tremble, yet gaily she sings,
> What is it to her? She has wings, she has wings!

'Wherever He went, in villages or towns or farms, they laid down their sick right in the roadway and begged Him that they might "just touch the edge of His cloak"' (v. 56, J. B. Phillips).

USING GOD FOR SELFISH ENDS. Comparing this scene —of multitudes of sick people clamouring for healing—with that of the handful of disciples at the Cross, we can recognize a widespread human failing.

People want Christ's healing, but not His lordship. They seek privilege without responsibility; to receive from God without responding to His service. The inhabitants of Gennesaret were happy to take, but not to give. Christ was to them merely a means to their own ends. But are we any better? How often we have pleaded for help from God, and forgotten to praise Him! Our prayers indicate how much we want things from God and how little we worship Him for His own sake, which is one reason why adversity undermines some people's faith.

The American theologian, Nels Ferré, after being in weeks of pain to the point of utter discouragement, was overheard by his mother as he prayed: 'Dear Lord, if Thou wilt ever have me well and use me again, Thy will be done; if not, Thy will be done anyway.' 'Nels,' she reproved, 'that's no way to pray. Thank Him and praise Him; thank Him and praise Him.' 'This I did,' said the scholar. 'Then I better understood what adoration meant. God's will is constantly for the best, whatever happens. Come what may, He is to be thanked and praised.' True, but our unrealized selfishness and self-pity often keep us more concerned about God's gifts than about the Giver Himself. The chief end of man is to love God and to enjoy Him for ever.

MARK 7: 1-13

'You drop what God commands and hold to human tradition' (v. 8, Moffatt).

RELIGION GONE WRONG. In today's reading, Jesus levelled two charges against the Pharisees and Scribes.

He accused them of hypocrisy (v. 6). The reason was that they had made all-important the Law's outward observance, with the inevitable result that ceremonial cleanness had replaced purity of heart, and religious ritualism taken priority over right relationships. Whenever people think more of appearances than attitudes, pretence is never far away. The Pharisees' reputation for piety did not prevent Jesus from recognizing that their lip-service to God was a cover for hearts that dishonoured Him. This means, of course, that hypocrisy is determined by motive, by secret intention. Christ's second charge against these profoundly religious Pharisees and Scribes was equally serious.

He accused them of 'making the word of God of none effect' through their traditions (v. 13). Men have always tried to reduce the laws of God to accommodate human frailty; and their ingenuity has often managed to justify, in the name of religion, the consequent lowered standards. For instance, to get round the possible inconvenience of caring for ageing parents, the elders of Israel had established the tradition of Corban: a man could be excused his filial responsibilities by pleading that the money he would have used to provide for his parents had been dedicated to God (v. 11).

Selfishness is never happier or more firmly entrenched than when parading as piety, which is one reason why our selfish prayers are far less conscious than our selfish deeds.

MARK 7: 14–23

'Listen to Me now, all of you, and understand this. There is nothing outside a man which can enter into him and make him "common". It is the things which come out of a man that make him "common"' (v. 15, J. B. Phillips).

THINGS ARE NOT SINFUL. We saw previously that the Pharisees were primarily concerned about such matters as clean and unclean foods, hand-washing and freedom from the taint of innumerable unholy things. Cleansing, according to the traditions of the elders, was entirely dependent upon the fastidious observance of prescribed ceremonialism. Christ challenged such surface sanctity with teaching that was truly revolutionary.

A man was clean only to the extent his heart was pure. It is, He taught, not what a man does, but what he is that determines whether or not he is a sinner. Before we take this truism for granted, let us be sure that we too are not falling into the error of making doing more important than being. The Pharisees sincerely believed that a man was religiously clean if he 'performed' the Law; and don't we tend to feel self-satisfied if we do certain things

—attend a place of worship, read the Bible, teach in Sunday-school, visit the sick? Such activities are excellent in themselves, but, inferred Jesus, they do not guarantee purity of life. 'For it is from inside, from men's hearts and minds', he said, 'that evil thoughts arise' (v. 21, J. B. Phillips).

There are no sinful things, only sinful people. Adverse circumstances are not sinful in themselves, but possibly provide an easier excuse for sinful hearts to reveal themselves. So often, like the Pharisees, we blame things for our failings, for our spiritual and moral uncleanness, while the real explanation is our own secret life. It is there that Christ wants to rule.

MARK 7: 24–30

'She was a Gentile woman ... and again and again she begged Him to expel the demon from her daughter' (v. 26, Weymouth).

WHEN GOD DOESN'T ANSWER. On this occasion Jesus appears to be unlike Himself—harsh and even rude to an anxious mother, but we know enough of Him to realize that there must be some meaningful explanation. According to Matthew's account of this incident, Jesus initially answered the woman 'not a word'; and probably we know something of this kind of experience in prayer—our petitions are met with a stony silence. Why? Christ's dealing with this Syro-Phoenician can help us to understand.

He wanted to give her more than she was asking. She sought only healing for her daughter. He purposefully slammed the door in her face: 'It is not meet to take the children's bread, and to cast it unto dogs'. (Dogs was usually an expression of contempt, but here it is a diminutive, meaning family pets.)

Notice, however, that Jesus had already said, 'Let the children first be fed'; but only first. He wanted her to understand that the time had come for Gentiles also to be offered the gospel; and the woman now saw this. 'Yes, Lord, I know,' she replied, 'but even the dogs under the table eat what the children leave' (v. 28, J. B. Phillips).

In such a manner was this woman led to perceive that she could belong to Christ's spiritual household. Healing certainly came to her daughter; but more than that—the woman came to the Healer, in a way beyond her first imaginings.

'The man's ears were opened, the impediment to his speech was removed, and he spoke clearly' (v. 35, Rieu).

SENSITIVE TO OTHERS' FEELINGS. Christ travelled from Tyre to Galilee in the south by way of Sidon in the north, a roundabout journey probably undertaken to give Him undisturbed time with His disciples. In the region of Decapolis, a deaf and dumb man was brought to Him, and Jesus used what to us is an unhygienic method of healing. In the ancient world, however, human saliva was reckoned to have healing properties. For our meditation we should look beyond the method to the manner in which Christ healed, recognizing that the spirit in which we serve is always more significant than the service itself.

Jesus, considerate of the man's feelings and possible embarrassment, 'took him away from the crowd by himself' (v. 33, J. B. Phillips). How easily we serve at the expense of other people's feelings! In *Private World of Pain*, Grace Stuart describes a visit from a minister of religion: 'Having depressed me considerably more than I was already depressed, having actually taken away from me some of my power of physical and personal recovery, he disappeared ... never to come back again. Fortunately!'

Have we become cold and 'official', even officious, in our service? Christ, loving people, was always sensitive to the heart needs of individuals, which is a good test of genuine love.

'My heart yearns over the people; for this is now the third day they have remained with Me, and they have nothing to eat' (v. 2, Weymouth).

PRACTICAL COMPASSION. Why had this crowd of 4,000 suddenly gathered around Jesus in the region of Decapolis? One possible explanation is that the cured Gadarene demoniac, told by Jesus to witness at home among his own people (Mark 5: 19), had created this widespread interest. Such is the influence of individual faithfulness. But to concentrate upon Christ in His feeding of the multitude:

His compassion led to practical sympathy. Some people give the impression that piety and consideration for the menial are irreconcilable. They fail to see that true spirituality is never so absorbed with thoughts of the next world that it overlooks the details of routine obligations in this one. Christ shows us that Christian compassion is observant, considerate and down-to-earth.

His compassion overcame practical difficulty. How like some of us were those first disciples. Hearing of plans to meet the needs of the people, their immediate reaction was, 'It can't be done.' We also want to wait for ideal circumstances before we do anything. But Christ told His disciples that if, under His guidance, they would faithfully do the best possible with what they had, just seven loaves, the people's need would be met. Here is a message for us.

MARK 8: 11–21

'While He was warning them to watch and be on their guard against the yeast of the Pharisees and the yeast of Herod, they were arguing with one another about the bread they had not brought' (vv. 15–16, Rieu).

LEARNING FROM LIFE. The Jew generally thought of leaven as representing evil; and the leaven of the Pharisees and of Herod (v. 15) was their false idea of power. They both wanted an earthly kingdom, the former through God's spectacular intervention, and the latter through the building up of his own might. The only power they could imagine was force, visible and irresistible.

Jesus, however, reveals that the one redemptive power in the world is suffering love, despite its often apparent helplessness, and that to depend upon any other power is to be contaminated by evil ideas. Yet the disciples did not hear this vital lesson.

They were too occupied with personal trivialities. Of more importance to them was their next meal (v. 16). Not that food was unimportant. Jesus recognized its necessity by providing for the multitude. But it was not important to the extent of keeping a man's mind away from more crucial matters. Few things in life make greater demands of us than the working out of value priorities, and then our sticking to the right order. On the occasion of today's reading, even Christ was amazed at His disciples' spiritual blindness and deafness (v. 18): 'How is it that ye do not understand?' He asked.

They were learning nothing from life's experiences. Despite having recently shared Christ's provision for thousands of hungry people, they still doubted His ability to provide for them. We, too, often forget the evidence of past mercies in the face of present trials.

MARK 8: 22–26

'He began to see, and said, "I can make out people, for I see them as large as trees moving"' (v. 24, Moffatt).

A GRADUAL MIRACLE. With the same sensitive considerateness for the feelings of another that we have noticed already, Jesus took this blind man away from the prying crowd before restoring his sight. Again He used spittle as the method of healing, knowing that this would be understood by the blind man and therefore would most readily help his faith. Christ always starts with people where they are, going from the known to the unknown; and our evangelism would be more effective if we did likewise.

There is symbolic meaning for us in the fact that this miracle is the only recorded one that happened gradually. Exactly why this was so we shall never know, but it does serve to remind us that God requires time fully to heal a soul. We are usually in such a hurry, wanting to be made saints overnight. But conversion, though wonderful and necessary, is never more than the beginning of a long journey. We too shall often (with our spiritual eyes) 'see men as trees, walking', for none of us has the capacity to perceive the whole of God's truth at once. The nearer we live to Him the more this becomes apparent; indeed, our Christlikeness can perhaps best be measured by the intensity of our longing to be more like Him. Our spiritual pilgrimage is living and vital only to the extent we recognize how much further we have to go to a perfect knowledge of the Son of God.

MARK 8: 27–33

'But what about you—who do you say that I am?' (v. 29, J. B. Phillips).

SUBTLE TEMPTATION. In this well-known incident, Peter, impulsive and lovable, identified Jesus and himself, thereby illustrating two subtle temptations against which we must be constantly watchful.

His confession of faith reveals the danger of half-understood orthodoxy. Peter gave the right answer, but it had the wrong ideas behind it. When he and Jesus used the same word—Messiah—

they had in mind totally different functions: One thought of a spiritual Kingdom established by suffering love, the other of a material kingdom established by supernatural might. To express belief about God 'correctly' is not nearly as important as having in the heart the right ideas about God. And see where Peter's half-understood orthodoxy led him!

His contradiction of Christ reveals the danger of unenlightened love. This well-intentioned disciple was unconsciously tempting his Master to unfaithfulness; and the vehemence with which Jesus reacted surely indicates the power of the temptation. How often have people been led into sin by heeding their loved ones' well-meaning advice!

Peter called himself a follower, but right to the end of his Leader's earthly life he thought he knew best. Indignantly he protested at the feet-washing, and he never would accept the warning from Christ that he would be guilty of disloyalty and cowardice. Always he thought he knew better than Jesus! Are we any better?

MARK 8: 34-38

'If any man has a mind to come My way, let him renounce self, and take up his cross, and follow Me' (v. 34, Knox).

THE WAY TO SUCCESS. So often we associate success in life with material prosperity and personal prestige. Jesus had other ideas, some of which are clearly outlined in these verses:

Real success is giving the achievement of noble ends priority over the enjoyment of present pleasures. 'What shall a man give in exchange for his soul?' He asked; and an honest answer from each of us will define the values we hold in highest regard. 'Getting on' in life is not necessarily a matter of improving our circumstances, but of refining our character through costly loyalty to spiritual values.

Real success is the ability to say 'No' to oneself. 'Whosoever will come after Me,' said Jesus, 'let him deny himself,' which means saying 'No' to himself in the secret places of his life. Nothing could be more demanding, as Jesus emphasized when He warned that discipleship involved habitual and ruthless self-renunciation. He never misled would-be followers by underestimating the price of faithfulness; their unconditional surrender was a minimum requirement.

138

We only really fail in life when we are disobedient to God's will. The New Testament makes it unmistakably clear that God never judges success by appearances, but by obedience; never by results, but by faithfulness.

MARK 9: 1–13

'This is My Beloved Son; to Him, then, listen' (v. 6, Knox).

CHRIST WANTS MORE THAN OUR ADMIRATION. When Jesus said: 'Believe Me, there are some of you standing here who will know nothing of death until you have seen the Kingdom of God coming in its power' (v. 1, J. B. Phillips), He could not have been speaking, as sometimes imagined, about the Second Coming, otherwise He would have been proved wrong. The fact is that within the lifetime of some of those who listened to these words, Christianity spread from the obscurity of Jerusalem to the Gentile centre of Antioch and marched on through Europe. This was the Kingdom of God come with power!

The Transfiguration is full of significance, coming as it did shortly after Peter's confession of faith and contradiction of Christ at Caesarea Philippi. Moses and Elijah, representing the Law and the prophets, added their testimony, as Luke's account makes even more explicit, that the Cross was to be God's way of accomplishing His purposes; and this was further confirmed by the words: 'This is My Beloved Son: hear Him' (v. 7). Says T. W. Manson in *The Servant-Messiah*: ' "Hear Him" does not merely mean "Listen to what He has to say". It means much more than that: "Listen to His instructions, and obey".'

Christ wants not our admiration, but our obedience.

MARK 9: 14–29

'I have brought You my son. He has a dumb spirit in him. . . . I begged Your disciples to expel it, but they had not the power' (vv. 17–18, Weymouth).

WHY DO WE FAIL? As we saw yesterday, the Transfiguration confirmed how Christ was to save mankind. After this mountain-top experience, He descended, immediately to meet the needs, not of the world, but of a father and his son. Make no mistake—it is easier to think lovingly of a crowd than actually to love an individual man, woman, or child into the Kingdom.

Like these first despondent disciples, we must often ask, 'Why did we fail?' Back comes this answer: 'Nothing can drive out this kind of thing except prayer' (v. 29, J. B. Phillips). Jesus was saying that we fail Him because we do not live close enough to God.

Fellowship with Him must be safeguarded by secret prayer. 'Right relation between prayer and conduct', wrote William Temple, 'is not that conduct is supremely important and prayer may help it, but that prayer is supremely important and conduct tests it.' True, yet how often in our experience is prayer the first casualty in times of domestic and business pressure?

Secret prayer involves stern self-discipline. 'Fasting' means keeping bodily appetites in subjection to spiritual necessities. 'Prayer and self-indulgence will not go together,' insisted Teresa of Avila, which was what Bede Frost underlined when he wrote: 'To enter upon a life of prayer and, much more, to persevere in it, demands a firm determination, a resolute will and a great confidence in God.'

> We kneel, and all around us seems to lower;
> We rise, and all, the distant and the near,
> Stands forth in sunny outline, brave and clear;
> We kneel, how weak! we rise, how full of power!

MARK 9: 30–37

'If any man wants to be first, he must be last and servant of all' (v. 35, J. B. Phillips).

TOO ASHAMED TO ANSWER. Jesus secretly left Galilee at the beginning of His journey to Jerusalem and the Cross. His immediate concern was further to prepare His disciples for their responsibilities beyond His death and Resurrection. And how like some of us they were in their attitude and ideas.

The disciples were afraid to hear the truth (v. 32). Jesus told them plainly about what was to happen to Him, but, though 'they understood not that saying', they 'were afraid to ask Him'. Why? For the same reason that some people refuse to see a doctor; they were afraid of finding out the truth. What little these first followers of Christ did understand of His teaching was so frightening, being utterly contrary to their expectations, that they preferred not to hear any more. We behave in exactly the same way when we hang on to our peace by ignoring disturbing revelation.

The disciples were afraid to speak the truth (v. 34). Jesus asked them about what they had been disputing, but they were too ashamed to answer. Here, then, is a test for each one of us regarding what we say: would the repeating of my words or even the naming of the subjects I have discussed cause me shame in the presence of Christ?

MARK 9: 38–50

'Whoever receives one of these little ones in My name receives Me' (v. 37, Moffatt).

DOING ORDINARY THINGS WELL. The dismembered body (vv. 43–48) is clearly symbolic of the cost of single-minded devotion to Christ. It cannot be repeated too often that such faithfulness involves the renunciation of every hindrance to spiritual maturity. Some hindrances are possibly legitimate in themselves, but, warned Jesus, tolerance of them could cost a man his soul. Individually—and no one else can do this for us or even know exactly what needs to be done—we must root out any friendship, pastime, or habit that compromises our obedience to God's will.

But more than heroic renunciation is required. We are also called to heroic service; and it is heroic because it lacks the excitement we all crave; we are to go through life giving 'cups of cold water' in Christ's name (v. 41). In our desire to do great things for God, we frequently overlook the little things close at hand. Or perhaps we feel so useless that we sincerely think ourselves incapable of doing anything worthwhile in God's service. But He is not concerned about great accomplishments, but great faithfulness; and it is always far harder to do ordinary things well than to respond only to the extraordinary.

Such a 'little' thing as a man's attitude to children was, inferred Jesus, more revealing than his attitude to, for instance, his employers. Indeed, to offend 'little ones' was, He said, to warrant stern judgment (v. 42). We are sure to be stumbling-blocks to faith when we show to those who can do nothing for us less consideration than we show to those whose favour we covet.

MARK 10: 1–12

'What God has joined, then, man must not separate' (v. 9, Moffatt).

CHRISTIAN MARRIAGE. John Galsworthy tells of a soldier

during the first world war who was being tried for attempted suicide. His excuse was that he could not bear to be separated from his wife. Most people laughed, but one of the jurymen began to think. He had caught a glimpse of a treasure he had never known—a love and sympathy he had never experienced. He went home longing to go to his wife and say: 'I've learned a lot today. I've found out things I've never thought of. Life's a wonderful thing, a thing one can't live all to oneself—a thing one shares with everybody so that when another suffers we suffer too. It's the first time I've ever felt the spirit of Christ.'

Describing marriage, Joseph Newton said: 'It is a struggle for adjustment, an experience in unselfishness, an adventure in self-sacrifice ... a discipline in patience, kindness, sympathy, renunciation, and utter devotion, not to oneself, but to another—else it fails.' In the first century world, divorce was so widespread that some women were hesitating to marry on the grounds of marital insecurity. Jesus' call to fidelity was, however, more than a moral challenge. He desired that men and women should see marriage as a sacred and mystical union, unbreakable because God Himself 'hath joined together' (v. 9). This is the Christian ideal, and its fulfilment, as in all harmonious relationships, is as rewarding as it is demanding of daily unselfishness.

MARK 10: 13–16

'The man who does not accept the Kingdom of God like a little child will never enter it' (v. 15, J. B. Phillips).

CHILDREN HELP US TO UNDERSTAND OURSELVES. When Martin Luther looked round at his family in 1538, he remarked: 'Christ said we must become as little children to enter the Kingdom of Heaven. Dear God, this is too much. Have we got to become such idiots?' On this occasion the great reformer was exasperated, not serious.

However, Christ was never too busy to overlook children. Pearl Buck, the American novelist, tells of a boy's bitter disillusionment. His hero was Charles Lindberg, and when it was announced that the famous flier was to visit China, where the American boy lived, excitement ran high. 'At exactly the planned moment, when Lindberg was within a foot of him, the little boy shouted in a mighty voice, "Hullo, Lindy!" Lindberg looked down blankly into the boy's face and went on without speaking. He was, I suppose, absorbed in his own thoughts.' The novelist concluded: 'Ah, well, I suppose we are all guilty sometime or other of inflicting such wounds upon the innocent.'

But not Jesus! The disciples understandably pushed the children away, thinking that their Master, on His way to death, would not want to be bothered. He took the children into His arms and blessed them. Our attitude to children, and theirs to us, is often revealing!

Christ used a child to illustrate spiritual qualities. Look at just one of them—the 'openness' of little children, a combination of trust and freedom from deceit. They live gaily in the light of the truth, which accounts for their genuine humility. And this explains why in the presence of little children (note the 'little'), our sophisticated ways can make us ashamed.

MARK 10: 17-22

'You still lack one thing. Go, sell all that you have, and give it to the poor and you will have treasure in Heaven. And come! Follow Me' (v. 21, Barclay).

SEEKING AND SURRENDERING. This man was young, rich and religious, but still he was unsatisfied; hence his appeal to Jesus. The incident is full of meaning for us.

It illustrates the difference between religion and Christianity. The young man was respectable, but not reconciled to God. His religious training had emphasized a series of moral prohibitions, with the not surprising result that he thought of himself as good simply because he was not bad. This outlook reveals a negative religion, which can save a man from sin, but never to sanctity; and because of its spiritual associations, it often actually stands between the misguided believer and his hearing the call to adventurous Christian living.

This conversation between Christ and a respectable seeker also illustrates the difference between seeking Christ and surrendering to Him. He obviously had noble desires, but they were not strong enough to overcome his basic self-centredness. In his devotional classic *A Serious Call*, William Law insists that we fail 'through the want of a sincere intention of pleasing God in all our actions'. In other words, lack of predominant desire, of this central loyalty to live for Christ, explains our lack of spiritual achievement. We are too half-hearted to be pure in heart. We seek Christ, but rarely wholly surrender our riches, whatever their nature, to Him.

'How difficult it is for those who have great possessions to enter the Kingdom of God' (v. 23, J. B. Phillips).

HUMAN JUDGMENTS REVERSED. The contemporaries of Jesus, like their forebears and innumerable people today, thought of material prosperity as a sign of God's approval. That was why they put their trust in riches. Christ, however, brought a new judgment, which we must be careful to understand:

Jesus did not condemn riches. In the parable of Dives, the rich man, and Lazarus, the beggar, Jesus made Abraham's bosom the opposite of Hell; yet Abraham was possibly one of the richest men in the Bible! Self-evidently, riches in themselves do not necessarily lead to spiritual impoverishment or to God's condemnation.

Jesus stressed the danger of riches. Money being power and influence, a man of wealth was inclined to think of himself as self-sufficient, and of this material world as his one home. But, corrected Jesus on numerous occasions, only the individual whose treasure is first in the invisible world can live to the glory of God in this one. The development of this truism must have been breathtaking for His first hearers.

Jesus taught that human success was no guarantee of divine commendation. The next world is going to be full of surprises, for God's judgments are often so unlike man's. 'Many who are first now', said Jesus, 'will then be last, and the last now will then be first' (v. 31, J. B. Phillips). Why? Because we foolishly give undue importance to the externals of life.

'Whoever has a mind to be great among you, must be your servant, and whoever has a mind to be first among you, must be your slave' (v. 43, Knox).

TRUE GREATNESS. Having again listened to Jesus talking about His own death, James and John were primarily concerned about their position and prestige. But if they completely misunderstood Him, they also implicitly trusted Him, for in spite of His strange talk, which must have sounded to them like defeat, they still thought in terms of His establishing a Kingdom. He answered their request by outlining the essential qualities of spiritual greatness.

Greatness is measured by humility (v. 45). 'There is a hunger for humiliation', says Thomas Merton, 'that is nothing else but a hunger for admiration turned inside out.' With such self-deceit in mind, William Temple wrote: 'There is nothing big enough to hold a man's soul in detachment from the centre of himself through all the occupations of life except the majesty of God and His love; and it is in worship, worship given to God because He is God, that man will most learn the secret of real humility.'

Greatness is measured by willingness to sacrifice (v. 38). Was Thomas à Kempis right as far as we are concerned when he said, 'Jesus hath many lovers of His heavenly Kingdom, but few bearers of His Cross. All desire to rejoice with Him, few are willing to endure anything for Him, or with Him'?

Greatness is measured by lowly service (v. 44). This is not, note carefully, a question of what we do, but of the spirit in which we do it.

MARK 10: 46–52

'What do you want Me to do for you?' (v. 51, Moffatt).

THE MAN WHO KNEW WHAT HE WANTED. 'God's free gifts are generally proportioned to our desires,' wrote Bede Frost in *The Art of Mental Prayer*. 'We get what we really desire in our spiritual life.' But what do we 'really desire'? The question that Bartimaeus was called upon by Jesus to answer would possibly find us lost for words. True, we ask God to bless our loved ones, our nation, the world! But what do we actually want or expect Him to do? Could it be that such an indefinite and easy petition is but a camouflage for our lack of desire? We do not care deeply enough to know what to ask of God in explicit terms; and this, of course, accounts for our lack of persistence in prayer.

Bartimaeus kept asking because he knew precisely what he wanted. We cannot always be so sure, but our uncertainty, even about our own spiritual needs, is more often the result of unconcern than unavoidable ignorance. 'We pray against some evil habit in our lives,' says Dr. H. E. Fosdick, 'while at the same time we refuse to give up the practice that makes the habit easy, or the companionships in which the habit thrives. We go through the form of entreating God to save us from sin, but we do not want the answer so keenly as to burn the bridges across which the sin continues to come. Our petition is a lame and ineffective whim, without power.' How would we answer Christ's question to Bartimaeus?

'Those who went before Him and followed after Him cried aloud, Hosanna, blessed is He who comes in the name of the Lord' (v. 9, Knox).

CONDITIONAL WELCOME. As He rode into the city, Jesus was greeted with cries of 'Hosanna', which was not an expression of praise, but of need; the word means 'Save now'. The reason for this plea was the people's longing for deliverance from the power of Rome. And who but the Messiah could defeat such a conqueror? These 'common people' believed that Jesus was the One who is coming, but they completely misunderstood the nature of His kingdom. They greeted Him as the militant Son of David; He came as the Prince of Peace.

He was welcome only so long as He would do their will. We are like them when, for instance, we make our prayers for guidance a 'spiritual' justification for following our own preferences, or withdraw our service because we cannot have our own way. We want Jesus only as a divine means to our own selfish ends.

This was why the devout pilgrims waved their palms and shouted their Hosannas. But He withstood the temptations of popularity, and suffered the heartache of disappointing good—if misguided—people. Whatever the cost, His Father's will, not the people's, must be done, and this explains the secret of His own habitual serenity—though rarely free of outward conflict, Jesus knew the inner peace of God because His obedience kept Him at peace with God.

'Whatever you ask for in your prayers, believe it granted and it will be granted' (v. 24, Rieu).

HOW TO BEAR FRUIT FOR GOD. These two separated readings are full of mystery, for here is a picture of Jesus which is seemingly out of character. Why should He curse a fig tree for not having fruit, when the 'time of figs was not yet'? One explanation is to interpret this incident as an acted parable. Another, as William Barclay suggests, is to see it as a 'kind of continuation' of the similar parable recorded by Luke (12: 1-9).

What can be said, however, is that fruitlessness in God's service results in spiritual disaster. 'Every branch in Me that beareth not fruit', said Jesus, 'He taketh away' (John 15: 2). But what is spiritual 'fruit'? William Temple made the comment: 'No amount of ascetic discipline or spiritual fervour is a substitute for the practical obedience which alone is "fruit".' How often in Scripture we stumble across this same truth—God is not concerned about the results we achieve so much as the obedience we offer!

Fruitfulness in God's service and faith go together. Peter's incredulous observation that what Jesus had said would happen to the fig tree had happened is answered by Christ: 'Have faith in God.' How? 'Whatever you pray for and ask, believe you have got it, and you shall have it' (v. 24, Moffatt). This paradox contains a major secret of victorious living. We receive what we believe we have!

MARK 11: 15-19

'Is it not written, My house shall be known among all the nations for a house of prayer?' (v. 17, Knox).

THE NEED FOR REVERENCE. Referring to the cleansing of the Temple, William Temple wrote: 'The Lord dominates the multitude by the righteousness of His energy and the energy of His righteousness.' The meek Son of God's fierce anger against these desecrators of God's house was provoked by two primary causes.

They lacked reverence for God. 'We are anxious', said W. E. Orchard, 'about those who do not go to worship; we ought to be much more anxious about those who do. Suppose that what is intended for inspiration is turned into a self-satisfying enjoyment; suppose what was meant to open the eyes only closes them in sleep, and what ought to stir the will only drugs the conscience. That this does happen is deplorably obvious; for there are many who have a temperamental desire for worship who remain under it all, ignorant of God and deaf to His call.' In this unconscious development, the basic reason is a cheap familiarity with sacred things.

They lacked reverence for people. Religious pilgrims were exploited: they were compelled to change their money into Temple coinage at an exorbitant rate of interest and buy their sacrifices at inflated prices from sellers within the Temple. Even the piety of others was used for self-gain. This spirit of cynicism and contempt follows naturally from an absence of reverence in spiritual worship. Perhaps this accounts on occasion for our own unchristian attitude toward others.

'Jesus said to them, "I am going to ask you a question. Answer this, and I will tell you what authority I have for acting in this way" ' (v. 29, Moffatt).

LIES IN THE SOUL. These representatives of the Sanhedrin asked their question of Jesus not to elicit information, but to secure evidence to use against Him. They wanted not the truth, but confirmation of their own unconscious bigotry. He responded by confronting them with an insoluble dilemma, insoluble because the obvious answer would have undermined their position.

They preferred a lie to being proved wrong. Lies in the soul make it almost impossible for truth to penetrate. Said Somerset Maugham of an acquaintance: 'I do not think he ever had an inkling that he was an outrageous sham. His whole life was a lie, but when he was dying, if he had known he was going to, which mercifully he didn't, I am convinced that he would have looked upon it as well spent. He had charm, he was devoid of envy, and though too selfish to do anyone a good turn, he was incapable of unkindness.'

Few of us are wholly free of self-deceit, which is one reason why Thomas Merton noted that some of the people who worship 'with glistening eyes are very often the ones with the worst tempers'. This is bad enough when the failing is recognized, but when it is called righteous indignation, or zeal for truth or fiery conviction, the position is nearly hopeless.

'He still had one messenger left, His own well-beloved Son; Him He sent to them last of all' (v. 6, Knox).

GOD'S PATIENCE IN JUDGMENT. We noted above that fruitlessness in God's service brings its own judgments, and this reading underlines this truth. The vineyard was Israel to whom God had sent innumerable prophets and finally His Son, but the people, rejecting them all, had proved themselves unworthy of such high privilege. Judgment was to follow and the vineyard entrusted to others. The parable is full of spiritual lessons, but here are two.

Evil always tends to grow. The husbandmen beat the first servant, stoned the second and killed the third. Of sin, Professor J. S. Stewart wrote: 'It is, as Thomas à Kempis said centuries ago, first a simple suggestion, then a strong imagination, then delight, and then assent. And you remember Thackeray's fourfold progression—an act, a habit, a character, a destiny. That means that evil is never so easy to destroy as at its first attack.' The second lesson should drive us to our knees in worship.

Despite His judgment of sin, God is infinitely patient with our waywardness. The history of Israel is similar to the history of our own souls, for we too have repeatedly rejected the light. Yet God's persistent love has given us chance after chance, as it does still.

MARK 12: 13–17

'Give to Caesar what belongs to Caesar, and to God what belongs to God' (v. 17, J. B. Phillips).

MODEL CITIZENSHIP. In a genuine clash of viewpoint, it is possible, as these Pharisees and Herodians illustrate, to be more concerned about scoring a point than discovering the truth. These men confronted Jesus with what they imagined was an inescapable dilemma; whatever the answer, there would be cause for His condemnation! In His masterly reply, Jesus stressed man's obligations to the State and to God, an answer which can be stated for us in explicit terms.

The Christian should be a model citizen. Far too often have people, in the name of religion, withdrawn from the world, leaving its affairs in the hands of godless individuals. 'Those of us', said Keir Hardie, 'who, for many years, have practically deserted the religious platform have not done so because our faith and religion have grown less, but because, since the Church thought fit to specialize on what it most unfairly calls the spiritual side of Christianity, it became necessary for us to concentrate on the human side by way of restoring the balance.' The ideal is, of course, for the Christian eagerly to meet his obligations in this world (his vote, taxes, community service and possibly political leadership) because he knows himself to be a citizen of the next.

Nevertheless—the Christian's first allegiance is to God. He meets the wishes of the State only in so far as they are not in conflict with his loyalty to Christ's kingdom. Recognition of this truth made the Church in Germany the strongest, perhaps the only effective, opponent of Nazism. Thanks be to God for those German Christians who proved their model citizenship by choosing death rather than compromise.

'When people rise from the dead they neither marry nor are given in marriage; they live like the angels in Heaven' (v. 25, J. B. Phillips).

LIFE AFTER DEATH. At some time many of us may have felt like the poet Tennyson:

> Ah, Christ! that it were possible
> For one short hour to see
> The souls we loved, that they might tell us
> What, and where they be!

The Sadducees, not believing in life beyond the grave, asked Jesus a question which they imagined pointed in itself to a confirmation of their own view. His answer did the exact opposite.

Jesus affirmed the fact of immortality. God 'is not the God of dead people,' He said, 'but of living' (v. 27, Moffatt); for not even death can break the personal relationships that His love creates. ' "God is love" appears to me nonsense in view of the world He has made,' said Archbishop Temple, 'if there is no other.' Belief in God's love is our strongest reason for believing in life beyond the grave.

Jesus asserted the nature of immortality. In thinking of life after death, we tend, like the Sadducees, to imagine it in physical and material terms. This explains why people the world over have conceived of Heaven as a place empty of the things of which they disapprove, and as symbolic of the things they personally hope to experience. But, as Moffatt translates 1 Corinthians 2: 9—'What no eye has ever seen, what no ear has ever heard, what never entered the mind of man, God has prepared all that for those who love Him.'

'Thou shalt love the Lord thy God with the love of thy whole heart, and thy whole soul, and thy whole mind, and thy whole strength. ... Thou shalt love thy neighbour as thyself' (v. 30–31, Knox).

HOW TO LOVE PEOPLE. 'We cannot know whether we love God, although there may be strong reasons for thinking so; but there can be no doubt about whether we love our neighbour or no,' said Teresa of Avila. 'Be sure that in proportion as you advance in fraternal charity, you are increasing in the love of God.' Yet how difficult it is to advance in 'fraternal charity'!

'Probably the most difficult command to obey in the New Testament', wrote J. G. McKenzie in *Nervous Disorders and Religion*, 'is: Love thy neighbour as thyself. To love people is very hard and few there be who can do it. Those few are those who love God with mind, heart and soul. They love people because God loves them and because they see even the most debased as God's children. That relationship of love to God which feeds their own soul and motivates their love to man is an experience as real as that of sense perception.'

This love is not necessarily a matter of feeling. It must be directed by the will and brain, otherwise, when we cease to feel, we give up loving or praying or serving.

MARK 12: 35–44

'These are the men who grow fat on widow's property and cover up what they are doing by making lengthy prayers' (v. 40, J. B. Phillips).

SHAM PIETY. 'If David called the Messiah "Lord",' said Jesus, 'how is it that the Scribes call Christ (the Messiah) David's Son?' Far from merely playing with words, Jesus was trying to help the people to see the difference between their understanding of the title Messiah (a heavenly potentate who would establish an earthly kingdom) and His own (a suffering Servant whose sovereignty would be in the hearts of men). But there is another part of today's reading more challenging.

Jesus issued a further warning against sham piety. The Scribes looked religious enough, but their secret aims were for reputation, respect and prominence (vv. 38–39). They said 'long prayers', but never actually prayed, for prayer basically is thinking about God, and the Scribes, despite their parade of devoutness, were too self-centred to do this.

Their unrelieved, though personally unrealised, self-centredness also accounted for the way they could unashamedly fill their pockets by exploiting the religious sentiments of certain women (v. 40). Of course, the reason for spiritual pretence is always pride. 'The root from which the weaknesses in modern Christianity springs is pride,' said Florence Allshorn. 'For the devil's use, a proud Christian is of much more value than an atheist or a pagan.'

And the only antidote to pride, the saints unite to testify and illustrate, is to haunt Calvary.

MARK 13: 1–13

'He will be saved who holds out to the very end' (v. 13, Moffatt).

OVERCOMING CYNICAL HALF-HEARTEDNESS. In this reading there are prophecies about the fall of Jerusalem, which took place in A.D. 70, the persecution of Christians, and the Second Coming, about which see below. For the moment, consider the quality that Jesus said should characterize the Christian —endurance (v. 13).

It is easier to start than to continue. This applies to almost every experience in life, but most particularly to Christian discipleship. Indeed, there are few, if any, more demanding proofs of faith than to maintain our spiritual enthusiasm, to safeguard our zeal from the temptations of drab conformity and cynical half-heartedness. A bishop said to one of his clergymen: 'I suppose you're proud and pleased with yourself at converting a Communist. But I wouldn't be in your shoes for anything! That man has served the Communists for years. He has sold *The Daily Worker* at street corners and submitted to insults for doing it. He's given his life and his money to a cause he believed in! And now, you've got to transplant him into a congregation of dull, ordinary Christians. Why, I don't know a church in my diocese where a man like that will be at home.'

Christian endurance faces a stern test in unrelieved routine. To overcome that, and arrive at the end with our faith eager for new discoveries, is truly to have endured and therefore to be saved.

MARK 13: 14–27

'Now you take care!' (v. 23, Moffatt).
'You must keep your eyes open!' (J. B. Phillips).
'You must be on your guard' (Knox).

THE SECOND COMING. In pondering this sometimes neglected doctrine, we need to remember that Christ spoke about it in a picture language which His contemporaries would understand much more readily than we do. But even if some of this symbolism and imagery is confusing to our twentieth-century minds, and therefore does not lend itself to incontestable interpretation, two vital truths stand out.

Christ did say that He was coming again. It is futile to speculate as to the manner or, as He Himself stressed, the time of His coming; but we lose sight of a profoundly significant factor if we ignore these words because of their difficulty. They point to the fulfilment of Christ's purpose in history, to a triumphant winding-up by God of the affairs of men. Life is not empty of meaning or uncertain of achieving its rightful end. In this H-bomb age, such a realization can put steel girders into our faith.

Christ did say that the Christian's primary responsibility was to be ready for the Second Coming. People who spend their time in idle speculation are denying the spirit of His words. In speaking of His coming again, Christ was calling men to live—to work out their values and make all their decisions—against the background of the eternal. Only then could they always be ready!

MARK 13: 28–37

'Watch: I say it to you, and I say it to all' (v. 37, Moffatt).

HOW TO WAIT. Jesus said of His coming again that 'of that day and that hour knoweth no man, not the angels which are in Heaven, neither the Son, but the Father' (v. 32). Therefore when, just previously, He said, 'This generation shall not pass, till all these things be done' (v. 30), He could not have been referring to the Second Coming. What He had in mind was the fall of Jerusalem, which in fact did take place within the generation of those who heard His words. Characteristically Jesus concluded His prophecies with a word of practical counsel, mentioned three times in the final five verses of our reading.

The Christian must be watchful. J. B. Phillips renders this reiterated warning: 'Keep your eyes open' (v. 33); 'keep a look-out' (v. 35); 'keep on the alert' (v. 37). Now watchfulness is purposeful waiting. Nels Ferré put it like this: 'Real waiting is concerned waiting. It is more than interested watching. It is feeling and knowing oneself involved in the outcome. . . . Real waiting is also expectant waiting. Love never fails. Christian concern hopes all things. . . . Real waiting is also victorious waiting. We have unsolvable problems, but God has none. We have permanent problem children, but He does not. We die and do not see the fruits of our labour in this life, but God never dies, and beyond this life we shall see the reward of every deed done in the body.

Real waiting is victorious waiting because though our warfare seems constant the outcome is certain.' To watch is to wait in this spirit!

'Let her alone. . . . She has done a beautiful thing to Me. . . . She has done all she could' (vv. 6–8, Moffatt).

WHAT CHRIST WANTS ABOVE ALL. The Passover, commemorating Israel's exodus from Egypt, and celebrated on about April 14th, was immediately followed by the Feast of Unleavened Bread, a minor festival, which lasted for seven days and also marked the ingathering of the barley harvest. Every Jew living within fifteen miles of Jerusalem was compelled to attend the Passover, but devout pilgrims came from all parts of the world. Obviously there was not accommodation for all of them in the city, so they lodged in such places as Bethany, where Jesus received hospitality from Simon the leper.

Apart from Jesus Himself, the central characters in today's reading are the woman, who broke the box of ointment, and Judas, the traitor. They have so much to teach us, but this above all.

Christ wants nothing more than our love, which is the only guarantee of our loyalty. A father may have an otherwise perfect son, but if there is no love between them the father is wretched indeed. The rich young ruler brought to Jesus his moral goodness and his sincere religion, but not his love. If we do the same—and how easy it it to mistake this for Christian discipleship—we actually crucify Jesus afresh. His reaction to extravagant love can be seen in His words that the memory of this woman would be perpetuated.

Notice too His majestic confidence in His cause—facing imminent death, He spoke of His gospel being preached 'throughout the whole world' (v. 9). What a rebuke to our pessimism!

'He also took a cup and . . . said to them, "This means My covenant-blood which is shed for many" ' (vv. 23–24, Moffatt).

THE LAST SUPPER. Jesus was obviously an efficient organizer. Just as He had arranged in good time for an ass to be obtainable, so He guaranteed the availability of this Upper Room. True sanctity never overlooks practical details. The man with the pitcher would be conspicuous, as women usually performed such a duty, and he was to guide the two disciples.

During what we now call the Last Supper, Jesus told the Twelve that one of them was going to betray Him. The reaction of the innocent was an example for all of us. Far from looking accusingly at each other, they asked of themselves, 'Is it I?' We possibly prefer to discuss the failings of others than to look into our own hearts.

Christ also instituted a new covenant (v. 24). The old covenant, meaning bargain or relationship, was entirely dependent upon Israel's keeping of the Mosaic Law. This new covenant was dependent upon Christ's shed blood. In other words, the new relationship between God and man was dependent upon, not human obedience, but divine love. Someone has said that Jesus came not so much to preach the gospel as that there might be a gospel to preach. And here is the gospel—the Cross reveals that men are no longer only under God's law, but within God's love. Realization of this one truth makes slaves into sons, and transforms dull religious ceremonialism into the exciting exploration of divine love.

MARK 14: 27-31, 66-72

'When she noticed Peter warming himself, she looked at him. "Ah," said she, "you were with the Nazarene too, with Jesus!" ' (v. 67, Moffatt).

WHY PETER FAILED. In our understanding of this familiar story, we have possibly done Peter less than justice.

The Apostle was courageous. Granted, the opposite view is more general, but surely not valid. In the Garden of Gethsemane, Peter drew his sword to defend Jesus to the death. He was courageous enough to take on, if needs be, the cohort of soldiers single-handed. And would anyone but a truly brave man have followed his Leader right into the enemies' camp? Yet Peter was in the courtyard of the High Priest's palace. Whatever his failings, this disciple was not a coward. Then why did he deny Jesus? The answer, in the light of his rugged character, is most significant.

The Apostle was beaten by the taunts of a servant girl. She was doubtless mildly amused that One so 'weak' as Jesus (people had

even spat upon Him) should be accused of making claims to kingship. Some King! And here was one of His deluded followers. Was
she 'pulling Peter's leg' more than identifying a criminal in her
accusation? This much can be said with confidence—ridicule has
caused more denials of faith than danger. In such subtle ways does
the enemy of our souls undermine our loyalty. He knows that
generally it is easier to stand violent persecution than to be
laughed at. Peter, tough and so full of bold intentions, was brought
low by a girl's jesting.

MARK 14: 32–50

' "Dear Father," He said, "all things are possible to you.
Please—let Me not have to drink this cup! Yet it is not what
I want but what you want" ' (v. 36, J. B. Phillips).

GETHSEMANE. Even in the agony of Gethsemane, Jesus
was concerned about the needs of others. He left His wrestling
with God, and warned the disciples of their need to watch against
temptation. This characteristic longing to save people from evil
at least partly explains the mystery of our text for the day. He was
not trying to escape the Cross, nor was He afraid of the physical
suffering involved. His whole life had been one of intense and
almost unrelieved suffering, for the reason that His weeping over
the city of Jerusalem reveals.

Jesus was desperate to save His persecutors from the consequences of the terrible evil they were about to commit. He desired
not a different purpose, but, if possible, out of compassion for
those soon to be implicated in the world's greatest sin, a different
means to its fulfilment.

Herein is the nature and the cost of love! Even when itself
innocently suffering through sin, it remains first of all concerned
about the sinner, so concerned that it pleads with God on the
sinner's behalf.

MARK 14: 51–65

'What more evidence do we want? You have heard His
blasphemy for yourselves. What is your mind?' (v. 64,
Moffatt).

'PLAYING ABOUT' WITH THE TRUTH. The young man
who slipped out of 'a linen cloth' to escape arrest was almost certainly John Mark. He was too humble to mention himself by

name, but this incident, which is unique to Mark's gospel, could explain how we know so much about the agony of Jesus in Gethsemane. The disciples slept, but not this 'young man'. He saw and heard—and wrote!

The remainder of this reading is commentary upon the assertion that character is most accurately revealed in its attitude to truth. Hearing that the historian Penty was propounding a theory that Roman law was the cause of all sorts of evil, Lord Justice Slessor, with a very considerable knowledge of the subject, pointed out to him that in certain particulars at any rate his facts were wrong. 'They can't be wrong,' replied Penty, with the utmost seriousness, 'I'm sure of that, because if they were my theory would fall to the ground.'

This outlook was also the Sanhedrin's in its campaign against Jesus. Whatever the contrary evidence, these devoutly religious men were determined to hang on to their own 'theory'. And we are as bad when, in challenging situations, we 'play about' with the whole truth for the sake of personal comfort or convenience, or because of our cowardice.

MARK 15: 1–20

'Pilate questioned Him again. "Have you nothing to say? Listen to all their accusations!" But Jesus made no further answer—to Pilate's astonishment' (vv. 4, 5, J. B. Phillips).

THE SILENCE OF CHRIST. The previous reminder that character is revealed by its attitude to truth is now further emphasized by Pilate, who, though knowing that the Jewish religious leaders were motivated by envy (v. 10), nevertheless preferred to act upon a lie rather than face the consequences of doing the truth.

Jesus met this outlook with—silence (v. 5). 'Singular as it may seem,' wrote General Albert Orsborn, 'it is nevertheless a fact that Christ had nothing to say to certain types of men. This is still true of Him. A man's attitude of heart makes a difference when he wishes to approach the Lord, and only certain conditions of soul will draw replies from Him. Some men set out toward Christ with critical minds, prepared for argument, stocked with questions, prone to disbelief, and desiring least of all things to know the truth. To such men the Master reveals nothing, save the vanity of their own conceptions.'

Spiritual perception is always in proportion to our moral

stature and purity of motive. Dr. John A. Hutton had a man in his first parish of somewhat easy morals, who came to him with a thoughtful frown, 'I have great difficulties about the deity of Christ.' Whereupon his impatient pastor blurted out, 'But are you not a little weak also on the Ten Commandments?' The silences of Christ are eloquent to the pure in heart. But to the wilful sinner they are often pointers to his self-inflicted spiritual deafness.

MARK 15: 21–39

'My God, My God, why hast Thou forsaken Me?' (v. 34).

THE CROSS. Adoration is the only spirit in which this passage can be studied for, other considerations apart, this cry of dereliction from the Cross is finally beyond our understanding. Here is mystery, but not to bewilder; our wonderment should lead naturally to worship.

Someone has suggested that if Jesus was actually forsaken by God, then no good man can ever again be sure that he will not be deserted by God at the very moment he needs Him most. Yet this is surely to overlook a central meaning of the Cross. 'Up to this moment', writes William Barclay, 'Jesus had gone through every experience in life, except one—He had never known the consequences of sin. Now if there is one thing sin does, it is that it separates from God. It puts up between us and God a barrier like an unscalable wall. That was the one human experience through which Jesus had never passed because He was without sin. It may be that at this moment that experience came upon Him.'

Whatever our interpretation, and dogmatism would be foolish, this much can be said with certainty—having, though sinless, passed through this dreadful experience, Jesus is able to understand us when our sin separates us from God. In His name we can penitently approach the Father.

MARK 15: 40–47

'There were women there, who stood watching from far off. ... These used to follow Him and minister to Him when He was in Galilee' (vv. 40–41, Knox).

DANGEROUS LOYALTY. Here is a study of costly devotion to Christ:

The women remained dangerously with Him to the last (vv. 40–41, 47). True, they stood 'afar off', but they were there, which is more than can be said for most of the men disciples; and we shall never fully know what their presence meant to Christ. In *Doctor's Case Book and the Bible*, Paul Tornier writes: 'I received recently a letter from a woman doctor who told me of an experience she had just had. Called to the bedside of a man with a lung disease, who was able to speak only with difficulty, she realized that he did not want a flood of words from her, nor exhortation, nor even sympathy; he wanted real, deep, burning companionship.' These women at the Cross offered Christ the only thing they had—their loving companionship.

Joseph gave Jesus greater devotion after His death than during His life (vv. 43–46). How often we do this with our loved ones. An old man said to a Salvation Army officer, 'My wife died three months ago, and now I realize that I wasn't always kind to her. But it's too late.' Joseph can remind us that people need 'bouquets' before they die. Devotion to the dead is poor compensation for disloyalty during their life. We must be thoughtful now.

MARK 16: 1–8

'Are you looking for Jesus the Nazarene, who was crucified? He has risen: He is not here' (v. 6, Rieu).

THE LIVING CHRIST. Samuel Azariah, the first native Indian bishop, was once asked, 'If you were in a village where they had never heard of Christ, what would you preach about?' He answered without hesitation, 'The Resurrection.' After some condemned Christians had been driven to the place of their execution, their Nazi guards found scrawled into the paintwork of the truck: 'Jesus Christ is Lord!' 'Christ is alive!'

This is the breathtaking message of Easter Day. 'There is a Man', wrote Lacordaire, 'whose ashes after nineteen centuries have not grown cold; who daily lives again in the thoughts of an innumerable multitude of men.' True, but only partly true. For Christ is more than a perpetual memory lingering in the thoughts of men. He is a living Presence.

'Go your way,' the women at the sepulchre were told, 'tell His disciples and Peter' (v. 7). Poor, ashamed, self-despairing Peter had this special word of hope; and so have we. If we fail to hear it, it could be because, like these devoted women on their way to the sepulchre, we are too concerned with our problems and doubts.

'Who shall roll us away the stone?' they worried. But the stone was no longer there.

MARK 16: 9–20

'Go the whole world over, and proclaim the Good News to all mankind' (v. 15, Weymouth).

KNOWING CHRIST FOR OURSELVES. Scholars generally are agreed that these verses were not the original ending to Mark's gospel, for, apart from their marked change of style, they do not appear in any of the oldest manuscripts. Nevertheless they still have significance for us.

The disciples wanted first-hand confirmation of the Resurrection. All of us initially believed in Christ probably because of what somebody else (like parent or Sunday-school teacher) taught us. The danger always is that our faith could stop there. What we need is a personal encounter with the living Christ, whom we know about, without necessarily knowing. The disciples were right to make this emphasis, but wrong to assume that such an experience could come only by sight.

Wrote Alexander Whyte to a seeker: 'Act faith if you do not feel it. If you cannot think spiritually about Christ, think naturally of His work, a passage in His history, a word of His sayings. . . . Though cold and faithless at first, love and faith will come. Do not wait for a surge of feeling, think of Him at once. . . . There is nothing more that I can say. Christ is before you to take freely; accept Him, trust Him, believe what He says, assume that you are His, and behave as if you were.' In such ways do we come to know Christ for ourselves; and then we shall want to accept His commission to witness (v. 15).

THE GOSPEL ACCORDING TO LUKE

The Wideness of God's Mercy

INTRODUCTION

One tradition suggests that Luke, 'the beloved physician', was also a painter. Certainly he was an artist in words and his gospel has been described as 'the loveliest book ever written'.

He was also a serious historian, checking his sources with the meticulous care of a scholar, but this did not detract from the attractiveness of his style. As the only non-Jewish writer in the New Testament he saw Jesus, not only as the promised Messiah, but as Saviour of the world.

'Fully know the truth of what you have been taught by word of mouth' (v. 4, Weymouth).

THE HEART AND MIND'S DELIGHT. At the very start of his gospel Luke made clear his reasons for writing. One was that the individual whose identity was hidden under the pseudonym of Theophilus should be given 'full and reliable knowledge' (Barclay) about 'the matters in which you have already had instruction' (J. B. Phillips). The twentieth century believer may also be confident that he has not been tricked into accepting some cunningly devised fable but, as D. E. Nineham has said in his Penguin Commentary on St. Mark, can be 'virtually sure that what the tradition is offering us are the authentic deeds, and especially the authentic words, of the historic Jesus'. It was certainly not the New Testament writers who dreamed up the story of God Incarnate, but Jesus Himself who provided the facts they felt compelled to set down.

Luke's second reason was that his anonymous friend should find in this story the truth which would make him wise unto salvation. 'The certainty' (v. 4) of which the Authorized Version speaks is one which embraces head and heart. As Gerhard Kittel wrote: 'The Jesus of history is valueless and unintelligible unless He be experienced and confessed as the living Christ. . . . And the Christ of faith has no existence, is mere noise and smoke, apart from the reality of the Jesus of history.' It is the fact that the Christian gospel is based upon God's unique self-revelation of Himself in a particular person at a particular point in time which gives the saving message its lasting foundation and its present power.

'In the days of Herod king of Judaea there was a priest named Zechariah' (v. 5, N.E.B.).

ETERNITY AND HISTORY. Two statements appear in today's reading which, in many religious traditions, would have nothing to link them. A specific period in history is picked out—'the days of Herod king of Judaea'—and a man's role in the public worship of his nation is described. What has the worship of the eternal and unchanging God to do with the flux and turmoil of human history? Is not the very purpose of worship to escape the transient flow of events into the purer air of the spirit? The answer is 'No'—not for the Jew nor yet for the Christian. For the eternal God is also the God of history, the God who is concerned with the destiny of the human race and the destiny of each individual.

'Christianity', writes Karl Rahner, 'is an historical and a very concrete and sturdy religion, a stumbling-block to the proud, who really—at least in religious matters—do not wish to be human beings, but it is grace and truth for those who with the humble hearts are willing to be human beings in space and time even when they are adoring the God of eternity and infinity.'

This does not mean that worship is less important to the Christian than it is to, say, the eastern mystic. It simply means that the Christian engages in worship in order to clarify the action he must undertake in everyday life, to reinforce his spirit so that he becomes a co-worker with the God who is at work in human affairs.

LUKE 1: 18–25

'You will lose your powers of speech, and remain silent until the day when these things happen to you, because you have not believed me' (v. 20, N.E.B.).

ENFORCED SILENCE. Why did Zechariah temporarily lose his speech after his vision in the temple? We can hardly regard this as divine punishment, or the result of a fit of angelic pique on the part of Gabriel because his message was received with some incredulity. In one sense it was merciful that Zechariah was unable to communicate a vision about which he obviously had some doubts, and his dumbness enforced a period of solitude in which he could ponder the meaning of the vision and prepare himself for the responsibilities of fatherhood.

How often we hear people claim that a period of enforced silence or solitude has enabled them to make new spiritual discoveries! How sad that we cannot organize our lives so that we do not need misfortune to make this possible! Thomas Merton has said that 'the world of men has forgotten the joys of silence, the peace of solitude which is necessary, to some extent, for the fulness of human living. ... All men need enough silence and solitude in their lives to enable the deep inner voice of their own true selves to be heard at least occasionally. When that inner voice is not heard, when man cannot attain to the spiritual peace that comes from being perfectly at one with his own true self, his life is always miserable and exhausting. For he cannot go on happily for long unless he is in contact with the springs of spiritual life which are hidden in the depths of his own soul.'

LUKE 1: 26–38

'In the sixth month the angel Gabriel was sent from God to a town in Galilee called Nazareth' (v. 26, N.E.B.).

WHERE TO BEGIN. G. K. Chesterton pointed out how misleading was the statement that popular journals print above the closing chapters of their serial stories, 'You may begin the story here'; misleading because the only place to begin reading a story is at the beginning. And where shall we begin the Christmas story —with a stable, oxen, shepherds and a birth? The New Testament writers, each in their own way, affirm that that is not the beginning. However much the story of angelic visitations may puzzle our twentieth-century minds, they underline this important truth: in the coming of Jesus the initiative was with God. This story begins, not at Bethlehem, but in the divine purpose for man's redemption.

There is food for reflection in G. A. Studdert Kennedy's observation that 'advent, the coming of God, is a more accurate and significant name for the creative process than evolution'.

Yet the birth we celebrate each year was no violent intrusion from another sphere. Even in the Incarnation God waited upon Mary's willing surrender—'I belong to the Lord, body and soul. Let it happen as you say.'

What was true of the birth of Jesus provides the model for all spiritual life. Wilbur Chapman, the American evangelist, once felt such a failure that he wrote out his resignation. Before posting it he happened to read some words by Dr. Meyer: 'It does not matter so much what we do for God: but it matters a great deal what God does through us.' He tore up his resignation and began again with an act of total surrender.

LUKE 1: 39–56

'Yes, from this day forward all generations will call me blessed, for the Almighty has done great things for me' (vv. 48 and 49, Jerusalem Bible).

A BLOW TO PRIDE. One of the positive gains arising out of

the dialogue between Roman Catholics and Protestants is the recognition that exaggerated claims for Mary, the mother of Jesus, on the one hand have led to equally exaggerated reactions on the other. Her part in the story of redemption has been somewhat neglected by Protestants. Yet, as we saw yesterday, the Incarnation required her submission and at so many points in the gospel story her example is worth contemplating.

Both in Elizabeth's greeting and Mary's exalted response we meet the word 'blessed'. If we would discover the full meaning of this quality we must look at the Beatitudes where Jesus gives a detailed portrayal of who are the 'blessed'. Significantly, they begin with a recognition of our poverty before God, and they breathe a spirit of humble self-forgetfulness. Although the gospel narratives tell us little about Mary we may be sure that humility was one of her chief virtues. Could God have entrusted so responsible a vocation to one in whose heart there was any trace of arrogance?

That the Christ should be born to a woman of such lowly origin is a blow to all our social pretensions and intellectual pride. Mary's song of praise, which we call the Magnificat, sounds more like a revolutionary manifesto than a religious hymn. Modern man, says Niebuhr, believes that religion is 'consciousness of our highest social values'. Nothing could be further from the truth, he insists. 'True religion is profound uneasiness about our highest social values.'

LUKE 1: 57–66

'People turned the whole matter over in their hearts, and said, "What is this child's future going to be?"' (v. 66, J. B. Phillips).

DOUBLE-EDGED DISCOVERY. Obeying the heavenly messenger who foretold the birth of their son, Zechariah and Elizabeth gave the baby the name John, meaning 'Jehovah is gracious'. The circumstances surrounding this birth cause widespread speculation about the boy's future. Obviously God had some special purpose for him to fulfil. Yet is it not also true that every child should be regarded with wonder and hope?

In recent years the paramount importance of infancy has been increasingly recognized. To be securely loved in childhood is the greatest boon we can be granted. Like many discoveries, however, this realization is double edged. Parents spend years in bitter regret at what they now see to be the mistakes made in rearing their children. Adults who did not have a very good start in life harbour resentment against their parents. 'There are some childhoods which are invitations to unconscious remorse', writes Roger Schutz. 'One always wants to start all over again in order to do better.' Brooding regret kills the creative impulse and makes life sterile. We must tackle life from where we now are by the help of God, and not waste our energies wishing we were somewhere else.

If vain regrets constitute one danger, smug complacency is another. If we ourselves have been loved into security and well-being, how much do not we owe to those around us who are insecure and unloved.

LUKE 1: 67–80

'In the tender compassion of our God the morning sun from heaven will rise upon us . . . to guide our feet into the way of peace' (vv. 78 and 79, N.E.B.).

PASSING UNDERSTANDING. Dr. Paul Carlson, the medical missionary who was killed by rebels in the Congo, had been the only doctor serving a hundred thousand people. He treated hundreds of patients every week and performed at least one major surgical operation each day. His wife said that she believed the only way he was able to stand up the strain of such a volume of work was that he kept close to God through prayer and meditation upon the Bible. The day before his execution Paul Carlson wrote in his New Testament a single word—'Peace'.

Zechariah's hymn of praise, since used so often in the worship of the church, looked to the 'morning sun from heaven' which would 'shine on those who live in darkness, under the cloud of death' and 'guide our feet into the way of peace'. Perhaps even more at Christmas than at any other time we are acutely and painfully aware of the divisions and conflicts which rend mankind and endanger the future of the race. No Christian can merely be content with 'peace of soul', turning his back upon a needy world. He is pledged to strive for harmony and reconciliation against all odds.

Yet we must not lose sight of the truth that the coming of Christ can mean for each one of us that deep peace of heart which passes understanding and is not dependent upon circumstances. The birth of Jesus is God's message of love and pardon to every individual; that a large part of the world rejects this message does not mean we should forfeit our inheritance as believers.

'As there was no place for them inside the inn, she wrapped Him up and laid Him in a manger' (v. 7, J. B. Phillips).

TENDER APPEAL. Nothing is as vulnerable, or so utterly dependent, as a baby. And the Christ Child 'was not merely helpless, as all babies are. He also lacked a home, He was threatened by powerful enemies, His parents were people without wealth or influence, an artisan couple as politically and socially defenceless as their child was physically vulnerable. This refugee family lacked even the feeble support and companionship of others in a similar plight. In their terrifying predicament they were utterly alone.' In reminding us of this fact, Rosemay Haughton points out that such helplessness always evokes powerful feelings in the beholder: from the strong a sense of protectiveness and concern, but in the weak feelings of fear or even panic.

Those who have been deeply wounded by being deprived of love may positively resent anything which reminds them of their own vulnerability, or appeals to tender emotions they have found it necessary to repress. This is why the weak and helpless sometimes find themselves, not protected, but attacked. Both these reactions—protectiveness and rejection—are seen in the story of the first Christmas.

How significant it is that God should choose to come in such a way, appealing to our love! The appeal of irresistible power or dazzling splendour is wholly laid aside. The fear we feel before the Christ child is the fear that our own love is inadequate and that we shall be carried out of ourselves into costly, compassionate concern. Yet this is a fear which we now can conquer—for Christmas reminds us that as we are loved of God we can afford to let go our defensive isolation.

LUKE 2: 8–14

'Suddenly an angel of the Lord stood by their side, the splendour of the Lord blazed around them, and they were terror-stricken' (v.9, J. B. Phillips).

STARTLING PROXIMITY. For the shepherds the most astonishing thing about that night which was so full of surprises must have been the commonplace scene at the manger. Surely the splendour of the angelic appearance, and the ecstasy of the heavenly chorus, must have been but the prelude to something more 'out of this world'. But no! Bethlehem had nothing more unusual to show than a mother weary from the labour of child-birth, an anxious, vigilant father, and a Baby unfortunate enough to be born in a stable. Yet in this ordinary situation the shepherds did not experience an anti-climax—they discovered God.

Could they ever again regard the circumstances of their daily lives in quite the same way? If the divine could once break through so unexpectedly must it not be much nearer than they thought? And is this not one of the lessons which this passage has for us? The tragedy of Christ's coming was that so many who were looking for Him completely missed Him because they needed the spectacular to convince them. God in ordinary life they overlooked.

We all need the reminder contained in these lines of G. K. Chesterton:

> Step softly, under snow or rain,
>   To find the place where men can pray;
> The way is all so very plain,
>   That we may lose the way.
>
> Go humbly; humble are the stars,
>   And low and large and fierce the Star;
> So very near the manger lies
>   That we may travel far.

LUKE 2: 15–20

'So they came as fast as they could and they found Mary and Joseph—and the baby lying in a manger' (v. 16, J. B. Phillips).

THE FAMILY. When the shepherds came to the stable they found, not only a Baby, but a family. Christmas is traditionally the season of the family, and we may at present be congratulating ourselves on the strength of the family tie. Yet few would deny that in the modern world family life is a frequent casualty. Even in the happy home where breakdown is unlikely we need to be-ware lest the rush of modern life and too great a reliance upon TV entertainment prevent us from really knowing our family at depth.

Trevor Huddleston claims that because the Bethlehem stable

shelters a family, 'Christianity asserts that a social order which ignores or debases the true dignity of family life is in fact destroying society itself. The stable shelters a family, a very ordinary artisan family of the largest tribe of David. But if that family is in fact the chosen way of God's entering human society, the family itself and the ties which bind it together have a meaning and a purpose which are also infinite.'

In the light of the love manifested at Bethlehem can we examine our family relationships and the standard of home life we are setting before our children and those who visit us? As J. S. Hoyland has written:

A home
Is the armoury of God
In His battle to the death with the evil, cruelty, lust . . .
A home
Is a treasury of God
Wherein purity, beauty and joy
Are stored for His purposes, inviolate.

A home
Shall be potent
Through the world and beyond it
To scatter abroad the love and the knowledge of God.
For a home
Is in itself the triumph of God,
Banishing night and chaos and necessity,
Indwelling this lifeless clay
With the spirit divine of freedom and joy
Overcoming to all eternity
Evil with good.

LUKE 2: 21–24

'The time came for circumcising the child and He was called Jesus, the name given Him by the angel before His conception' (v. 21, J. B. Phillips).

WARM AND CLOSE. In John Galsworthy's novel *The Forsyte Saga* there is a scene where the whole family has gathered to bury the much-beloved dog, Balthasar. A young boy is there, puzzled about death and wondering about the God of whom he has heard very little in his family circle. 'Do you believe in God?' he asks his father. 'Of course,' the father replies, 'if by God one means the power which is behind everything that exists, or if by God one means the sum of human goodness.' 'That leaves out Christ, doesn't it?' the son perceptively replies.

The name given to the Christ-Child was Jesus and that means: Yahweh helps. To the father in Galsworthy's novel, God was a vague indefinable power, of little consequence in the everyday affairs of life. Yet even to many earnest seekers and mystics God is hidden in dark inaccessibility. The Christian does not minimize the mystery of God but for him the mystery has become warm, close and loving in Jesus. He dare not 'leave out Christ' for if he did God would once again disappear into abstraction or confusion. Jesus brings God into sharp focus, and the name He bears reminds us that the infinite God is yet to be loved, trusted and obeyed.

LUKE 2: 25-35

'This Child is destined to make many fall and rise in Israel and to set up a standard which many will attack—for He will expose the secret thoughts of many hearts' (vv. 34 and 35, J. B. Phillips).

THROUGH HUMILIATION TO TRIUMPH. Like most of his contemporaries, Simeon saw the 'salvation of Israel' in terms of national liberation and a restoration of the glories associated with the reign of David. When at last he held the Christ-Child in his arms, and the spirit of prophecy came upon him, he glimpsed the truth that the way to glory lay through humiliation and suffering—for both the Messiah and His would-be followers.

Concerning Simeon's prophecy the most natural interpretation is that many in Israel will fall before they rise again, not that some will fall and some rise. 'For in the actual event,' as G. B. Caird has commented, 'it was not true that the coming of Jesus meant the fall of some and the rising of others. Even His best friends had to be humbled by failure, and then it was only because He had chosen to share their humiliation that they were able to rise at all.'

Do we imagine there is some easy path to humility? Or that it is a virtue that can be isolated from action? Baron von Hugel, Roman Catholic scholar and mystic, claimed that 'there is no humility without humiliation'. The Christmas story should leave us more prepared to follow Christ on His path of humiliation to glory, no longer seeking the short cuts which pride would desire.

'A widow . . . their own city Nazareth' (vv. 37, 39).

OBSCURE NAME AND OBSCURE PLACE. Setting legend aside, little is known of Anna, and the text is not clear whether she had been left a widow for eighty-four years, or whether that was her age when she returned thanks in the Temple for the coming of Jesus (see note, N.E.B.). But neither her personal sorrow nor her great age had dimmed her spirit's expectancy or closed her eyes to the identity of the One who was held in Mary's arms. Those who are young in heart will always be awake to new truths, to respond to new duties, to receive new blessings. As with Moses, their eye will not be dim nor their natural force abated. In the spiritual life high noon is not a matter for the calendar.

If our judgments sometimes need correcting on the comparative values of age and youth, they also often need correcting on the relationship between size and importance. 'The largest conurbation in industrial England' or 'The most swiftly growing city in the mid-West', some public announcement will read. The justified comment is: so what?

The Authorized Version calls Nazareth a city; the N.E.B. a town; we might describe it as a village. Nathanael, who came from Cana some three or four miles away, thought nothing of it (John 1: 46). But just as we ought to be wise enough not to write any man off, so we ought not to write any place off. There are encyclopedias which do not give Abraham Lincoln's birthplace; just that he was born in Kentucky. And who, in a 'Top of the Form' session, could give the birthplace of Albert Schweitzer— Kayserberg in Upper Alsace? These are but warnings that it has pleased—and still pleases—God to choose 'things which are not to bring to nought things that are'.

LUKE 2: 41-52

'Jesus increased in wisdom and stature' (v. 52).

THE CHILD JESUS. Luke provides the one authentic story which we have of the boyhood of Jesus, and it is a welcome relief from parallel incidents to be found, for example, in the apocryphal gospel of Thomas. Nor is there overmuch foundation in this particular passage for Mrs. S. Z. Kaufman's line that Jesus 'taught the learned doctors'. This could owe more to Hofman's painting 'The finding of Christ in the Temple' where the Lad is portrayed standing almost authoritatively among the Jewish elders as if He were teaching them, whereas what Luke says is that He was 'listening to them and asking them questions' (v. 46, R.S.V.).

Clive Sansom has described the possible feelings of one of the watching rabbis.

> Marking a sympathetic face,
> I found myself addressing him
> And had deliberately to avoid
> The Lad, lest others, following my glance,
> Should cause Him such embarrassment
> As again only youth can suffer.

Mary was reproachful when at long last she and Joseph found Jesus once again. They had been 'worried to distraction' (v. 48, Barclay). But there was nothing unfilial in His reply. Why had they been searching the city for Him? They should have come straight to the Temple. That was the one place where He was likely to be—'in My Father's house' (R.S.V. and N.E.B.). Is this the first hint we are given of the awareness of Jesus of the unique bond which linked Him to the Father? His personal dedication to the will of God which was eventually to take precedence over all family ties was already a factor in His life.

Luke 3: 1–6

'All mankind is to see the saving power of God' (v. 6, Knox).

A UNIVERSAL APPEAL. When Bernini, the Roman sculptor, was commissioned to make a statue of Charles the First, the artist Vandyck drew three portraits for him on one canvas. One drawing showed the king's face viewed from the left, another from the right and the third showed him full face. Similarly, each of our gospels shows Jesus from a different viewpoint. One characteristic of the Lucan portrait is that the writer shows Jesus as the Saviour of all mankind. Christ's appeal is universal. So Luke begins his account of the ministry of Jesus by setting it in the context of world history (v. 1). And he carries his quotation from Isaiah one verse further than the other gospel writers to include the words, 'All mankind shall see God's deliverance' (v. 6, N.E.B.).

The life of Jesus has world significance and His character universal appeal. Said a Tamil, whose only introduction to Jesus had been reading one of the gospels, 'This Jesus gets into my heart.' Writing of his experience teaching in a Chinese university A. B. Starratt says that the students read the Bible just as a Christian might read the book of another religion. Yet they 'recognized the authority of the way of love not because of prior acceptance of the authority of the Bible or of the Church or of any theological opinion about Jesus, but simply because the value of His teaching and life are self-authenticating'.

Christ's appeal is not only to all races of men but to men of all ages. This is why our charter still is to 'make disciples of all the nations'.

LUKE 3: 7-14

'See that you do something to show that your hearts are really changed!' (v. 8, J. B. Phillips).

GENUINE REPENTANCE. The familiar scenery of the Jordan valley, which is covered with thick shrub, provided John with vivid metaphors of the judgment he proclaimed. The fate of the unrepentant would be like that of snakes fleeing in panic before a grass fire or as a doomed tree at which the woodcutter lays his axe while taking a rest. Genuine repentance, however, would avert judgment.

Repentance means a changed attitude to other people. To each class of people John spelt out in simple terms the meaning of repentance, and in each case it meant a revision in their way of regarding their fellows. That the Baptist sought to destroy the false security which the Jews felt in their racial inheritance is also significant (v. 8). Nothing prevents genuine human encounter so much as personal pride and status seeking, whether social, intellectual or religious.

Repentance must be specific. A general but vague desire for improvement achieves nothing and can even be an evasion of the need for particular action. For instance, an abstract 'love' for mankind can coexist with callous indifference for those near at hand. Mrs Jellyby, in Dickens's *Bleak House*, was absorbed with schemes for the improvement of the African but sadly neglected her own family. 'She was a pretty, very diminutive, plump woman, of from forty to fifty, with handsome eyes, though they had a curious habit of seeming to look a long way off. As if . . . they could see nothing nearer than Africa!'

174

'It was while all the people were being baptized that Jesus was baptized too, and stood there praying' (v. 21, Knox).

THE KING WHO SERVES. Why was Jesus baptized? John's baptism was for the forgiveness of sins, yet the uniform witness of the New Testament is that Jesus had no sins of His own to confess (Acts 3: 14; 2 Corinthians 5: 21; 1 Peter 1: 19). All we know of Jesus, particularly His scathing attacks on empty ritual, assures us that He was incapable of taking part in a meaningless ceremony. The clue to the meaning of His baptism is found in the words addressed to Him, 'Thou art my Son, my Beloved; on Thee my favour rests' (v. 22, N.E.B.). This is a composite quotation from Psalm 2: 7 and Isaiah 42: 1. The first phrase proclaims the ascension of a king and the second describes the Suffering Servant of God. At His baptism Jesus was being anointed to both these offices. He was a king—but He was to reign in patient and self-forgetful service.

At His baptism Jesus fully identified Himself with the people He came to save. Aloofness or condescension found no place in Christ's character for He was perfect love. Describing the part of the Jordan where Jesus is supposed to have been baptized, J. E. Fison wrote, 'It is perhaps the lowest, dirtiest, muddiest, most barren and desolate place on the earth's surface.' George Adam Smith said the Jordan was 'mostly silent and black in spite of its speed ... muddy between banks of mud, careless of beauty, careless of life.' All of which is something of a parable of the love of Christ. He did not disdain to join the thronging multitude seeking release from guilt in the grimy waters. That is what made Him truly their Saviour.

LUKE 3: 23–38

'Which was ... which was ... which was' (v. 24, or any other verse in the reading!).

SON OF ADAM, SON OF GOD. What good purpose do these lengthy genealogies serve? Paul Tournier, the gifted Swiss Christian doctor, has described how in his youth he used to be wearied by these long lists of names which, in certain Old Testament books, occupy whole chapters and here, in the Authorized Version of Luke's gospel, run to upwards of five hundred words. But with maturing judgment Tournier came to see that these lengthy lists were declaring that, in the sight of God, no man was just a thing, or an abstraction, or a unit in a mass— but a person. As such he was the object of God's love who, as Augustine said, loves us each as if there was only one of us to love.

This truth is underlined by the name given to the one to whom Luke dedicated this gospel (1: 3). Theophilus is made up of two Greek words which mean 'beloved of (or by) God' or 'dear to God'. Wolfgang Amadeus Mozart was first christened Theophilus. His parents later changed this to its Latin form—but the meaning remained unchanged. We are all God's chillun—the Congolese as well as the Canadian; the aborigine as well as the Arab.

We are irreplaceable only to those by whom we are loved. An employer is not irreplaceable, nor is an employee. President will follow president; general will succeed general. But a wife, a husband, a child—these are irreplaceable. Even if there are several children in a family the loss of one leaves a vacant chair which none of the others can fill. This is what makes each of our lives unique. As Frank Crossley of the Star Hall, Manchester, used to say: 'The good news is not just that God loves men but that He loves me.'

LUKE 4: 1–8

'From the Jordan, Jesus came back full of the Holy Spirit, and for forty days He was led by the Spirit in the desert, while the devil tempted Him' (v. 1, Moffatt).

NO EXEMPTION. The account of Christ's lonely conflict with temptation in the wilderness came from the Master's own lips. That the story is a highly picturesque way of describing an inner conflict we may be sure: we cannot, for instance, imagine Jesus tempted to worship a visible embodiment of the Evil One. Jesus may have shared this experience with His disciples after Peter had recognized His messiahship. It would help to disabuse their minds of any notion that He was a popular nationalistic leader.

Holiness brings no exemption from the struggle with evil. This is one lesson we may learn from the fact that Christ was tempted. True, the thorough-going egotist who is taking the first faltering steps in learning to love will encounter different temptations from the saint. This is because temptation changes its form as we mature; indeed, our struggles with evil are an indication of our inner growth. But even the saint does not escape spiritual conflict. And, because He was truly human, our Lord was frequently tempted.

The temptations of Jesus remind us that sin is a failure to trust God. Christ was tempted to abandon trustful dependence upon God and faith in the triumph of goodness. The devil urged Him to demand miraculous confirmation of His Sonship and to bring in God's kingdom by unworthy means. Whenever we doubt the power of love, and let us admit that life often suggests such doubts, we are in danger of abandoning the only way of life which harmonizes with the nature of God.

LUKE 4: 9-13

'And when he had exhausted every kind of temptation, the devil withdrew until his next opportunity' (v. 13, J. B. Phillips).

NO DISCHARGE IN THIS STRUGGLE. The temptations of Jesus remind us that evil is tremendously subtle. Evil usually masquerades as good, which may be the secret of its attraction. This is true even of the temptations of a saint, even of the temptations of Christ. G. B. Caird has observed that at His baptism Jesus had 'heard a voice saying, "Thou art My Son"; now He hears another voice, "If you are the Son of God . . .", and He must decide whether or not it comes from the same source.' Skilfully using Scripture the devil made his suggestions highly attractive to One who was utterly dedicated to bringing God's Kingdom on earth. Yet each suggestion involved the betrayal of trust and love. Long after we have outgrown the appeal of blatant selfishness or evil indulgence our lives can be marred by subtle compromise or unconscious egoism.

Few temptations can be disposed of once for all. They reappear, though in different forms. The Gospel records that the devil 'withdrew until his next opportunity'. When Peter later tried to divert his Master from the way of the Cross the violence of Christ's reply, 'Away with you, Satan' (Mark 8: 33, N.E.B.), was an indication that Christ recognized the old temptation in a new form. And surely the doubt-insinuating words of the tempter, 'If you are the Son of God . . .' were echoed in that last grim struggle when the onlookers mocked the crucified Jesus, 'If you are the king of the Jews, save yourself' (23: 37, N.E.B.).

There is a Scots proverb that 'the devil's boots don't creak'. Remembering that he can disguise himself as an angel of light, we must always watch—and pray.

'He has sent Me to proclaim release for captives and recovery of sight for the blind' (v. 18, Moffatt).

CHRIST'S PROGRAMME. Following the temptations Jesus returned to Galilee 'armed with the power of the Spirit' (N.E.B.). Spiritual conflict, when fought through with integrity, greatly adds to a man's moral strength. Luke placed today's story at this particular point, although Mark has it later, because the Scripture passage which Jesus read in the Nazareth synagogue beautifully outlined the programme upon which He was embarking. The synagogue must have evoked many memories for Jesus. It had been His school as well as His place of Sabbath worship. Boyhood teachers and friends were no doubt present, expecting from Jesus an explanation of His aims.

Christ's manifesto was, and is, a programme of healing and liberation. Like the Baptist, Jesus also sounded a note of warning— but this was never His primary emphasis. In Him God's power to make men whole and to set them free was breaking through. Good news indeed! Writing of the power of the gospel to help nervous sufferers Paul Tournier has said 'Religious salvation lies in the re-discovery of the divine purpose. ... No doubt that purpose is never fully realized in this world. But case after case has shown that the road to health both for the person and for society lies in a genuine experience of the grace of God.' Because God's grace was perfectly manifested in Jesus He was able to set men free. Nor has His touch lost its ancient power.

' "Today", He said, "in your very hearing this text has come true" ' (v. 21, N.E.B.).

DISTORTING PRIDE. The synagogue service contained two Scripture readings: one, from the law, was from a fixed lectionary and the other, from the prophets, was probably chosen by the reader. Any suitable person could be asked to preach the sermon which was delivered seated. At Nazareth Jesus did not simply read the Scripture portion. He made it a proclamation and declared its prophecy fulfilled in His own ministry. His sermon pleased His listeners until He suggested that God's goodness was extended to the Gentiles. The enraged congregation tried to anticipate Calvary and destroy One who offended their national conceit.

There is a profound contrast between John the Baptist's opening words (3: 7–9) with their warning of doom and our Lord's of deliverance. The one told men what they must do for God, the other of what God could do for men; the one urged people to achieve, the other to believe; the one warned men to flee from the wrath to come, the other wooed them to flee to the Love that had come.

Let us be sure that we understand these differences. Some of us fail to recognize the gospel as 'good news', viewing it rather as impossible idealism which makes life an insufferable burden. Christ is the power of God unto salvation, not the taskmaster of God unto distraction.

LUKE 4: 31–37

'Jesus rebuked the demon. "Silence!" He exclaimed; "come out of him" ' (v. 35, Weymouth).

POSSESSED BY EVIL. The ancient world believed that the air was full of evil spirits, which sought to enter the human body, often through food and drink, and were responsible for all disease. A raving lunatic, for instance, was simply possessed by demons.

'Modern thought', says Dr. Wm. Barclay, 'has been swinging round to the admission that perhaps there is something in demons after all. There are some troubles that have no bodily cause at all, as far as can be discovered. . . . Since there is no physical explanation some now think that there must be a spiritual one and that demons are not so unreal.'

What cannot be denied is that people are still possessed by evil, despite any appearance to the contrary. Having seriously examined his own inner life for the first time, C. S. Lewis confessed: 'I found what appalled me; a zoo of lusts, a bedlam of ambitions, a nursery of fears, a harem of fondled hatreds.' This from a respectable university don, who claimed to be typical of Mr. Everyman! There is only one answer to such 'demon possession', as C. S. Lewis soon afterward proved—the living Christ.

LUKE 4: 38–44

'As the sun was setting, all those who had friends suffering from every kind of disease brought them to Jesus and

He laid His hands on each of them separately and healed them. . . . At daybreak, He went off to a deserted place' (vv. 40, 42, J. B. Phillips).

THE BALANCED LIFE. The need for a balanced life—of worship and work—is obvious, but so many of us fail to achieve this in practice. We work for things that can only be accomplished by prayer, and pray for things that can only be obtained by work. We must learn to differentiate and to guard against our prayer-life being undermined by over-busyness.

When particularly busy, Martin Luther actually lengthened his time for prayer, explaining that otherwise he would be incapable of meeting all his commitments. Arthur Jackson, medical missionary in Manchuria, played strenuous games and was the soul of good company. One person described him as the 'manliest of men', another as the 'jolly doctor equally at home in his comic song and in the meeting-tent when he spoke for his Lord'. Wrote his biographer: 'His strength came from prayer. He won his chief victories upon his knees. He was Christ's man.'

Today's verses reveal that Christ recovered from (and prepared to face) a day of hectic activity, not by 'lying-in' in the morning, but by 'getting up' a great while before day to pray.

LUKE 5: 1-11

'As soon as they had brought the boats to land, they left everything and followed Him' (v. 11, N.E.B.).

MOMENT OF DECISION. Here is the story of a momentous and life-changing encounter. What the outcome of meeting this disturbing Man would be Peter could not have dreamed. And certainly Peter's obedience was immensely to influence the future of the Christian cause. We must always remember that this Gospel and the Acts constitute a single two-volume work. There is probably an implied connection between the command of Jesus, 'Put out into deep water', and Peter's later obedience in going to the house of Cornelius (Acts 10) and so launching the Church into the deep waters of the Gentile world.

Peter was the kind of man Christ wanted. Like his fellow fishermen, he had been disciplined by labour and hardship. Despite the heavy weariness of a night's fruitless toil Peter's immediate response to Christ's command was, 'If you say so, I will let down the nets.' Jesus loved the enthusiast, the man of energetic action, the man who was prepared to 'go out on a limb', to take risks. Such a man was Peter. Those of us who are temperamentally more cautious must beware lest our caution results in lack of commitment.

Jesus was the Leader Peter needed. Here was One capable of harnessing and directing all the energies of this colourful but contradictory character. Like us, Peter needed not a philosophy but a personal loyalty. He needed to see the truth embodied in a Man. As Werner Pelz once wrote: 'To the unavoidable human question: what must we do in order to live? there is no human answer—and the words of Jesus never attempt to supply one. "Leave all you have and all you are and follow Me" they say, and thereby insinuate that we are not so much in need of an answer as of an answerer.'

LUKE 5: 12–16

'Jesus stretched out His hand and touched him. "I am willing," He said. "Be cleansed" ' (v. 13, Barclay).

HOW TO HELP THE OUTCAST. An Irishman named Connell was found guilty of murder and sentenced to death. Philip Doddridge, the hymn-writer, unsuccessfully tried to prove that the man had been 120 miles away from the scene of the crime at the time it was committed. Granted a last wish, the condemned man asked that on the way to his execution—then a public spectacle—he be allowed to pause outside the hymn-writer's home.

Kneeling on the door-step, he cried, 'Mr. Doddridge, every part of me, every hair of my head, every throb of my heart, every drop of my blood, thanks you, for you did your best to save me.' The hymn-writer was willing, but not able to save the condemned man.

This leper was sure that Jesus was able to cleanse him, but unsure that He was willing. 'If Thou wilt, Thou canst,' he said. Jesus touched him, touched the untouchable, and he was healed.

Not only was the Saviour able and willing to help, but His hand went out in costly love to a social outcast. We must do likewise, reaching down to people shunned by society, but without humiliating them or congratulating ourselves. It takes a prayerful man to serve moral and social outcasts without thinking more of his own virtue than of their need.

'Some men came up, carrying a man who was paralysed. ... When He (Jesus) saw their faith, He said, "Man, your sins are forgiven you"' (vv. 18, 20, Moffatt).

HAVING FAITH FOR OTHERS. In the ancient world it was thought that suffering and sin were related, the one being an evidence of the other. This was why Jesus began by telling the man that his sins were forgiven. But let us concentrate upon another aspect of this story.

Jesus healed a man through the faith of his friends. When He saw their faith, He said to the one infirm, 'Arise,' and such faith, sometimes called expectant love, still gives Christ the chance to heal.

But do we provide Him with this chance? The question can probably best be answered by pondering some words of the Sinhalese Christian leader, Dr. D. T. Niles: 'Can you mention the names of the people—two or three perhaps—who are to you a cause of real sorrow because they are not Christians? They are good people, they are your friends, but always when you think of them there is a pain in your soul because they do not serve Jesus Christ. Are there such people in your life? If not, you are not an evangelist however much may be the evangelistic work you do.'

LUKE 5: 27–32

'Jesus answered them: "It is not the healthy that need a doctor, but the sick; I have not come to invite virtuous people, but to call sinners to repentance"' (v. 32, N.E.B.).

SALVATION BY ASSOCIATION. Tax collectors were banned from the synagogue and regarded as social outcasts. Not all were directly employed by Rome but all were branded as collaborators, and their regular contact with Gentiles placed them beyond the pale as far as the Pharisees were concerned. Mark records that Levi arranged his feast on one of the Pharisees' fast days—no wonder the virtuously hungry were angered. Most tax collectors had lined their pockets by oppressing the poor and this would be a sumptuous feast. Jesus certainly laid Himself open to criticism. He took the risk because, contrary to the Pharisees, He did not believe in salvation by 'spiritual quarantine'. He believed in salvation by loving association.

To Jesus sinners were not criminals to be punished but sick

people to be healed. The Master here anticipated many modern insights. We now know that much anti-social behaviour stems from deep mental conflicts. People often resist this idea for fear we will become too 'soft' with the criminal or provide excuses for lawless behaviour. Yet, in fact, this view does not remove all responsibility from the sinner and it is more true to the facts as we now know them. In His attitude to sinners Jesus replaced Pharisaic condemnation with loving acceptance and understanding. It is surely His example which lies behind the modern attitude to 'problem people'. 'Condemnation does not liberate, it oppresses,' wrote C. G. Jung, 'I am the oppressor of the person I condemn, not his friend and fellow sufferer.'

LUKE 5: 33-39

'No one pours fresh wine into old wineskins; otherwise the fresh wine will burst the wineskins . . .' (v. 37, Moffatt).

WHEN DISCIPLINE QUENCHES SPONTANEITY. Fasting was a natural expression of sorrow and penitence from early times but in the days of Jesus it had become regularized. The Pharisees, for instance, fasted twice weekly and encouraged their followers to do the same. To the criticism that His own disciples neglected this practice Jesus pointed out how inappropriate it would have been in their present joyful situation. One further difference between the religion of Jesus and that of the Pharisees is here highlighted. Jesus stood for spontaneity and reality against the dreary performance of mechanical routine. Formal fasting, carried on regardless of one's inner state of mind, makes for unreality.

How can we reconcile the need for spiritual discipline with a life of spontaneous expression? How avoid the blight of insincere formalism? In the first place we can test whether our self-denial has the right motivation by asking ourselves: Do I resent the liberty of those who do not accept my discipline? If so, I am like the Pharisees who were peevishly critical of the happy conviviality of Jesus' disciples. Such reaction indicates that discipline has become burdensome and vacant of spiritual meaning: it is maintained only by some morbid compulsion. On the other hand, healthy self-discipline is free from neurotic constraint, is positive in its aim, and is accompanied by joyful fulfilment.

'The Son of Man has even the Sabbath at His disposal'
(v. 5, Knox).

BURDENSOME RESTRICTIONS. The gulf between Jesus
and the Pharisees was rapidly widening. As the Sabbath was regarded as the most sacred Jewish institution it was inevitable that
the conflict would become most bitter on this issue. From the
Rabbinic point of view the disciples were guilty of reaping and
threshing on the Sabbath. Similarly, while saving life on the
Sabbath was permissible, orthodox Jews would argue that Christ's
healing miracle could well have waited until sundown.

Jesus valued the Sabbath for its opportunity for worship, as His
regular attendance at synagogue shows, but He opposed the
burdensome restrictions which hedged in this day. He was always
uncompromisingly positive both in His teaching and example. A
great eighteenth-century Jewish Rabbi described a dream in which
an angel took him to visit two men. The first Jew lived in a Gentile
environment, ignorant of Judaism, except that on the Sabbath he
gave his Gentile friends a joyful banquet. The reason, he said,
was that he recalled the happy Sabbath meals of his childhood.
The Rabbi wanted to instruct him in the law but his power of
speech departed. The angel then accompanied him to a strict
observer of the law who was consumed by anxiety lest his conduct
was incorrect and who spent the entire Sabbath 'as if he were
sitting on hot coals'. The Rabbi wanted to rebuke this man but
once again his power of speech departed. Upon waking the Rabbi
realized that negative religion which robs a man of joy, even if
accompanied by full knowledge of the law, is a great bondage.

'During this time He went out one day into the hills to
pray, and spent the night in prayer to God' (v. 12, N.E.B.).

TIDES FROM BEYOND. Luke was particularly interested in
prayer. Seven instances when Jesus prayed are recorded by Luke
alone, and only he preserves some of Christ's parables concerning
prayer. It is typical that, when mounting opposition demanded
some new response from Jesus, Luke records that the Master spent
a whole night in prayer. Following this, Jesus chose the twelve men
who were to constitute the 'New Israel', men who would receive

and treasure the teaching which orthodox Israel was rejecting.

Prayer enables us to tap resources of which otherwise we are deprived. Wrote Rufus Jones, 'Almost every person who has attained to a mature spiritual life has had experiences which convince him, at least in high moments, that he was more than himself. Help comes from somewhere and enables us to do what we had always thought could not be done. We find somewhere power to stand the universe when its waterspouts are let loose and even when they have gone over us. . . . No one can with certainty draw the boundary between himself and the beyond himself, any more than we can tell where the tidal river ends and the ocean begins, but we unmistakably feel on occasions that tides from beyond our own margins sweep into us and refresh us.'

LUKE 6: 20-26

'Then fixing His eyes upon His disciples, Jesus said to them, "Blessed are you poor, because the Kingdom of God is yours"' (v. 20, Weymouth).

STRANGE BLESSEDNESS. The sermon recorded in Luke 6 is the counterpart of Matthew's 'sermon on the mount'. Luke says Jesus delivered His sermon 'on a level place'—perhaps a small plateau on which a crowd could gather. At first glance Luke's version of the beatitudes seems less inward—for instance, he has 'Blessed are you poor' instead of 'Blessed are the poor in spirit'. The difference is more apparent than real. In many Old Testament passages the term 'poor' had a religious as well as an economic significance. In an unjust society the righteous frequently were poor.

Jesus found the ordinary working class people generally more receptive than those well-placed. Certainly the poor are less likely to idolize the *status quo* than those who are 'doing very well, thank you'. Perhaps the Church in the modern world will increasingly qualify for the blessedness of which Christ spoke. Compared with believers of some former ages we are poor. Much of which our grandparents were utterly certain has been taken from us. But it is in such a time of testing we discover what is of abiding worth.

Wrote Monica Furlong, 'I cannot imagine a more enjoyable time to be a Christian, except possibly in the first few centuries of the Church. For while the great holocaust is sweeping away much that is beautiful and all that is safe and comfortable and unquestioned, it is relieving us of mounds of Christian bric-a-brac as well, and the liberation is unspeakable. Stripped of our nonsense we may almost be like the early Christians painting their primitive symbols on the walls of their catacombs—the fish, the grapes, the loaves of bread, the cross, the monogram of Christ—confident that having done so they had described the necessities of life.'

LUKE 6: 27–38

'Love your enemies, do good to those who hate you: bless those who curse you, pray for those who abuse you' (vv. 27 and 28, Moffatt).

UNLIMITED LOVE. These verses seem to embody the most unpractical teaching in the world until we recognize that much more than non-violence is urged. Merely to forgo retaliation may be a sign of weakness and in some circumstances submission may even encourage aggression. What Jesus does here is not lay down hard and fast rules but show, by concrete illustrations, how love works. Each specific instance underlines the fact that the follower of Christ must set no limits to the exercise of love. In face of aggression the Christian does not merely submit, he seeks to overcome hatred by positive love. As G. B. Caird has said: 'He who retaliates thinks that he is manfully resisting aggression; in fact, he is making an unconditional surrender to evil.'

When the young Dick Sheppard was working in boys' clubs in the East End of London, the father of one of the lads was particularly hostile to Dick. One day the boy told Dick that his father had burned his hand and that it was 'blistered something cruel'. He also said how difficult it was for his dad to work. That afternoon Dick bought a good, stout, soft glove and early next morning, before four o'clock, he met the boy's father on his way to work. When Dick presented the glove to his 'enemy' the man was amazed. 'You got this for me?' he asked. 'You turned out, Mister, at four o'clock in the morning to give me this? You've got me beat, Mister.' There came a day, much later, when the boy from the club told Dick of the revised opinion which his father now held about Dick: 'Do you know, last night my dad said to mum and me, "Good Gawd, Mother, what should we do without 'im?" '

LUKE 6: 39–45

'Speck of sawdust ... plank ... figs ... grapes' (vv. 41, 44, J. B. Phillips).

WIT AND WISDOM. Both are to be found in this passage. Dean Farrar once observed that the gospels never record that Jesus laughed, though on one occasion it is said that He wept. But His wit must have provoked a grin—sometimes wry, sometimes cheerful—on the face of many a hearer. Verses 41 and 42 provide an example of this. Why try to get a splinter out of someone else's eye when there is a plank in your own? A man with a blind spot is hardly the one to teach his neighbour to think straight. Both will fall into the ditch of the self-appointed leader's prejudices.

Allied to a wit which was perhaps most searching when most gently expressed, was a homely wisdom which would have carried the judgment of many a listening peasant. Figs do not grow on thistles (N.E.B.) nor grapes on a bramble bush (Goodspeed). A man is what he does. His inner nature comes out in what he says.

To adapt a Barclay illustration, a stranger asking the way to his destination in an unfamiliar town might be told by one man that he should bear left after he has passed 'The Crown and Anchor'; by another—just before he comes to the church; by a third—immediately opposite the cinema; by a fourth—as he reaches the road sign which points to the motorway. A man reveals his natural bent not in some prepared statement but in his unstudied responses. We sometimes describe this as being caught on the wrong foot. But if the mind is filled with such things as are true, honest and lovely, we need not fear what may unexpectedly come to light.

LUKE 6: 46-49

'But the man who hears Me and does nothing about it is like a man who built his house with its foundation upon soft earth' (v. 49, J. B. Phillips).

A BOLD CLAIM. 'Nothing in the Gospel story is more startling,' writes Hugh Martin, 'or to some people more unwelcome, than the self-assertion of Jesus.' The popular picture of Christ emphasizes His meekness, but we must also reckon with His bold claims, not least the one implicit in this story. Many agree that Christ's teaching is sublime. Mahatma Gandhi, speaking to Indian students, said, 'I say to the seventy-five per cent of Hindus receiving instruction in this college that your lives also will be incomplete unless you reverently study the teaching of Jesus.' The parable of the two houses, however, claims that failure to carry out the teaching of Jesus results, not in incompleteness, but in disaster. Such a claim cannot be ignored.

The teaching of Jesus, founded upon the eternal principle of love, can be related to any environment. As an illustration of this, note how Luke adapts this parable to suit a Gentile geography. In Matthew the foolish man builds upon sand, not realizing that it it is a dry wadi, which in winter will become a rushing stream. Luke describes the man's folly as failure to dig down through the earth to the rock beneath. Luke had already begun the task, which the Church has carried on with varied success ever since, of relating the gospel to a new environment. That task is always unfinished. It is done most effectively, not by teachers and theologians, essential though their work is, but by those who live the gospel.

LUKE 7: 1–10

'Do not trouble Yourself, Sir; I am not fit to have You under my roof. . . . Just say the word, and let my servant be cured' (vv. 6 and 7, Moffatt).

SPIRITUAL RECOGNITION. The concern which this centurion showed for his slave, his attraction to the loftier religion of Judaism, his courteous recognition that a Jew might not wish to enter a Gentile household, and his sublime faith make him one of the most attractive figures in the gospel records. This incident is one of two occasions when Jesus healed at a distance: both miracles concerned Gentiles. The Early Church probably regarded these stories as prophetic of the future mission to the Gentile world. Jesus came personally to the Jews, to the Gentiles He came through the preaching of the word.

That this practical leader of men, imbued as he must have been with Roman ideas of power and authority, should recognize the superior spiritual authority of a humble Galilean rabbi was itself almost a miracle. This man's orders were obeyed because, as a centurion, he held a commission from Caesar. Similarly, the centurion saw that Jesus' authority lay, not merely in His own power to command, but in the higher authority invested in Him.

Why did this Gentile recognize an authority to which the religious leaders were completely blind? It could only be because consistent loyalty to truth had developed in him a sensitivity which the priests and Pharisees lacked. Spiritual perception, like musical appreciation and artistic taste, is the result of long training and inner discipline. Disloyalty to truth always blunts our perception; obedience refines and heightens it.

'When the Lord saw her His heart went out to her, and He said, "Weep no more".' (v. 13, N.E.B.).

THE ONLY MASTER OF DEATH. In his autobiography *In Search of Myself*, D. R. Davies describes how John Morley, Chancellor of Manchester University, journeyed to the city to deliver a lecture. 'He visited the Students' Union', recalls Mr. Davies, 'and it fell to my lot to hand him a cup of tea. I was immensely thrilled, in spite of the fact that he took not the slightest notice of me. Like his master, John Stuart Mill, he loved humanity in the abstract, but had little eye for the concrete specimen. He had none for us . . .'

Jesus saw the weeping widow and immediately she was the object of His strong compassion. Now such caring, which provides another glimpse of God's unchanging reaction to human need, is more than pity or sympathy. People, though moved by these two emotions, frequently are powerless to help. But divine compassion releases divine power, which is adequate for every situation.

True, our departed loved ones are not restored to physical life, but this incident points to an even more wonderful truth—that Christ is the master, the only master, of death. By His own triumph over the grave, He guarantees that death is the doorway into the more immediate presence of God. To have this assurance of Christ's compassion and His conquest of death is to be enabled to face the unknown future with confidence. As Hugh Redwood wrote: 'I think of life's last stages, not as a downhill journey, but as one over rising ground. What lies beyond the ridge is hidden but it is not in me to fear it.'

'John summoned two of his disciples and sent them to ask the Lord, "Are You the Coming One? Or are we to look for someone else?" ' (v. 19, Moffatt).

WHAT TO DO IN SPIRITUAL DARKNESS. Men of the strongest faith have been visited by doubt. Describing William Booth's vigil with his wife Catherine as she lay dying, Harold

Begbie wrote: 'At one moment he is at her bedside, holding her hand and singing with her:

> On this my steadfast soul relies;
> Father, Thy mercy never dies;

at the next he is on his knees in his study agonizing in spiritual darkness for strength to find, with hands groping through the gloom, the hands of God's Fatherhood.'

In his dungeon, John the Baptist also agonized in spiritual darkness about the identity of the One of whom he had already said, 'Behold the Lamb of God.' But he was wise enough through two of his disciples to take his doubts to Jesus, who wasn't in the least shocked or offended. Indeed, almost immediately afterward He publicly paid tribute to John's greatness.

The New Testament never condemns honest doubt, only dishonest belief. Jesus answered John's question not with a reprimand or a wordy claim to divinity. He simply pointed to the evidence of healed lives, evidence which, to those with sufficient insight, indicated the presence of God's Kingdom. Yet in our 'spiritual darkness' we tend still to search frantically for a spectacular sign. We can best combat our spiritual doubts by getting on with building the Kingdom of God, which exists wherever love seeks to meet human need.

LUKE 7: 29-35

'But the Pharisees and the experts in the Law frustrated God's purpose for them, for they refused John's baptism' (v. 30, J. B. Phillips).

POMPOUS REBELLION AGAINST GOD. Augustine tells the story of a man who complained to Almighty God about one of his neighbours, saying, 'O Lord, take away this wicked person', whereupon God said, 'Which?' It could have been that the critics of Jesus were similarly self-deceived. In the name of righteousness they accused Jesus of being too human and John the Baptist of not being human enough! Surely with a twinkle in His eye Jesus answered that they were incapable of being pleased—just like spoilt children. No one could win with them!

Then the Master's sword flashed! 'Wisdom is justified of all her children.' J. B. Phillips translates: 'Wisdom's reputation is entirely in the hands of her children.' By this we are to understand that God could have compelled men to do good, but His love took a calculated risk—that of allowing men to frustrate Him. Where, however, there is an eager, glad response, divine wisdom is doubly vindicated. It shines in the light of its own intrinsic worth, and those who follow it possess an inextinguishable light which shines more and more unto the perfect day.

LUKE 7: 36–39

'Having learnt that Jesus was at table in the Pharisee's house she brought an alabaster jar of perfume, and, standing behind close to His feet, weeping, began to wet His feet with her tears . . .' (vv. 37 and 38, Weymouth).

SEEING BENEATH THE SURFACE. At oriental banquets the guests reclined on low couches, their heads near the table and their feet behind them. Doors were often left open and beggars in search of food or spectators in search of interesting conversation would enter. The woman who took advantage of this freedom to express her gratitude to Christ became an acute embarrassment to the respectable but loveless Pharisee.

Nothing exposes our superficiality as much as our judgment of others. Simon saw in this woman nothing but a sinner who had gone seriously astray. He had neither sensitivity to recognize his own need of forgiveness, or the imaginative insight to allow for the mitigating factors which may have contributed to the woman's downfall. Jesus saw beneath the exterior to the warm, generous nature and the penitent heart. Writes Leslie Weatherhead, 'So often we label people according to some outstanding failing, forgetting that very rarely does a label account for the whole bottle, unless the label says "the mixture".' As Søren Kierkegaard searchingly remarked, 'The majority of men are subjective toward themselves and objective toward all others, terribly objective sometimes, but the real task is in fact to be objective toward oneself and subjective toward all others.'

LUKE 7: 40–50

'That is why I tell you, Simon, that her sins, many as they are, are forgiven; for she has shown me so much love. But the man who is forgiven only a little will love only a little' (v. 47, J. B. Phillips).

MUCH FORGIVEN. 'We all make mistakes,' said the dying Beethoven, 'but everyone makes different mistakes.' It is when men forget this truth that they sometimes assume attitudes of superiority like that of Simon the Pharisee. In contrast to the warm, spontaneous gratitude which the woman showered upon Jesus, Simon had received his guest with but formal politeness. The reason, said Jesus, was that the woman knew she was much forgiven. The implication was, not that Simon had less need of pardon, but that he was unconscious of his indebtedness to divine grace. 'Oh, Pharisee,' commented Augustine, 'thou lovest little because thou supposest that little has been forgiven thee: not because little is forgiven, but because thou thinkest that which is forgiven to be but little.'

Near the end of his life, when his strength was ebbing away, Augustine asked one of his friends to paint on the wall opposite his bed the words of the thirty-second psalm: 'Blessed is he whose transgression is forgiven, whose sin is covered. Blessed is the man unto whom the Lord imputeth not iniquity.' The joy of the forgiven is something which adds lustre to life's happiest experiences and it is a supreme solace when the clouds are heavy overhead. Pardon is not granted to those who convince themselves they are comparatively guiltless: it belongs to those who have ceased to trust in their own righteousness and have all their faith in God's mercy.

LUKE 8: 1–8

'And when He had said this, He called out, "Let the man who has ears to hear use them!"' (v. 8, J. B. Phillips).

HOW RECEPTIVE ARE WE? Both Mark and Luke agree that we have here a turning-point in Christ's ministry. Official opposition seems to have closed the synagogues to Jesus and increasingly He now addresses vast crowds in the open air. The parable of the sower reflects this situation, explaining as it does why Jesus' teaching met with such a poor response in some quarters. This is the only parable to which an explanation is appended in Luke. Jesus rarely interpreted His parables—'an explained parable is as flat as an explained joke'.

The quality of our lives is revealed by the reception we give to the word of God. This is the primary lesson of this parable. Of course, parables were usually meant to crystallize only one truth and the analogy of the soil and the human heart must not be pressed too far. The earth can do nothing to make itself more hospitable: we can.

Our capacity to absorb new truth increases as we attentively listen to the words of Jesus and obey each new relevation. The deepest joys of listening to great music come to those who, in addition to their native talent, train themselves to a keener discrimination. The same is true of the appreciation of art and literature. If we have reason to fear that our reception of God's truth has been sluggish and unfruitful we can begin to change this situation—today. As Nietzsche once observed, 'On the mountains of truth you can never climb in vain: either you will reach a point higher up today, or you will be training your powers so that you will be able to climb higher tomorrow.'

LUKE 8: 9–18

'Nobody lights a lamp, to hide it away in a jar or under a bed; it is put on a lampstand' (v. 16, Knox).

SPREADING TRUTH. It is inconceivable that Jesus created His timeless parables to hide the truth. How then shall we understand the statement, 'the others have only parables, in order that they may look but see nothing, hear but understand nothing' (v. 10, N.E.B.). These words from Isaiah were often used by the Early Church to explain Israel's rejection of Christ. We would state the same truth differently by saying that disobedience to truth leads to spiritual blindness. The Jews, believing everything to be divinely preordained, tended to regard God as responsible for the process of spiritual hardening. The parables of Jesus were meant to convey truth, but in such a way that only the earnest seeker, as distinct from the merely curious listener, would grasp the message.

We increase our grasp upon the truth as we share it with others. This is one implication of the saying about the light set on the lamp stand. In a phrase of G. B. Caird, 'God's revelation begins as a private discovery and ends as a public trust.'

In 1605 an intrepid Spanish explorer, Pedro Fernandez de Quiros, set out in search of the great southern continent which he believed to exist. He actually landed on the islands which fringe the coast of Australia and saw the great continent at a distance. Returning to Mexico he spent eight years pleading with the authorities to fit out an expedition. He met only with scorn. 'There is no southern continent,' travellers affirmed. Always he replied, 'There is. I know there is. I have seen it.' We too must witness to the truth, and our witness will strengthen our own convictions.

'Who is this, who gives His command to wind and water, and is obeyed?' (v. 25, Knox).

THE MASTERY OF EVIL. Many travellers in Palestine have commented on the uncertain temper of the Sea of Galilee. Twelve hundred feet below sea level the lake can suddenly be whipped into fury by a wind which is funnelled down the narrow gullies surrounding it. Unless we take account of the mental climate of Christ's day we will not only fail to understand this story, we may well minsinterpret its message. We might, for instance, assume that being a disciple of Jesus exempts us from physical harm. But discipleship is no insurance policy against natural disaster. What lesson then did the New Testament writers see in this story?

In Jesus the Kingdom of God was manifested. In place of the chaos caused by sin God was beginning to restore order and harmony. To first-century Jews storms were the work of demons. No gospel writer would have differentiated, as some modern studies do, between Christ's healing miracles and the nature miracles. Sin, disease, the desolation of the wilderness and the viciousness of the sea were all the work of forces hostile to God. The stilling of the storm, no less than the healing of the sick, manifested Christ's lordship over evil. Furthermore, the Bible writers asserted that God made man lord over nature. It was because of his sin that man lost his authority. But in Jesus that lordship was restored. By fellowship with Christ, and by receiving His Spirit, we also may increasingly become masters, not over the physical elements, but over adversity and evil.

'When they reached Jesus, they found the man from whom the devils had been driven out sitting there, clothed and restored to his wits, at Jesus' feet; and they were terrified' (v. 35, Knox).

WHERE A MAN'S RELIGION IS MOST EVIDENT. It demanded rare courage to talk to a raving maniac among the tombs, but Jesus did not hesitate and learned that the man's name was Legion; six thousand soldiers comprised a Roman legion, and it is probable that this fierce maniac imagined himself to be possessed by such a number of demons.

Some people have found the destruction of the herd of swine a stumbling-block, but this surely is to misunderstand the beliefs of

G

the ancient world and to underestimate the value of a human soul. Certain commentators have suggested that the herd stampeded because of the maniac's ravings, and that Jesus used the stampede to convince the man that he was healed. This, of course, is possible, but a literal acceptance of the story surely does not offend reason.

Who would wish to deny that the soul of a man, not to mention his happiness and that of his loved ones, is worth infinitely more than a herd of swine? And if Jesus did use this particular method to restore a poor, sick mind, does not the end justify the means? However, whatever our interpretation, the fact remains that a social outcast, mentally deranged, was restored to sanity and to his family. He naturally wanted to stay with Jesus, but was sent home to witness there; and he did, judging by the welcome later given to Christ by people previously hostile. A man's religion is what he does with his private life, particularly at home.

LUKE 8: 41–56

'When the woman realized that she had not escaped notice she came forward trembling, and fell at His feet and admitted before everybody why she had to touch Him, and how she had been instantaneously cured' (v. 47, J. B. Phillips).

A HARD LESSON. 'My own experience', wrote D. R. Davies, 'confirmed so wonderfully the truth of the Bible . . . that no man or woman can pass from death to life without first realizing utter self-despair. No one can find God as Redeemer who still flirts with the possibility that one can redeem oneself.' He continued: 'Despair of self is not to be feared. It is to be prayed for . . . I can ask no greater blessing for my wearied, disillusioned generation than the blessing of despair; for in it they will meet Him who can save them to the uttermost.'

This was clearly the experience of both Jairus and the woman sick for twelve years. The measure of the desperation of the synagogue president can be judged by his willingness to ask the help of the One who was frowned upon by the religious leaders of his race. And the woman, ceremonially unclean through the nature of her sickness, risked breaking the law to get near to the Saviour. A sense of personal helplessness and utter dependence resulted in both their needs being met. Only as we accept the need to be delivered from our illusory independence can faith become savingly effectual.

'So they set out, and went from village to village preaching the gospel and healing people everywhere' (v. 6, J. B. Phillips).

THE NEW ORDER. How we wish we had a detailed account of the disciples' mission tour! What were their feelings when Christ commissioned them to evangelize the villages of Galilee? Did Thomas overcome his natural caution sufficiently to speak the word of healing? What kind of sermons did Judas preach? Such questions lead to a flood of speculation. What is important is to note that preaching and healing were both ways of announcing the coming of the Kingdom. Preaching was more than moral exhortation—it was proclamation. Healing was more than acts of pity—it was the manifestation of power.

The perfect reign of God belongs to 'the age to come'. But in the ministry of Jesus, as in the mission of His Church, 'it breaks through into this age, penetrating it with the shafts of another order, as the rays of the sun light up the sky before its rising.'

In a *Reader's Digest* article Clarence Hall described a visit to the traditional site of Christ's burial for an Easter Day sunrise service. He asked his guide, a Christian Arab, if the darkness would never pass. 'Never fear, my friend,' replied the Arab. 'The day will come. You can't hold back the dawn.' Christians know that nothing can hold back the dawn of God's perfect reign. But in this interim period we are faced with a daily decision. Shall we live as those who are well content with the night or as those who wait for the dawn?

'Taking the five loaves and the two fishes, He looked up to heaven, said the blessing over them, broke them, and gave them to the disciples to distribute to the people' (v. 16, N.E.B.).

A FAREWELL FEAST. The gospel writers obviously considered the feeding of the multitude highly significant—it is the only miracle reported by all four evangelists. It has puzzled some modern commentators who have suggested that what happened was 'a miracle of fellowship rather than a miracle of multiplication'—the example of Jesus led to others sharing their provisions until all were fed. To focus all our attention on the miraculous element in the story, however, is to misunderstand the gospel writers. Their spotlight falls, not on the miracle, but upon the symbolic meaning of the meal.

Jewish literature frequently compares the Messianic age to a great banquet and Jesus Himself spoke of the Kingdom of God in this way (5: 34; 6: 21; 13: 29–30; 22: 15–18). It has been remarked that it was natural that a people who had lived with privation should picture God's brave new world in such imagery, sometimes even to the point of discussing the menu. Jesus was now leaving Galilee, probably because Herod Antipas, who had murdered the Baptist, was threatening Him. Before saying farewell to His many loyal supporters there He celebrated with them a symbolic feast, just as later He was to arrange a special meal for His disciples in the Upper Room.

Why celebrate a Messianic banquet before the establishment of God's perfect reign? Jesus pointed out in a hundred different ways that, for His followers, God's provisions do not await a future age of perfect fulfilment. They can be enjoyed now. They are a foretaste, and a very liberal one, of the joys which are to come.

LUKE 9: 18–27

'If any man has a mind to come My way, let Him renounce self, and take up his cross daily, and follow me' (v. 23, Knox).

THE WAY OF THE CROSS. The importance of this passage lies in its summing up both of Christ's mission and of Christian discipleship. What a mighty influence Jesus must have had upon the twelve disciples! He conformed to none of their traditional concepts of a Messiah yet all but one of them eventually joined Peter in accepting Him as the Christ of God. Outside this apostolic band people speculated about Jesus but none seems to have considered Him the Messiah. Close fellowship with Jesus, however, gradually transformed all Peter's ideas so that he was able to make his great confession. Even so, Jesus wasted no time in insisting that the Messiah must tread a path of suffering and that His followers must likewise expect no easy path to glory.

Fulfilment is found, not in self-aggrandizement or self-indulgence, but in loving self-sacrifice. Rufus Jones described the budding self-affirmation of a little child. One day the youngster, to everyone's surprise, asserts his will. 'I am somebody and I am resolved to be more of a somebody,' is what he is trying to say. All this is delightful and necessary. But by itself self-affirmation is 'a self-destructive principle. Made into a universal law it would produce a monster. .... If self-sacrifice is, as we are told, "glorious madness", then certainly undeviating self-assertion is inglorious madness.' The apparent conflict between self-assertion and self-denial is resolved in the experience of love. Love-motivated sacrifice is self-affirmation of the highest kind. That is why Jesus called His followers to find their lives by losing them for His sake.

LUKE 9: 28–36

'A voice came from the cloud, "This is My Son, My Chosen one; listen to Him." When the voice ceased, they found themselves alone with Jesus' (vv. 35 and 36, Moffatt).

AN UNTRODDEN WAY. The glory experienced on the mount of transfiguration was an impressive confirmation both of Peter's confession and of Christ's decision to tread the path of suffering. For the disciples it resolved any tension which existed between past tradition and God's new revelation in Christ. The whole mental world of the disciples had been fashioned by what these two figures from the past, Moses and Elijah, represented. The radically new insights of their Master must have created some conflicts for them. Any doubts as to where their final loyalty lay was banished by the voice which said, 'This is My Son, My Chosen one, listen to Him.' No tradition, however hallowed and apparently sacrosanct, can displace the Christian's primary loyalty to Christ.

For Jesus the transfiguration marked the beginning of a lonely road. Until this point in His ministry He had travelled a well-marked path. He stood in the long tradition of Hebrew prophets. Now God called Him to a way untrodden by human feet. Moses and Elijah were left behind and Jesus was to fulfil His own unique vocation. He is to walk alone, with only His Father's presence to sustain Him, and even His certainty of that will be denied Him toward the end.

Christians today are similarly called to step out along untrodden paths. There are no precedents in history for some of the tasks and challenges the Church now faces. The same may be true of us as individuals, but we can share the courage of Jesus born of a trust in God.

'They were all struck with awe at the majesty of God' (v. 43, N.E.B.).

AN UNDISTINGUISHED COMPANY. The lonely great-ness of Jesus is further emphasized in this part of the narrative. The account of the transfiguration, in which the radiant majesty of Christ shone in all its splendour, is followed by four incidents which reveal the weakness of the disciples' faith, their slowness to learn, their self-seeking and their intolerance. Note also, in passing, that no sooner had 'the majesty of God' been exhibited in Christ's healing of the epileptic boy than Jesus makes His second prediction of His approaching death. The disciples were allowed no dreams of worldly success. The Messiah's path led straight to a Cross.

Compared with their Master the disciples here appear as a weak and undistinguished company—as Plummer has com-mented, 'the chosen three are blinded by the light, the remaining nine baffled by the powers of darkness'. They are, in fact, exactly like ourselves. The record of their slow and stumbling progress should make us very tolerant of others—and ourselves. Christ does not choose ready-made saints, but ordinary human beings for His followers. Nor should we imagine that after Pentecost these men suddenly shed all human weakness and fallibility. Neither the Acts of the Apostles nor the epistles supports such a contention. Immeasurably empowered as they were by the Spirit's baptism, growth and development were still necessary—and, because they lived in fellowship with Christ, gloriously possible.

'Jesus said, "Forbid him no more; the man who is not against you is on your side" ' (v. 50, Knox).

THE EVIL OF INTOLERANCE. Today's passage is cer-tainly a reminder of the honesty of the gospel writers. No attempt was made to whitewash the mistakes and weakness of the first disciples. Here they are seen giving way to personal rivalry, in-tolerance and bigotry. These sins have done more than any others to discredit the Christian Church in the eyes of the world for, as T. W. Manson has said, 'Those who are concerned about their rights want to have exclusive rights; but Jesus regarded as an ally anyone who was fighting evil.'

Intolerance results from a narrow vision of God's activity. Like the disciples who rebuked the man casting out devils, the intolerant want to confine God's activity to the 'proper channels'. They resemble the parson in *Tom Jones* who said, 'When I mention religion, I mean the Christian religion; and not only the Christian religion but the protestant religion; and not only the protestant religion, but the Church of England.'

Intolerance also results from a defective understanding of God's love. In the Jewish Talmud there is a story which illustrates this fault. 'An aged man, whom Abraham invited to his tent, refused to join him in prayer to the one spiritual God. Learning that he was a fire worshipper, Abraham drove him from his door. That night God appeared to Abraham in a vision and said, "I have borne with that ignorant man for seventy years; could you not have patiently suffered him one night?" '

LUKE 9: 57–62

'Any one who puts his hand to the plough and then looks behind him is useless for the Kingdom of God' (v. 62, J. B. Phillips).

CALL FOR DECISION. In his book, *The Secular City*, Harvey Cox reminds his readers that a hundred years ago Christendom and European culture were so intertwined, often in a way that distorted the gospel, that genuine discipleship was extremely difficult. But now 'more and more, being a Christian is a conscious choice rathe than a matter of birth and inertia. The change can hardly be viewed as unfortunate.' What Jesus said to the three candidates for discipleship stresses this element of deliberate decision.

The most difficult decisions to make are not between good and evil but between the good and the best. A stable home life in which the responsibilities of love are faithfully carried out is, in normal circumstances, wholly desirable. But the call of Jesus can sometimes cut right across all lesser loyalties and the disciple must be in no doubt about his response when this happens. In any lives it is the good which is the worst enemy of the best.

True discipleship demands not one decision but many, and every one is important. 'Good and evil both increase at compound interest,' wrote C. S. Lewis. 'That is why the little decisions you and I make every day are of such infinite importance. The smallest good act today is the capture of a strategic point from which, a few months later, you may be able to go on to victories you never dreamed of. An apparently trivial indulgence in lust or anger today is the loss of a ridge or railway line or bridgehead from which the enemy may launch an attack otherwise impossible.'

It has been well said that 'there is a tragic waste represented by the gifted who remain uneducated. There is an even more tragic waste represented by the educated who remain uncommitted.'

LUKE 10: 1–12

' "There is a great harvest," He told them, "but only a few are working in it—which means you must pray to the Lord of the harvest that He will send out more reapers" ' (v. 2, J. B. Phillips).

THEIR WITNESS, AND OURS. The mission of the seventy, recorded only in this Gospel, was probably regarded by Luke as symbolic of the later mission to the Gentile world. Seventy was considered the number of nations upon the earth. Christ's instructions to His emissaries emphasized the urgency of their task. Reaping rather than sowing was now called for and delay could spell a ruined harvest. Consequently the disciples were to travel light, avoid the time-wasting intricacies of oriental etiquette, and abandon any scruples about unclean food which would prevent them eating wherever food was offered. They were to announce, not some future act of judgment or salvation, but the presence of the Kingdom here and now.

Though the mission of the seventy was in certain respects unique, it can also serve as a model for our Christian activity. Urgency is here. A missionary who reached China was told, 'You have arrived in the nick of time.' 'I was told that seven years ago when I landed', was the reply. 'Well, time is getting nicker every day', came the response.

Simplicity is here—of dress, speech and approach. We shall commend the gospel by our honesty and straightforwardness. As Paul Tournier has written, 'We can help others by telling them of our experiences, but let us be frank enough to speak of our failures and doubts as well. Above all, we must beware of the natural inclination to think that others must come to faith by the same road as ourselves.'

LUKE 10: 13–16

'Even wicked Sodom will be better off' (v. 12, Living New Testament).

PRIVILEGE CARRIES RESPONSIBILITY. Chorazin is

mentioned here, but nowhere in the four gospels is there any account of 'the mighty works' which Jesus said He had done in this lakeside town, the ruins of which have been tentatively identified some two or three miles north-east of Capernaum. This is interesting testimony to the fact that there is much about the ministry of Jesus of which we are ignorant. This need not trouble anyone. What we do know of His words and deeds is enough to provide the most serious food for thought—as in this passage, which is a commentary upon the truth that our own behaviour condemns us if we prefer darkness to light (John 3: 19).

This is a biblical principle. 'For you alone have I cared among all the nations of the world; therefore will I punish you for all your iniquities' (Amos 3: 2, N.E.B.), was the word of the Lord of Israel. This is also the point of the parable of the wicked husbandmen (Matt. 21: 33–46). Messenger after messenger was sent with entreaty and warning and, last of all, the owner's own son. What more could the lord of the vineyard have done? The illegal tenants could only expect what was coming to them.

This is what has been called the law of proportionate responsibility. Applied to individuals it means that those who have had the privilege of a godly upbringing might do well to come down from their judgment seat on the irreligious and make certain that their own house is in order. Applied to peoples, it means that nations who proudly describe themselves as Christian should remember that by the adjective which they claim they will most certainly be judged. To whom much is given, from him will much be required.

LUKE 10: 17–24

'He said to them, "I watched, while Satan was cast down like a lightning-flash from heaven" ' (v. 18, Knox).

THE CHRISTIAN VIEW OF EVIL. The deep significance which Jesus attached to the mission of the seventy is reflected in His vision of Satan's fall from heaven and in His exultant prayer offered 'at that moment'. His disciples' success in casting out demons was, for Jesus, a faint reflection of that cosmic victory over the powers of evil which was being accomplished through His ministry. All religion, and all philosophy, have to grapple with the problem of evil. The Christian attitude to this dark mystery is quite unique, as today's passage well illustrates.

Christians affirm that the decisive victory over evil has already been won—by Christ. On the face of it this is an illogical claim. For instance, Martin Buber described the difference between his Judaic faith and Christianity by asserting that the fate of the Jewish people 'standing, bound and shackled, in the pillory of mankind' demonstrated 'the unredeemedness of the world'. He placed the conquest of evil wholly in the future. Is he more realistic than the Christian? Or is the difference of viewpoint largely one of emphasis?

The accomplishment of Christ was of such magnitude as to tip the scales decisively in the conflict between good and evil. In Him God's love shines forth convincingly to assure mankind that compassionate concern, not careless indifference, is at the heart of things. In His life the true stature of humanity was fully achieved. In Him man is reconciled to God. This is why Christians believe that the essential encounter has already taken place. The warfare is by no means ended but the issue of the conflict is no longer in doubt.

LUKE 10: 25-37

'Love the Lord your God with all your heart, with all your soul, with all your strength, and with all your mind; and your neighbour as yourself' (v. 27, N.E.B.).

WHO IS MY NEIGHBOUR? This conversation between Jesus and the lawyer exposes the sharp difference between two views of morality. The lawyer wanted his duty precisely defined and therefore limited: Jesus expounded the limitless obligations of love. Jews agreed that a man should love his neighbour, but they included in that category only those they were inclined to love anyway. No Gentile, for instance, was regarded as a neighbour. The story of the Good Samaritan, one of the best known in all literature, hinges upon the fact that the traveller was left half-dead. To determine whether he was dead or alive the priest and the Levite would have had to touch him and so risk ceremonial defilement.

To ask 'Who is my neighbour?' is to reveal the deficiency of our love. P. A. Sorokin has defined what he calls the five dimensions of love. We might well use his analysis to test our own capacity for love. (1) Intensity: Where do I stand on the scale which runs from complete indifference to the level of a man who gives his life for a friend? (2) Extensity: How wide and inclusive is the circle of my concern? (3) Duration: How long does my

affection last? Is my love fickle? (4) Purity: Is my love unmixed
with motives of greed or the desire to dominate? (5) Adequacy:
Does my love bring to those for whom I care enrichment and
fulfilment?

LUKE 10: 38–42

'**Martha, my dear, you are worried and bothered about
a great many things. Only a few things are really needed,
perhaps only one. Mary has chosen the most important
thing . . .**' (vv. 41 and 42, J. B. Phillips).

THE BEST MENU. Although the Middle Ages found
authority in this passage for valuing the life of the contemplative
monk more than the life lived in the world, we should note that
Jesus did not disparage Martha's practical bent, nor encourage a
wholly passive spirituality. Martha's chief fault lay in her self-
pity. Good works must be self-forgetful to be of real value. When
we become resentful that others do not make the same sacrifices
it is time we scrutinized our motives. J. Alexander Findlay
translates Jesus' words: 'Martha, Martha, you are working yourself up and worrying about getting a lavish meal; one course is
enough. Mary chose the best menu for us both, and she shall not
be dragged away from it.'

Although temperament may incline us either in the direction
of Mary or of Martha our aim should be to balance action and
contemplation. However, modern life so stresses the active virtues
that we are more in danger of forgetting the need for quiet meditation and prayer. Rufus Jones used a ship in a lock as a parable of
prayer. 'Here the ship is, shut in by great gates before and behind.
Its driving engines have slowed down. Its speed has diminished to
nought. It is no longer going anywhere. And yet all the time the
water is rising underneath the ship, and when the gate in front
swings open, and the ship emerges from its period of full stop, it
will go out for its journey on a higher level and carry its burden of
freight henceforth on a new plane.'

LUKE 11: 1–13

'**When you pray, say, "Father, Thy name be hallowed . . ."**' (v. 2, N.E.B.).

THE SPECTRUM OF PRAYER. Communion with His
Father was so obviously the secret of Christ's amazing courage
and endurance that we can well understand the disciples'

request, 'Lord, teach us to pray.' We, too, would make the same request, for we have learnt that reliance upon our own resources leads only to frustration and defeat. The prayer Jesus gives to us is a model upon which to shape our own communion, not a form of words to be thoughtlessly repeated. Evelyn Underhill has commented on the fact that in 'the Lord's Prayer' the followers of Jesus 'have found the material of those vain repetitions which He has specially condemned'. Rather should we see in this model prayer a standard by which to test our own communion with God, a spectrum which displays the varying hues which constitute true prayer.

This does not mean that repeating the actual words of this model prayer is necessarily a vain repetition. At one point in her spiritual quest Simone Weil was able to write, 'Until last September I had never once prayed in all my life, at least not in the literal sense of the word.' Then she discovered 'the Lord's Prayer' and found it full of deep meaning. She began saying it through with absolute attention each morning and it had an extraordinary effect upon her. 'Sometimes', she wrote, 'it comes about that I say it again out of sheer pleasure.'

As a Japanese Christian has said, 'Every just man needs the seven things for which this prayer—or this scheme of prayer—asks.'

LUKE 11: 14–23

'Some of them said, "It is through Beelzebub, the prince of devils, that He casts the devils out" ' (v. 15, Knox).

HIDING BEHIND SLANDER. There are some people who react even to fair comment by abusing their critics. They try to hide their own failings behind a cloud of extravagant charges against their opponents.

Confronted by the ungainsayable evidence of the power of Jesus to deal with devils, His critics sought to cloak the weakness of their case by maligning His character. He was Himself, they say, in alliance with the powers of darkness. The slander was, of course, an obvious contradiction in terms. Would the prince of devils fight against his own kind? Would he wage a civil war to set a single one of his prisoners free? Even to suggest the possibility was to reveal its absurdity.

There is no account of the reaction of our Lord's hearers to this particular point. Maybe they continued to prefer prejudice to the truth. But they are not the only guilty parties. 'When we talk uncharitably', wrote Ronald Knox, 'we always imagine—too often, I'm afraid, with justice—that our company enjoys it. So much the worse if they do. But you are lowering the standard of fraternal charity with every word you say and, if you are talking in front of people younger than yourself or less important than yourself, you are setting them an example they may be only too ready to follow ... the moment you have left the room.' The more excellent way is: if you can't be kind, be quiet.

LUKE 11: 24-28

'When the evil spirit comes out of a man ... it says, "I will go back to my house from which I came." When it arrives, it finds it cleaned and all in order. Then it goes and collects seven other spirits more evil than itself' (vv. 24-26, J. B. Phillips).

NEGATIVE RELIGION. A little girl was learning to ride a bicycle and felt drawn toward everything that would obstruct her path or throw her off balance. Then the old Scots gardener who was teaching her said, 'Don't look where you don't want to go; keep your eye on where you do want to go.' John G. McKenzie, in his *Nervous Disorders and Religion*, likens negative conscience to a car driver who, instead of watching for the turning of the road he wants, 'keeps watching the roads down which he must not go.'

When Jesus told this story of an evil spirit returning to its former dwelling with 'seven other spirits more evil than itself', He was emphasizing the folly and danger of negative religion. Some people think that they are saints because they are not sinners; that they are good because they are not bad. They seek to be saved from vice, not to virtue, and measure their spiritual growth by how many 'Thou shalt nots' they obey. In prayer, they brood over their failings, some of them merely the reflections of a forbidding conscience, and suffer agonies of doubt and self-condemnation. They need a positive religion, one that by filling life with what is good, honest, lovely and of good report, keeps evil at bay. What could be more positive than a life of commitment to the service of Christ?

> Lord, when I think about Your life,
> Your work from day to day,
> I'm sure you loved the morning skies
> Better than twilight grey;

So when upon my spirit
Falls the awful pall of doubt
Draw near and be Yourself my Light
And drive this darkness out.

LUKE 11: 29-32

'This is a wicked generation; it asks for a sign, and the only sign that will be given to it is the sign of the prophet Jonas' (v. 29, Knox).

LIVING FAITH. These verses tell us a good deal about the nature of faith. The Jews wanted Jesus to prove His claims with a spectacular sign. His reply was to explain that just as Jonah was a sign to the people of Nineveh, so He was a sign to the people of 'this generation'.

The people of Nineveh believed Jonah, not because he performed a sign, but because their insight enabled them to recognize that he himself was the sign from God. In a similar way, the Queen of Sheba acknowledged the wisdom of Solomon, not because of his ostentatious royalty, but because her perception was sufficiently developed: she heard him and was convinced of his wisdom.

To those with eyes to see and ears to hear, Jesus Himself is sign enough of His true identity. Faith in Him at depth is rarely, if ever, created by spectacular means. No matter how beautiful a picture, no viewer truly believes it beautiful simply because some expert tells him it is so. He must see the beauty for himself, see it with more than his physical eyes. And when this happens, though probably lost for words, he will know. So it is with faith in Christ. We look at Him, ponder His words, share His fellowship, and sooner or later, He becomes for us God's sign. We just know!

Alfred N. Whitehead said that Mary who pondered in her heart the strange things said about Jesus had the deepest kind of knowledge. Just so. This is living faith.

LUKE 11: 33-44

'Alas for you Pharisees! ... You are like unmarked graves over which men may walk without knowing it' (v. 44, N.E.B.).

UNRECOGNIZED SOURCES OF POLLUTION. Jesus accused the pious Pharisees of being like 'unmarked graves', and they knew well what He meant. In the ancient world, to touch a grave was to become ceremonially unclean and consequently debarred from all religious worship for seven days. This was why graves were sometimes whitewashed, to protect pilgrims journeying to religious festivals from touching a grave unknowingly or accidentally; and the Pharisees, said Jesus, were similarly an unrecognized source of pollution. Under their influence, the innocent were unknowingly contaminated by wrong ideas about God and therefore about how to live!

The influence of every person's life and thought makes it easier or harder for others to believe in God and be good. It was said of Rufus Jones, Quaker writer and preacher: 'It is always a pleasure to meet Rufus Jones—he has such gusto. His friends are the best friends a man ever had. Today is the greatest day that has ever been. The job in hand is the most important job that has ever been undertaken.' Our lives can have the same infectious gaiety.

LUKE 11: 45-54

'I do blame you experts in the Law! For you pile up back-breaking burdens for men to bear, but you yourselves will not raise a finger to bear them' (v. 46, J. B. Phillips).

THE FUNCTION OF TRADITION. Why were these Scribes, these experts in the Law, so roundly condemned by Jesus? This reading suggests two reasons:

Even allowing for good intentions, the Scribes complicated religion by their multitude of rules. Sadly, some were past-masters at the art of evasion. They taught others while devising for themselves legal means of escaping the burdens of their own teaching. They pointed the way without personally following it. Old Richard Baxter had this sin of professionalism in mind when he wrote: 'Take heed to yourselves lest you perish while you call upon others to take heed of perishing; and lest you famish yourselves while you prepare their food. ... Many a tailor goes in rags, that maketh costly clothes for others; and many a cook scarce licks his fingers, when he hath dressed for others the most costly dishes.'

Another evidence that the Scribes were spiritually blind was that the only prophets they revered were dead ones. They made pilgrimages to their tombs, but still persecuted living prophets whose views did not conform to their own. Religion for them was only real if it was old and orthodox.

Tradition, excellent in itself, is like a map; and a map is not the destination, but a guide to it. Some maps are better than others, but they should never be confused with the destination. Our beliefs are vital and indispensable only in so far as they help us to love God and our neighbour.

'Be on your guard against yeast—I mean the yeast of the Pharisees, which is sheer pretence' (v. 1, J. B. Phillips).

APPEARANCE AND REALITY. Why did Jesus go to such lengths to dissociate Himself from the Pharisees and to warn His disciples against their influence? The reason was that, passionately devoted and apparently self-sacrificing, they appeared nearer to Him than any other religious party. The fatal flaw in their religion was that they had parted company with truth. Most of them were not consciously deceitful, but outward appearances had become so important they lost touch with their true selves.

Self-deception is the first step to a life of pretence. Long before the advent of modern psychology wise men recognized that in the depths of human personality there are tendencies we would all rather not face: aggression, naked ambition and ruthless self-concern. 'Looking down through the jade-green water, you see the monsters of the deep playing on the reef,' wrote Dag Hammarskjöld. 'Is this a reason to be afraid? Do you feel safer when scudding waves hide what lies beneath the surface?' Undoubtedly we do feel safer, and so are tempted to concern ourselves only with outward appearance.

The opposite of hypocrisy is repentance. This does not call for morbid introspection and poking around in the depths—it does mean an honest scrutiny of our own reactions in the hurly-burly of daily life. These will provide us with plenty of opportunities for self-knowledge. Such honest facing up to ourselves, always in the light of God's unfailing love, is the best way to reality and growth.

'Anyone who speaks a word against the Son of Man will receive forgiveness; but for him who slanders the Holy Spirit there will be no forgiveness' (v. 10, N.E.B.).

IS ANY SIN UNPARDONABLE. 'I feel terribly distressed,' wrote one person to a pastor, 'I am worried about the unforgivable sin. My thoughts are bad even when praying. .... They haunt me, and force themselves on me. Do tell me that I have not committed the unforgivable sin.' More people have suffered this kind of distress than is sometimes imagined. Usually they come into the categories of the excessively timid or the emotionally sick. One thing needs to be said quite categorically. To be worried about the possibility of having committed the unpardonable sin is absolute proof that one has not done so.

Mark and Matthew link this saying with the incident I found in Luke 11: 14–23 when the critics of Jesus attributed His healing, miracles to demonic influences. They were guilty of that terrible moral confusion which calls white black, and black white. In such a state a man feels no need for forgiveness and has placed himself beyond even God's grace. Such sin is unpardonable, not because God's mercy is limited but because a man becomes insensitive to his own need. The fish that swim in the farthest recesses of the Mammoth Caves of Kentucky are utterly blind. The structure of their eyes is perfect, but the optic nerve has completely shrivelled. Man also may choose spiritual darkness, but blindness is the ultimate penalty of such a choice.

LUKE 12: 13–21

'Keep clear of covetousness in every shape and form' (v. 15, Moffatt).

THE GREAT ILLUSION. The late Bishop Edwin Hughes was taken to task by a rich parishioner for a sermon he preached on 'God's ownership'. The wealthy man walked the bishop through his extensive estate and then demanded, 'Now are you going to tell me that all this land does not belong to me?' The bishop smiled and replied, 'Ask me that same question a hundred years from now.'

Jesus made this same point, in the parable of the rich fool, after having refused to take part in a family dispute over a legacy. Christ regarded with horror the illusion that abundant life can be found in material possessions. Clearly He thought it was better to be the victim of injustice than fall into such error. Surely the rich fool represents the great illusion of our own time, at least in the affluent countries. Material possessions are not evil in themselves and may be used for life's enrichment. But the greatest wealth is that which cannot be touched by death.

Wrote W. E. Sangster, 'When things become the chief purpose of living, when money (the key to the rest of them) is seen as life's chief good, every precious thing is in danger—the integrity of the individual soul, the decency of the community, the soundness of all human life.'

LUKE 12: 22–31

'Make it your first care to find the Kingdom of God, and all these things shall be yours without the asking' (v. 31, Knox).

THE HAVE-NOTS. Previously we noted the spiritual perils of wealth. But, if reliance upon possessions is the temptation of 'the haves', debilitating anxiety is the snare set in the path of 'the have-nots'. Jesus pointed out that anxiety about physical needs is both pointless and pagan. A man cannot increase his height or, what is the more likely meaning, cannot extend the span of his life by anxiety. And, what is more, needless concern reveals lack of trust in God. Many who live in affluent countries need the reminder implicit in this passage that the real necessities of life are fewer and simpler than we often imagine.

The real cure for needless concern over material needs is to have a true scale of values. Fulton Sheen writes, 'To conquer anxiety does not mean eliminating our desires but, rather, arranging them in a hierarchy, as Our Lord reminded us when He said that life is more than the raiment. This pyramid of values places things at the bottom—and things include everything material in the universe, from a star that inspires a poet to wheat used for the baker's bread. Above things comes man, and at the peak of the pyramid is God. A religious man orders his life by the pattern of the pyramid. He overcomes anxiety by making all material things subject to the human, by disciplining the body until it is subject to the spirit, and by submitting the whole personality to God.'

LUKE 12: 32–40

'Your heart is sure to be in the same place as your treasure' (v. 34, J. B. Phillips).

TRUSTFUL AND WATCHFUL. Christ's teaching about trustfulness leads up to a statement of infinite reassurance, 'Have no fear, little flock; for your Father has chosen to give you the Kingdom.' The man whose wealth is only material is harassed by fear of robbers and, in a land where hoardings were often in the form of exquisite rugs and tapestries, by moths. The life of trust is possible only to those who have invested in eternal values. But trustfulness does not mean an apathetic fatalism. Trustfulness is here linked with watchfulness and both are rooted in a deep confidence in God. The master may long delay at the lengthy wedding festivities but his servants await his return with alert anticipation.

Trustful and watchful: these are typically Christian attitudes. The believer knows that Christ will ultimately weave all the tangled threads of his life and of human history into a satisfying design.

Hilaire Belloc described a dreadful night he spent with a friend in the Pyrenees. Caught in a violent storm they barely managed to hold on to the mountain side. After many hours, when the tempest seemed at its worst, Belloc's friend, who was new to the experience, shouted, 'Isn't this terrible; it seems like the end of the world.' Back came the reassurance of the seasoned traveller, 'This is how the dawn comes in the Pyrenees.' In the darkest night of the spirit, and in the worst storm of affliction, Christian faith similarly enables a man to hold on. The dawn is sure.

LUKE 12: 41–48

'Much will be expected from the one who has been given much, and the more a man is trusted, the more people will expect of him' (v. 48, J. B. Phillips).

SERVING GOD WITHOUT BEING A SERVANT. Few people can handle prosperity and success; talents are used for self-display, promotion feeds pride, and improved standards of living encourage snobbery. In the parable here considered, the servant placed in a position of authority took advantage of his master's delayed return to lord it over his fellow-servants. There can be few more searching tests of character than the opportunity to use privilege for personal gain.

Jesus taught that privilege and responsibility belonged to each other; that the greater a man's opportunities to do good the more severe his judgment by God. Christ measured spiritual greatness by the extent to which a man, whatever his prestige or authority, was a servant. Haven't we already discovered how much easier it is to serve than to be a servant? And this explains why we get so

quickly discouraged and 'righteously indignant' at people's ingratitude and their refusal to respond in the ways we think good
for them. We want to serve (after the manner of our own choosing),
but not to be servants. Having received much, from us much is required—in service, but first of all as servants. Working for God is
no substitute for living with God.

LUKE 12: 49–53

'Fire ... baptism ... division' (vv. 49–51).

THE COST TO JESUS—AND TO OURSELVES. John
Wesley understood 'the fire on earth' (v. 49) to be the fire of
heavenly love. William Manson thought of it as 'the flame of
righteousness' which would inspire a nationwide repentance.
Other commentators have regarded it as the fire of judgment—
and vv. 51–53 would seem to support this.

But whatever the nature of this baptism of fire, Jesus realized
what would be the cost to Himself of kindling it. 'O that My task
was completed', translates *The Living Bible*. We can understand
Jesus as saying: 'Would that it were over!' Such a cry is of a piece
with the prayer in Gethsemane or the cry of dereliction from the
Cross. Yet such utterances are not to be taken simply as signs of
human weakness. The truly brave man is he who, conscious of the
severity of the ordeal that awaits him, nevertheless accepts and
endures it.

In this the disciple is not above his Lord. He too must recognize
that dedication will be costly. Father and son can find themselves
in opposite camps. A man's foes can be those of his own household.
Now as ever there can be circumstances in which the believer has
to be willing to write off all his attainments 'as a dead loss for the
sake of Christ' (Phil. 3: 8, Barclay).

LUKE 12: 54–59

'When you are going before the magistrate with your opponent, do your best to come to terms with him, while you have the chance' (v. 58, J. B. Phillips).

A MATTER OF URGENCY. In this illustration of a person
being taken to court, the assumption is that the accused will be
found guilty and punished severely. Jesus told the story to emphasize that every man has a weak case in the presence of God
and that therefore, if he is wise, he will make his peace with God
as quickly as possible.

Everywhere in the New Testament this note of urgency is sounded. We noticed this on pp. 210 and 211. Today we have the opportunity to consider a complementary truth, the other side of the same coin. Jesus nowhere identified urgency with feverish haste, the kind of urgency that expresses itself in frantic activity and anguish for speedy results. He likened the Kingdom of God on one occasion to a seed growing secretly, and spoke on another of the 'seed' of the gospel springing up rapidly because of shallow earth, only to wither and die.

The worst sin of some Christians is what Thomas Merton calls 'over haste'. They imagine that they are useful because they are busy. Of such people, Nels Ferré wrote, 'They lose the ease and joy of life.' He went on: 'We waste time by letting it dribble through our fingers or we are driven by it in the breathless attempt to snare it in a tight schedule. There is a better way. Those who live genuinely and joyously for God become free and alert to life.'

LUKE 13: 1–5

'Do you imagine that, because these Galileans suffered this fate, they must have been greater sinners than anyone else in Galilee?' (v. 2, N.E.B.).

SIN AND SUFFERING. Why did Jesus assert so positively that two well-known tragedies had nothing to do with the guilt of the people concerned, and then to warn His hearers: 'Unless you repent, you will all of you come to the same end'? The reason for this apparent contradiction is that the Master was affirming two equally important truths at the same time. He denied that individual sinners were punished in this life by particular tragedies. But He reaffirmed the prophetic doctrine that organizations and communities do come under God's judgment, which is worked out in history.

Personal tragedy is wholly mysterious. We gravely misrepresent God's character when we attribute accidents and misfortune to divine punishment. A minister who was suffering great distress dreamed he was to be granted a personal interview with Christ. 'Now I shall get an answer to all my problems,' he thought, and carefully prepared a questionnaire for the Master. Standing in the divine presence, however, he forgot all his questions and was simply content to know that there was an answer. This attitude is the only wisdom as far as personal misfortune is concerned.

Nations, churches and communities do come under the judgment of God in this life. Of the fourteen great civilizations which have already disintegrated, Professor Toynbee, in his ten volume historical survey, suggests that they were instruments 'which God could no longer use'.

LUKE 13: 6–9

'If it bear fruit, well; ... if not ...' (v. 9).

JUST AND MERCIFUL; MERCIFUL YET JUST. Some past expositors have attempted to find a meaning in each detail in this story. The vineyard was Israel; the vinedresser—Jesus; the three years—the length of His earthly ministry. But this is unnecessary and even confusing. The point of the parable is to stress the need for timely repentance.

In Palestine fruit trees were often planted in vineyards, turning them into a kind of orchard—but in this instance to no good purpose. The fig tree was eating up the goodness of the ground at the expense of the surrounding vines, but still bearing no fruit. So the owner instructed that it should be cut down. It was no more (comments T. W. Manson) than a glorified weed. However, the gardener pleaded for a year's respite. He would loosen the earth around the roots and manure it—trouble not usually taken with fig trees. The owner agreed. He would wait until the next harvest. But this could be the fig tree's last chance.

Without doubt the parable, when first spoken, related to the current situation. But its message is timeless. In His mercy God gives many a man another chance. But this should not lead anyone to presume upon God's goodness. There will be a last chance. The owner's patience was strained to breaking point with the barren fig tree. 'I wonder', mused Sir Winston Churchill once, 'what would happen if God lost patience with the world.'

LUKE 13: 10–21

'Jesus noticed her and called to her, "Woman, you are released from your weakness"' (v. 12, Moffatt).

THE COMPULSION OF LOVE. When criticized for healing on the Sabbath Jesus defended His action, not only on humanitarian grounds, but because the presence of the Kingdom demanded the woman's release from bondage. To express this divine necessity Christ used a word which He also used to explain the necessity for His Cross (9: 22). Both in His healing works and in the crowning sacrifice of His life Jesus recognized one over-riding necessity—the compulsion of love.

One of the early missionaries to Formosa was Thomas Barclay. He did not suffer martyrdom as did many pioneer missionaries but lived until he was eighty-five. Only after his death was the secret of his life of loving service discovered. Among his papers was found a solemn promise signed when he was a student in Glasgow on his sixteenth birthday, pledging his loyalty and love to Christ. It was signed on every subsequent birthday. Such was this man's recognition of the compulsion of love.

Luke links the parables of the mustard seed and the yeast with the healing of the crippled woman. Both mustard seed and yeast have potentialities which are out of all proportion to their apparent insignificance. Similarly, the healing acts of Jesus seemed to make small inroads upon the powers of evil, yet in them the Kingdom was present in germinal form and they held the promise of its final victory. In a lesser degree every truly loving action is both a revelation and a promise.

LUKE 13: 22–30

'Are there few that be saved?' (v. 22).

AN ACADEMIC QUESTION AND A REALISTIC ANSWER. While Jesus and His disciples were still on their way to Jerusalem an inquiry arose as to the number of those who would be saved. From the story it is impossible to tell whether this question was provoked by genuine concern for people, or was a patronizing attempt to discover how successful the mission of Jesus was proving to be.

But no matter; our Lord replied that the inquirer had better make sure that he himself was among the elect! He would have to struggle to get in through the narrow door (v. 24, N.E.B.). And as time was limited as well, he had better make sure now. Those who could have entered while the door was still open would knock in vain once it was shut. Useless then for a man to suppose he had any claim on Jesus just because he had listened to His words. He would find himself classed with the workers of iniquity (see Psalm 6: 8). 'Scoundrels' translates J. B. Phillips.

More often than not the values of the Kingdom contrast sharply with our own human judgments. Those who were children of Abraham felt that they had a prescriptive right to the joys of the

Kingdom. It was inconceivable that they should be shut out. But some were! For us today no privilege, or respectability, or religious status of our own will secure the blessing of eternal life. The passport to the Kingdom is repentance toward God and faith in our Lord Jesus Christ. Our prayer must be:

> Nothing in my hand I bring,
> Simply to Thy cross I cling.

LUKE 13: 31–35

'And He said unto them, Go ye, and tell that fox' (v. 32).

WHEN MEEKNESS BECOMES WEAKNESS. The fox, regarded by the Jews as the most sly and destructive of animals, was their name for a weak and worthless man. So Jesus left His hearers in no doubt about what He thought of Herod! Again we see how, as occasion arose, the meek Christ never minced His words; and let it be clearly understood that to speak in such terms of a king in the ancient world demanded rare courage.

Not to rebuke wrongdoers can bespeak weakness, not meekness. Some people keep quiet in the face of unashamed evil; when they should fearlessly reprimand they feebly excuse, not least themselves for their cowardly silence. It was said of a reputedly 'holy' man that he was often 'taken in' by unscrupulous people whom he never rebuked because, loving them so deeply, he believed the best about the worst. Of course, to err in this direction is far better than to be a carping fault-finder; but love that never rebukes is more indulgent than kind. As J. H. Oldham said about Florence Allshorn, 'The richer the possibilities she saw in a student the more drastic she would be about the weaknesses—provided she knew the student could stand it.'

Notice that Jesus' rebuke of Herod was another expression of the same yearning compassion that caused Him to weep over Jerusalem. Criticism without such a motive rarely helps and often seriously harms.

LUKE 14: 1–6

' "Well, is it right to heal on the Sabbath day or not?" But there was no reply' (vv. 3, 4, J. B. Phillips).

CRITICIZED FOR DOING GOOD. Malice was probably behind this courtesy to Jesus in the home of a leading Pharisee, for by this time the Pharisees were trying to trap Him into openly offending against the Law. But He accepted the invitation, though obviously aware that He was being watched with evil intent.

The fact of their hosility was added reason to Him to get along-side them in friendship, not separate Himself from them in resentment. Abraham Lincoln, accused of being too forgiving and kind toward his enemies, replied that the best way he knew of dealing with enemies was to turn them into friends. It is possible that the man with dropsy was a part of the Pharisees' scheming to get Jesus to incriminate Himself. Despite knowing this, and knowing also that His action would certainly cause Him to be criticized and even accused of irreligious behaviour, Jesus was true to Himself and healed the man.

Few people have the grace to do good under prying, disapproving eyes; and fewer still to serve others when the only reward is slander and bigotry. They manage it, however, because they are indwelt by the Spirit of Christ and, like Him, love the truth more than they fear the consequences of doing it.

LUKE 14: 7–14

'For everyone who makes himself important will become insignificant, while the man who makes himself insignificant will find himself important' (v. 11, J. B. Phillips).

THE SNARE OF SELF-IMPORTANCE. Those invited to a Palestinian dinner usually set out to the feast only when summoned by a servant. On arrival the guests sorted themselves out around the table but the host was free to rearrange them and to pick one guest to sit by his side in the place of honour. When the meal was finished this guest was expected to set the ball rolling in conversation. Probably it was this which gave Jesus the opportunity to point out that as in social etiquette, so in the spiritual realm, dignity and honour come only to those who do not attempt to grasp it for themselves.

A major fault in the Pharisees was their pompous self-importance. Elton Trueblood argues that, in an endeavour to save them from their own conceit, Christ used 'the strategy of laughter', exposing many of their positions to ridicule. 'Few features of official religion, of any particular faith, are more open to ridicule than is ostentation. The Christian faith, which began with an emphasis upon simplicity and humility ... has succumbed, in various generations, to the temptation to grandeur. Christ saw it coming and gave advance warning. . . .'

Ostentation is born of self-deception. It is an attempt to maintain the illusion that we are better than we really are. Far simpler, in the long run, to face reality. That is the only way genuine growth can take place.

LUKE 14: 15-24

'Go out to the highways and hedges, and compel people to come in' (v. 23, R.S.V.).

ARRESTING ATTENTION. This word 'compel' has resulted in misguided zealots trying to coerce people into the Kingdom of God, and even been used to justify the persecution and torture of the unconverted. Fanatics have argued that an individual's refusal to accept the gospel puts his soul in grave danger and therefore makes permissible the use of any means to encourage 'repentance'. Nothing could be further from the spirit of Christ.

When He talked about compelling people to come in, He was referring to the constraint of love, not the coercion of force. We have possibly heard a speaker who felt so deeply about his subject and presented it with such skill that we felt compelled to listen. His enlightened earnestness arrested our attention, making indifference impossible.

Now this is the commission that Christ lays upon us today. We are to command attention as we seek to persuade men of their need of God; and this requires primarily a spirit of desperate caring. Rudyard Kipling criticized the Founder of The Salvation Army for his unorthodox methods of evangelism. William Booth replied that if necessary he would play a tambourine standing on his head to compel attention. Only as we are constrained by the same love for Christ shall we really care whether or not our witness is arresting attention and demanding a response.

LUKE 14: 25-35

'A man cannot be My disciple unless he takes up his own cross, and follows after Me' (v. 27, Knox).

FOLLOWING JESUS. We have rightly stressed the tender compassion of Jesus, for nothing He ever did was inconsistent with love. There is a danger, however, that we overlook the uncompromising demand which Christ laid upon His would-be followers. 'The sentimentalized Jesus of our time is not One before whom men would fall on their faces,' writes Donald Miller, 'and certainly He would frighten away no devils! He is One whom nobody would crucify, and for whom few, if any, would be willing to die.' Of course, the claims which Jesus made, and makes, upon His disciples arose from His unique relationship with God. Upon the lips of a mere man they would have been arrogant presumption. This is why 'He is either God or He is not a good man.'

Loyalty to Christ must transcend every other loyalty. The words about hating father and mother must not be lightly dismissed, but neither must they be taken literally. It has been remarked that 'the semitic mind is comfortable only with extremes—light and darkness, truth and falsehood, love and hate—primary colours with no half-shades of compromise in between. The semitic way of saying, "I prefer this to that" is "I like this and hate that." Thus for the followers of Jesus, to hate their families meant giving the family second place in their affections.'

Today's passage challenges each Christian to ask himself, 'Have I substituted for the strong, challenging Son of God a weak and undemanding Jesus who is really a figment of my own imagination?'

LUKE 15: 1–10

'I tell you, there is joy among the angels of God over one sinner who repents' (v. 10, N.E.B.).

GOD IS THE SEEKER. 'This fellow welcomes sinners,' said the Pharisees of Jesus. What on their lips was a malicious slander has become the glory and impelling attraction of the Christian gospel. Eminent Jewish scholars, like Dr. Abrahams and Dr. Montefiore, agree that in His attitude to the outcasts Jesus was a pioneer. The Pharisees called publicans to repentance, Jesus went and sought them out. In answer to the Pharisees' criticism that His acquaintance with sinners was unbecoming Jesus affirmed that His attitude reflected the divine quest for all who are lost.

As Dr. Weatherhead once wrote, 'Before Christ, man was ever the seeker. . . . Now man knows himself to be the sought. Christ is the Shepherd and His search for us puts our half-hearted search for Him to shame.'

The ways in which God seeks the lost are infinitely varied. It may be happiness, or grief, a period of inactivity, or a heavy responsibility, which gives God His chance with a man. It was in a hospital ward, after receiving terrible injuries and being captured by the enemy, that Edward Howell was found of God. Suddenly there arose in his mind certain basic questions, 'What if there was a God? . . . Who could bring me home? Or bring home to me?' 'At that moment', he recalls, 'God spoke to me. Later, I lay in utter peace and quiet.'

LUKE 15: 11–24

'While he was still some distance off, his father saw him and his heart went out to him, and he ran and fell on his neck and kissed him' (v. 20, J. B. Phillips).

PRODIGAL'S RETURN. 'Nowhere in the gospel', wrote H. Balmforth, 'is the commentator's assistance less necessary than in this truly marvellous chapter.' The story of the prodigal son, perhaps the best-known story in the whole of literature, is a masterpiece of literary art and skilfully conveys its own message. Note, in passing, that no fate could be more degrading to a Jew than to feed pigs for a Gentile master. The returning prodigal, by intending to ask for a hired man's place, showed he had no idea of the extent of his father's love. Truly 'the love of God is broader than the measure of man's mind.'

Of all the sermons preached upon this passage perhaps the three main headings of the old Covenanting preacher have yet to be surpassed: 'First, sick o' Home; Second, Home-sick; and third, Home.' At Los Angeles airport, cargo-officials one day saw a flashlight shining from a crate which purported to hold a computer. Opening it they found, utterly exhausted, a twenty-year-old Welshman. He had emigrated to Australia ten months before, but became so unbearably home-sick that he devised this desperate method of getting back to Cardiff. Because the crate into which he had been nailed was diverted to America he almost lost his life.

The spiritual homesickness of the soul for God is not always as keenly felt, but it is eternally true—as T. S. Gregory observed— that the prodigal was more to the father than home was to the prodigal. The depth of the divine love for men unfathomably deeper than any human love for God.

LUKE 15: 25–32

' "My boy," said the father, "you are always with me, and everything I have is yours. How could we help cele-

brating this happy day? Your brother here was dead and has come back to life, was lost and is found" ' (vv. 31 and 32, N.E.B.).

TWO PRODIGALS—NOT ONE. This story has been misnamed the parable of the prodigal son. Its opening statement is 'there was once a man who had two sons'; it tells the story of two prodigals—not one. The father lost both his sons, one in the far country, and the other in a morass of self-righteous resentment. Writes F. W. Boreham, 'The curtain falls with the younger son in the father's house, and the elder son in a far, far country of his own! There are distances that cannot be measured in miles and furlongs and yards. I do not know how far it was from the father's house to the far country in which the younger son tended his swine; I only know that it was nothing like as far away as the chilly and gloomy country to which the elder son went.'

That Jesus concluded this story with the elder son sulking outside in the dark, unreconciled to his father and brother, implies a grave warning about the perils of a proud and unloving piety. We cannot remind ourselves too often that the heart of the Christian religion is a loving relationship with God. Anything which breaks that relationship, whether it be open rebellion or prideful independence, brings sadness to God.

LUKE 16: 1–9

'The master commended the dishonest steward for his prudence' (v. 8, R.S.V.).

CHRISTIAN PARASITES. This is not an easy parable to understand and many explanations have been offered. One of the most down-to-earth of these was given by Edgar H. Brookes in *The City of God and the Politics of Crisis*. 'The unjust steward, like some Christians today, made lots of friends on the basis of watering down his lord's demands and making things comfortable all round. So can we, and if we act otherwise we are liable to lose "friends" and to be hated.'

When Jesus condemned, but also commended the unjust steward for his profitable craftiness, He was not approving of or condoning such double-dealing. Rather He was making the point, among others, that 'the children of this world are considerably more shrewd in dealing with their contemporaries, than the children of light' (v. 8, J. B. Phillips). Another insight into the meaning of this same verse is provided by Moffatt's translation: 'the children of this world look further ahead . . . than the children of light'.

Christians are called upon to show the same perception, foresight, enterprise and ingenuity in the service of God as world-lings show in the service of success. If some believers gave to their spiritual welfare only half the time and thought they give to their material welfare, their lives and values would be transformed. So often the business 'go-getter' is the Christian parasite, giving to the concerns of the Kingdom of God only a fraction of the drive and interest given to his first loyalty. The parable has much to teach us all!

LUKE 16: 10-18

'You cannot serve God and money' (v. 13, N.E.B.).

THIS ONE THING I DO. Gathered around the irreconcilable alternatives of God and Money—note that the N.E.B. spells money with a capital 'M', investing it with the status of a god—are several utterances by Jesus on the obligations of a disciple.

Verses 9 and 10 elaborate the principle that he who makes good use of smaller opportunities of service will be entrusted with larger. The converse is also true. The man given to small 'fiddles' is likely to try his hand at more complicated (and remunerative) deals. And if (v. 11) a man is not to be trusted with that which moth and rust can corrupt, can he be entrusted with any of the riches of the Kingdom? Our responses to life must be single-eyed. Here is a clear cut either-or. The choice is between the service of God and the service of self.

Many Jewish scholars deny that the Pharisees were fond of money (v. 14). This was a Sadducean failing. Whether or not, the truth that God knows the human heart is a warning to all—particularly to those who are considering the acceptance of Jesus as Lord. They will have to make a genuine effort to enter the Kingdom; 'forcing their way into it', translates J. B. Phillips.

Then follows one of several of Christ's sayings concerning divorce (e.g. Matt. 19: 9, Mark 10: 11, 12) and these need to be studied together. What can be said about v. 18 is that Jesus is not so much laying down the civil law as stating a principle for His disciples to follow—and that can give us food enough for thought!

LUKE 16: 19–31

**'There was a rich man ... who feasted sumptuously.
... At his gate lay a poor man ... full of sores' (vv. 19, 20).**

THE SPIRIT OF UNCONCERN. In this parable Jesus made use of a familiar folk-tale found in other Jewish sources, from which two truths emerge. The first is that the point which our Lord was making had to do with this life, not the next. The parable does not offer a literal map of 'the other world'. Hell is separation from God, not a fixed location in space. This is why Mephistopheles, when asked how he could be on earth and yet in Hell at the same time, replied:

> Why this is hell, nor am I out of it:
> Think'st thou that I who saw the face of God,
> And tasted the eternal joys of heaven,
> Am not tormented with ten thousand hells
> In being deprived of everlasting bliss?

By a practical denial of the second of the two great commandments, a man shuts himself away from the presence of Him who is love—and that is Hell.

The second truth is that 'the sternest of all Christ's parables' (as Alexander Maclaren said) indicts those who ignore the needy and the dispossessed. It may be sound economics to come to the aid of the third world; it is most certainly a Christian duty.

Wealth is not the only factor that can separate a man from his neighbour and therefore from God. We may have time to spare. How much of it do we place at the service of the lonely? We may be blessed with an abundance of creature comforts. How much personal ease are we willing to forgo to help the less privileged? Dives need not have looked farther than his own gate, and we than our own street.

LUKE 17: 1–6

'If you had faith like a grain of mustard seed, you might say to this sycamore tree, Be rooted up, and planted in the sea, and it would obey you' (v. 6, Williams).

DOING THE IMPOSSIBLE. Having been challenged by their Master's words about the severe judgment awaiting those whose example encouraged others to stray (vv. 1–2); and also by His teaching regarding the need to forgive endlessly (vv. 3–4), the disciples understandably cried, 'Increase our faith.' Jesus then went on to talk about the power of faith, to talk about it with characteristically Eastern vividness.

Faith, He insisted, can accomplish the seemingly impossible. This truth is illustrated in every department of life, but pre-eminently in the realm of personal religion. Let us be sure, however, that we understand the nature of faith. Some people imagine that having faith in God is believing something that they suspect isn't true! Yet faith never contradicts reason; it transcends it, sees beyond it.

Faith gives God the chance to work. Professor Nels Ferré tells of being accompanied by his wife to a certain university to deliver a series of lectures. Just before the first lecture his wife looked at the large assembly, most of them ministers of religion, and said: 'Nels, as you think of the congregations these men represent, their young people, their Sunday-schools, and their contacts in the community, doesn't a chance like this to speak to them all seem most important?' He replied: 'It certainly does, let us pray harder.' Looking at him with 'soft eyes wonderously wise', she admonished: 'No, Nels, not harder, but easier, for it is not your prayer, but God who will do the work.'

This is the faith that 'moves mountains'!

LUKE 17: 7-10

'When you have done all that is commanded you, say, "We are unworthy servants; we have only done what was out duty" ' **(v. 10, R.S.V.).**

WHY THE SAINTS NEVER TALK ABOUT SACRIFICE. Here is a reminder that we can never put God in our debt, or under an obligation to serve us. At best we are unprofitable servants trying to meet our Master's legitimate claims upon us. Some people appear to think differently, their attitude suggesting that God has their patronage and should be jolly grateful for the honour.

How different is the spirit of the saints. When their sacrifice and suffering in the cause of Christ are most apparent (but never to themselves), they are lost in genuine wonderment that God should stoop to use such unprofitable servants as they know themselves to be. This explains why the saints, whatever their record of service, always feel unworthy. They know themselves to be incapable of satisfying the claims of God's love, or of theirs for Him;

and this is why those who sacrifice the most never talk about it. Indeed, they are not even aware of making sacrifice, for they are too preoccupied with its motive—their response to God's incredible love.

LUKE 17: 11–19

'And Jesus said to the man, "Stand up and go. Your faith has made you well" ' (v. 19, Living New Testament).

A GOSPEL FOR THE TOTAL MAN. There is a puzzling feature about this story. Jesus said to the Samaritan who returned to give thanks, 'Your faith has made you well'. In fact, the other nine were made well also. What can the words of Jesus mean, then, other than that his estimation of human well-being includes but is not limited to the physical? All ten lepers were healed physically. The Samaritan also entered a new relationship with Jesus of which his returning to give thanks was the sign. It is this 'new relationship' with Christ, which involves the total man, that is the supreme purpose of the gospel.

The missionary specialist goes out impelled by God's love. As a doctor or a teacher he does not consider his work limited to healing bodies or enlightening minds. It is his fundamental aim to bring Christ Himself to those to whom he ministers. This is not to say that the healing ministry and the education programme are preliminaries to the preaching of the gospel. They, with the offer of Christ, are the preaching of the gospel. Man is not so many parts; he is a whole—spirit, mind and body—and Christ is concerned with that whole. The Kingdom of God is a breakthrough into the realm of disease and ignorance in body and mind as well as the sin of the spirit.

LUKE 17: 20–25

'The Kingdom of God is not coming with signs to be observed . . . for behold, the Kingdom of God is in the midst of you' (vv. 20, 21, R.S.V.).

THE REIGN OF GOD IS HERE. These words of Jesus should caution us against a too literal interpretation of what He says later about His 'coming in clouds with great power and glory'. The emphasis here, which we should keep in mind, is on the real but unseen Kingdom already within and present among men. We ought not to think so much of an absentee Christ who is one day to return, but of a living Christ present now and coming to men all the time. The rendering above, 'in the midst of you', and the translation, 'within you' (A.V.), are both possible, and both are doubtless meant; the Kingdom in the heart, a spiritual experience; and the Kingdom among men, seen in the events taking shape before their eyes.

This is not to deny the fact of the End, the Consummation, the one 'divine event to which the whole creation moves'. C. P. R. Hanson has said that the Kingdom has come, is coming and is yet to come. This faith bears 'witness to the "finality" and all-sufficiency of Christ Himself'. Yet we ought not to fail to see the presence of the Kingdom in the events of today and also in our own personal experiences. Every loving deed, every endeavour made for others beyond the call of duty; every gesture of goodwill among men are signs of the present outworking of God's eternal purpose. As Gabriel Fackre has written: 'History is not "God-forsaken", illuminated only by the light at its end. It is also the theatre of God's present glory.'

LUKE 17: 26-37

'As it was in the days of Noah ... of Lot' (vv. 26, 28, J. B. Phillips).

DON'T BE TAKEN OFF GUARD. The emphasis here is not on the prevailing sinfulness of the people of Noah's day, but on their preoccupations. The sins of Sodom were a byword, but they are not mentioned here. They were eating, drinking, buying, selling, planting and building (v. 28, Moffatt). It was their indifference to the seriousness of their situation that proved their undoing.

The followers of Jesus must pray to be saved from any such complacency. Though it is true that no one knows when the Son of man may come, that hour will have decisive consequences for it will cut across any human distinctions. Men of the same household may be separated (v. 34) and women working at the same task (v. 35).

Various interpretations have been offered of the eagles (v. 37, A.V.) or vultures (N.E.B. and elsewhere). Some commentators have understood this to be a reference to the insignia of the Roman legions bearing down upon Jerusalem. Others—the swiftness with which carrion will attract birds of prey. More simply we may say that when the necessary conditions arise, certain events will take place. This just means that the believer must always be found with his loins girt and lamp burning.

'**He told them a parable, to the effect that men ought always to pray and not to lose heart**' (v. 1, R.S.V.).

WHY THE DELAYS? 'All the treasures of an infinite universe of goodness, truth and beauty are ours,' wrote Geoffrey Studdert Kennedy, 'if we will set ourselves with single minds to seek the highest. But we must ask and keep on asking; we must seek and keep on seeking; we must knock and keep on knocking. Only to those who persevere can the glory of the Kingdom be revealed. The difficulty, according to Jesus, does not lie in persuading God to give; but in preparing ourselves to receive'. That is a perfect commentary on the parable of the unjust judge.

The question, 'Why does God, who loves me, sometimes delay His answer to my prayers?' has taxed the minds, if not the faith, of many a good man. God is not reluctant to give to His children so that they have to wrest an answer out of His unwilling heart; nor does He delight in the 'much speaking' of His people: Jesus warned us against 'vain repetition' in prayer. There is a real mystery in our unanswered prayers, but it might help us to understand that the reason why the answers to some of them are delayed is that, as Studdert Kennedy said, 'the glory of the Kingdom can be revealed only to those who persevere.'

Our persistence in prayer is proof of the sincerity of our desire; it helps fit us to receive the answer. We cannot always see that in this case or that the answer we seek might result in our harm. But in this way God answers the pray-er, though not of necessity the prayer.

LUKE 18: 9–14

'**The tax-collector ... beat his breast and said: "God! Have mercy on me, the sinner"**' (v. 13, Barclay).

FACING THE TRUTH ABOUT OURSELVES. There is an episode in Nikos Kazantzakis's powerful novel *Christ Recrucified*, when five men are in prison awaiting execution, sentenced to hang by the Turkish overlord of the village as a reprisal for the murder of a member of his household by some unknown villager. In the shadow of the gallows one of the five goes to pieces and rails his companions about the lives of duplicity they have lived. He forces them to face the truth about themselves. It is an unpleasant experience, especially for the hypocritical village priest. He had never faced the truth about himself. 'And you, you sham, who'd make us confess, I'd like to know what sort of a face you'll wear when you present yourself before God . . .' the accuser rails.

It was the tax-collector's redeeming feature that he had faced the truth about himself. Bad though he was he did not pretend. The Pharisee, on the other hand, though he had kept all the rules, was self-righteous and hypocritical. He had never looked himself squarely in the face. Measuring himself by the tax-collector he obviously came out rather well. Measured by God's standard of sheer love he was, like all men, a 'miserable offender.'

It is never easy to face the truth about ourselves, but this is where Christian experience both begins and continues. We fail when we pretend. The way to Christian maturity is to see ourselves as we are when measured against God's standard and to recognize our need of His forgiveness.

LUKE 18: 15-23
'At these words his heart sank; for he was a very rich man' (v. 23, N.E.B.).

TOO HIGH A PRICE. Emphasis has been laid on the fact that the meeting of this wealthy Jewish religious leader with Jesus followed close upon our Lord's blessing of the babies brought to Him. When the disciples tried to prevent interested parents from doing so—'mothers of Salem' is William Hutchings' gloss upon the gospel story—Jesus rebuked them. Men would enter the Kingdom in the same trustful way as these infants accepted His smile and blessing.

Did this 'man of the ruling class' (N.E.B.) happen to notice what had taken place and, viewing the incident as a rebuke to his more sophisticated ways, run up impulsively to Jesus with his inquiry about eternal life? The Master accepted the newcomer's assurance that he had kept the commandments, but made one further demand.

It has been suggested that the command to 'sell all that you have' arose from the fact that this man's wealth was the final hindrance to his commitment to Christ. This may have been so. What is more to the point is that Jesus loved him (Mark 10: 21) and love always makes a total demand. Jesus was on His way to Jerusalem. In fulfilment of His redemptive mission He had broken every earthly tie. He did not even have a place to lay His head. Those who would share His mission must possess His spirit. Sadly the would-be seeker after eternal life turned away. What would we have done?

LUKE 18: 24-30

'**Believe Me, nobody has left his home or wife, or brothers or parents or children for the sake of the Kingdom of God, without receiving very much more in this present life—and eternal life in the world to come**' (v. 30, J. B. Phillips).

ENRICHED BY SELF-DEPRIVATION. 'What sacrifice you must have made', said someone to Thomas Chalmers, of New Guinea, 'in leaving your home and your native land and your Christian fellowship to live among debased and cruel cannibals.' 'Sacrifice,' replied Chalmers. 'Do you call it sacrifice when you see lives transfigured, savages turned into saints, men and women and children freed from degradation and made right-thinking, right-living members of a Christian community? There is no sacrifice there. On the contrary, there is joy unspeakable and full of glory.'

This missionary, his life an epic of heroic devotion, knew well what Jesus meant when He promised that, in the service of God's Kingdom, self-deprivation, no matter how costly, would always be less pronounced than unsought self-enrichment. The inevitability of this spiritual development was explained by the late Archbishop Temple when he said: 'There can be no such thing as sacrifice if the cause is big enough.'

LUKE 18: 31-43

' "**What do you want Me to do for you?**" ' (v. 41, R.S.V.).

ALLOWING CHRIST TO SERVE US. Lord Attlee once said that Sydney Webb, a one-time parliamentary colleague of his, tended to be more interested in statistics and institutions than in people. By contrast, Jesus, surrounded by an eager crowd and teaching as He walked, was not too preoccupied to hear and answer a blind man's cry.

There is plainly a whole world of personal need to which each of us must personally respond. But this does not mean—as Norman Pittenger has pointed out in *Goodness Distorted*—just 'membership on committees, often an Anglo-Saxon substitute for genuine love'. 'It is easier to give a subscription to a hospital', wrote D. T. Niles, 'than to stop on one's way and pick up a drunk who has fallen down and hurt himself and deliver him to a hospital. I found writing this address on Christian service', he continued, 'easier than to get up from my table and deal patiently with the beggar who had come to the door.'

But the question which Jesus asked of the beggar He also asks of us. For what matters first of all is not what we can do for Christ but what we will allow Him to do for us. To quote from Norman Pittenger again, 'Christian action is that which goes on inside us as we seek to realize more fully our manhood in and under God'.

Inasmuch as we are willing to be served by Christ with His love and grace and receiving the infilling of His Spirit, shall we 'realize more fully our manhood in God'.

LUKE 19: 1–10

' "Zaccheus, make haste and come down; for I must stay at your house today" ' (v. 5, R.S.V.).

THE JOY OF BEING WANTED. In one of his books Dr. Frank Boreham told how he once asked a young lady about her engagement day. 'Can you remember any particular thought that accounts for your ecstasy on that day?' was his question. She paused. 'I think,' she replied, 'it was the feeling that somebody wanted me.' It is a basic longing of all people to be wanted. When Jesus spoke to Zaccheus, saying, 'I must stay at your house today', His words gladdened the heart of the little man who, through his own greed, had become lonely and bitter. Nobody wanted him. He was the most unpopular man in Jericho, we might well think. Nobody visited his house socially, fine place though it doubtless was. But the Teacher said He wanted to and, Luke tells us, Zaccheus 'received Him joyfully'.

It is a wonderful thing to be wanted, to be accepted as we are. Nothing destroys inner peace and warps the personality more than the feeling that nobody cares; that we do not count with anybody. Said an old man, 'I can think of nothing sadder than to die and not to be missed'. When some time ago an old lady who lived alone was found dead, a diary at her side carried the same sad entry day after day, 'Nobody called'!

Let our thought be that God wants us. We are precious to Him and He accepts us, as Jesus accepted Zaccheus, just as we are.

LUKE 19: 11–27

'The man who has will always be given more; but the man who has not will forfeit even what he has' (v. 26, N.E.B.).

INOFFENSIVE USELESSNESS. This text comes at the

end of the parable of the talents, teaching which reminds us again of the awful possibility of being condemned for doing nothing. The man who received one talent did no harm; in fact, he did nothing at all. In consequence he lost even the possibility of doing anything. This is a law of life and can be seen working itself out in, for instance, the realms of music, sport, health and study: the non-practising musician finally loses his gift, and the sportsman his skill; lack of physical exercise produces a flabby body, and the absence of thought a flabby mind. No wonder our capacity to serve God is sometimes so limited!

We do well to ponder the words of Thomas E. Powers in *First Questions on the Life of the Spirit*: 'You know that everyone who learns chemistry (a few geniuses excepted) has got to learn it this way, by hard work. Everybody grumbles a little about this state of affairs, but nobody seriously questions the fact of it. Yet when we come to spiritual knowledge, learning about reality, learning about God, a strange conceit and an even stranger sentimentality appear. More often than not the candidate imagines that this kind of knowledge can be poured into him with no pain, no strain, no work, and certainly no hard work. This attitude, if it exists, is a considerable obstacle. It is based on the common assumption that since God is a loving Father, He must also be a silly old fool who would just as soon raise a brood of spoiled sons as a company of ... strong, gentle, brave, compassionate, free and triumphant sons.'

Inoffensive uselessness is often the end result of simply doing nothing!

LUKE 19: 28–40

'Then they threw their cloaks on the colt, for Jesus to mount, and they carpeted the road with them as He went on His way' (v. 36, N.E.B.).

DEMANDING A VERDICT. The entry of Jesus into Jerusalem on a donkey was His first open claim to Messiahship. Before this He had made no public claim. But now the time had come for Him to enact the fulfilment of the ancient prophecy: 'Rejoice, rejoice, daughter of Zion, shout aloud daughter of Jerusalem; for see your King is coming to you ... humble and mounted on an ass' (Zech. 9: 9). It was a challenge to the people of Jerusalem. They must now reveal what they thought about Him.

Christ still demands this kind of verdict from men. Debates, discussions and arguments about Him abound, and doubtless they serve some useful purpose. But in the final resort men must make up their minds about Him, not merely as a result of debate, not wholly on the testimony of others, but by a leap of faith.

In his book *The Need to Believe*, Murdo Macdonald writes, 'Neither argument nor authority can create the inner personal assurance we want. The mystics and saints have made the dangerous leap of faith, but no matter how unanimous their verdict, we cannot rest on that. There is no such thing as Christianity by proxy. We can never be certain until we make the leap ourselves. Only then will we find the support of the everlasting arms.'

LUKE 19: 41-48

'"If only," He said "you would realize on this day ... the things which would bring you real prosperity"' (v. 42, Barclay).

MISTAKES WE ALL MAKE. In this moving passage Jesus spoke of two grave errors the people of Jerusalem were making. Firstly, He said, they did not recognize where life's real values lay. This was illustrated by their rejection of Christ's way of peace. Rebellion was in the air; the people seemed determined on it. But that way, Jesus knew, would lead only to destruction. And it did; in A.D. 70 Jerusalem was totally destroyed. Christ's sorrow as He looked over Jerusalem was not that the people wanted emancipation—for that is a true human longing—but that they did not realize that political and material freedom could not of themselves lead to life. It is a truth men of all ages, including our own, seem slow to learn. Political emancipation and material well-being for all are worthy causes to which a man may justly give himself, but only if he recognizes the prior claims of the soul of man, which can find release and fulfilment only in Christ.

The other tragedy of the people of Jerusalem was *their failure to see and hear God in Christ*. Though they had for centuries looked for God's visitation, when He came they did not recognize Him. 'He came unto His own,' says a New Testament writer, 'and His own received Him not'. That is as tragic a text as any in the whole of Scripture.

It is a reminder to us to be ready to see and receive Christ when He comes and speaks today. Says D. W. Cleverley Ford, 'We must remember that we do not know when and in what form

Christ will appear to us. The need is to be ready for his recognition even in the secular movements of our time.'

LUKE 20: 1–8

"'If we tell Him it was from heaven", they said, 'He will ask, 'Then why did you not believe him?' And if we say it was from men, all the people will be ready to stone us . . .'" (vv. 5, 6, Knox).

UNCOMFORTABLE TRUTH. The Jewish religious leaders were in no small quandary when Jesus asked them about the authority of John the Baptist. This was no mere debating point. Many of the Jews believed in the Baptist as a man sent from God and knew that he himself had pointed to Jesus as the long-expected Messiah. To approve of John was therefore to acknowledge Jesus. But to question the authority of John was almost to provoke a riot! So the chief priests and scribes pretended ignorance (v. 7).

To play fast and loose with truth is to invite the kind of disaster which would overtake the captain of a ship who threw away his compass. Yet what a discomforting thing the truth often is, and how the men of truth have been hated. In his play *Curtmantle* Christopher Fry makes Henry II demand from Archbishop Becket obedience to certain legal customs. To which demand Becket replies, 'God said, "I am Truth," not "I am Custom."'

There may be situations when the whole truth cannot immediately be spoken. Kindness and responsibility for other's welfare can require a partial withholding of the truth. Dag Hammarskjöld, when he was Secretary-General of the United Nations, must have known delicate situations of this kind. But in his notebook was found this warning: 'The most dangerous of all moral dilemmas: when we are obliged to conceal truth in order to help the truth to be victorious. If this should at any time become our duty in the role assigned us by fate, how strait must be our path at all times if we are not to perish.'

LUKE 20: 9–18

'He will come and wipe out these tenants, and will give the vineyard to others' (v. 16, Barclay).

NO COUNTING ON PRIVILEGES. In *The Parables of the Kingdom*, C. H. Dodd says that this story could well have been based on a true-life incident. It was not unknown for the heir to a property to be murdered and the estate seized while the owner was abroad. The parable is more allegorical than most, identifying the landlord with God, the servants with the Old Testament prophets, the son with Jesus and the 'others' with the Gentiles. It was courageous of Jesus to tell it, for its meaning would be abundantly clear, and bound to exacerbate the feelings of hostility that were building up towards Him.

The Jews were being warned that by their attitude to Jesus they were forfeiting the right to be called the chosen of God. That privilege was to pass to the New Israel, the Christian Church. It did so. And if the Church as at present constituted fails in its purpose might not her privileges be taken away also? Might not God by-pass the Church and reveal Himself to men through other channels?

This has personal application. If by our disobedience, our rejection of truth and our slow response to God's Spirit, we fail Him, we might be in the tragic position of being 'officially' His representatives on earth and yet not be doing the work He requires of His people. God will not leave Himself without His witnesses, but we can be sure He will use us only if we are wide open to His love, grace and direction.

LUKE 20: 19-26

'He saw through their trick and said, "Show Me a silver piece"' (vv. 23, 24, N.E.B.).

WHO TAKES WHAT? The Jewish leaders now intensified their campaign against Jesus so that they might trap Him into some indiscreet utterance which might form the basis of a charge against Him before the Roman authorities. The poll tax—levied on every adult male in Judea since A.D. 6 and heartily disliked by all—gave them such an opportunity.

Jesus asked for a silver piece—the amount of the tax. This was the *denarius* (a shilling or 5 new pence) of Tiberius and bore (says Stauffer) an inscription which meant: 'Emperor Tiberius, august Son of the august God'. The coin was not only in general, but official, use. Each money-lender wore a *denarius* in his ear as a sign of his profession and their tables must have been loaded with such coins. The place and power of Roman authority could not be denied. Daily sacrifice was offered in the Temple for the welfare of the emperor. The Jewish people shared in the benefits of Roman rule. They were therefore to pay (i.e. render) to Rome what they owed to Rome. As we must. We share the blessings of community life; we must make an appropriate return to the community.

But there is also an appropriate acknowledgment to be made to God. Recognition of the one claim demands recognition of the other. Early believers did both. Said Christians on trial in Carthage in A.D. 180: 'We serve the invisible God. We have embezzled nothing. On every transaction we pay the due tax.' When sentenced to death the martyrs cried with one voice: 'We praise Thee, thrice holy God, Thy kingdom endures through all eternity.'

LUKE 20: 27-44

'It is of living men, not of dead men, that He is the God; for Him, all men are alive' (v. 38, Knox).

A FUTURE LIFE. The stock problem of the Sadducees was brought to Jesus in order to pour scorn upon this reality The Pharisees believed in a resurrection from the dead; the Sadducees did not—on the ground that there was no warrant for such a belief in the Mosaic law.

The incredible story they told would be sure to have raised a snigger from the crowd, but the questioners once again overreached themselves. Jesus answered that they were overlooking the nature of the world to come and, further, they were ignoring the teaching of their own sacred writings. There would be no point in the record's reference (Exod. 3: 6) to 'the God of Abraham ... of Isaac, and ... of Jacob' if the patriarchs were but dead corpses.

We know only in part concerning the life to come, but we know enough about God confidently to leave our future with Him. Brother Lawrence, despairing with doubts about his salvation and consequently dreading his possible rejection in the life beyond, found peace in the realization that nothing, not even existence in Hell itself, could stop his loving God; and this was all the Heaven he wanted.

When William Booth was dying, he pleaded, only half-consciously, 'Oh, I wish you would let me go—I want to go home.' His son Bramwell told him that he was there, in his own home at Hadley Wood, lying on his own bed. He listened and then exclaimed: 'But that is not home.' Heaven is home to the man who loves God; and to love God is Heaven.

'Beware of the Scribes! They like to walk about in long robes, they are fond of being saluted ... of securing the front seats ... they prey upon the property of widows and offer long, unreal prayers' (vv. 46, 47, Moffatt).

THE SPIRIT BEHIND RELIGIOUS OBSERVANCES. These teachers of the Law practised religion to glorify themselves. Their robes made an ostentatious showing of their piety; they expected to be addressed as 'Master' or 'Teacher', and to be given an honoured place at every gathering. It was considered an act of great piety to support a rabbi; and this gave the Scribes an opportunity to prey upon the wealth of pious and lonely women.

In contrast to this religious professionalism, the widow who gave her only half-farthing practised religion to glorify God. He measures giving always by its quality, never its quantity or public acclaim; His concern is not how much we give, but why we give and how much we have left. When John Wesley was an undergraduate at Oxford, he had £30 a year; he lived on £28 and gave £2 away. His income increased to £60, £90, £120, but he still lived on £28 and gave the rest away. His rule was 'to save all he could and to give all he could'.

'Most men, it is to be feared', observed Alexander Whyte, 'have no principle and no method in their giving. They dole out their contributions and subscriptions as if it were a cruel intrusion and a real injury they suffer just to be invited to give. And thus, life goes on, and wastes away, and they neither get the good nor do the good that intelligent, conscientious, methodical giving always brings with it.'

'And when you hear of wars and insurrections, do not fall into a panic. These things are bound to happen first; but the end does not follow immediately' (v. 9, N.E.B.).

HOPE—THE ANTIDOTE TO PANIC. Jesus spent much of the last week of His earthly life teaching in the temple, and though Mark (13:1 ff.) sets the dialogue on the far side of the Kidron valley, the conversation is virtually the same. His disputes with the authorities show Him to be both a fearless and a formidable controversialist (20: 9-47). In this reading Jesus launches into a long discourse about the upheavals of history, both those which would follow His death and those which lead up to 'the end'.

Christians believe that God is working His purpose out in the processes of history. Sometimes, usually long after the actual events, this providential ordering is apparent. At other times faith has to be clung to in the teeth of contradictions. Teilhard de Chardin, that great Christian scientist who did so much to increase our knowledge of the distant past, wrote, 'I am persuaded that at all costs we must cling to a faith in some direction and in some destination assignable to all this restless human activity.'

The Christian sets the worst that history can do constantly in the context of the best that God can do. The chorus in an ancient Greek tragedy sings: 'Tragedy is restful; and the reason is that hope, that foul, deceitful thing, has no part in it.' Nothing could be further from the Christian point of view. Our fellowship with God in Christ has given us an indestructible hope. No upheaval, and no tragedy, can defeat God's purpose of love.

LUKE 21: 10–19

'You will be handed over even by parents, and brothers, and kinsfolk and friends; some of you will be put to death; and you will be hated by all for the sake of My name. But not one hair of your head will perish. By your endurance you will win your souls' (vv. 16–19, Barclay).

OVERCOMING DESOLATION. Jesus never tried to hide the brutal truth from His followers; their loyalty to Him would often lead to persecution and even to martyrdom. But He promised to save them in their tribulations. African Christians in Mau Mau country, understanding this, bravely prepared for the worst. In their message to fellow-Christians, they requested with rare insight for converts so young in the faith: 'Do not pray that we shall be kept safe, but that we shall be kept faithful!'

Christ is never more with us than in our troubles, when desolation would deny His presence. A Lutheran minister, Paul Schneider, imprisoned by the Nazis, and starved to death in a concentration camp, wrote shortly before his death to his sorrowing wife: 'Be comforted and faithful; fear not. I hold you close in my heart. In God we are not separated ... Let us be thankful for this beautiful period of preparation for harder trials. New sorrows should bring us new experiences of our God and a new glory. Christ says: "I am with you all your days".'

Jesus never promised always to still the storm, but He did promise always to stay on board the ship of life with us!

LUKE 21: 20-28

'Men's courage will fail completely as they realize what is threatening the world. . . . But when these things begin to happen, look up, hold your heads higher, for you will soon be free' (vv. 26, 28, J. B. Phillips).

WHAT TO DO IN ADVERSITY. With the insight of one who sees life from God's point of view and is therefore able to read the signs of the times, Jesus knew that Jerusalem was heading for terrible disaster, the kind that follows national forgetfulness of God. He told His disciples what they should do in this situation, but His words can help us in more general terms.

When confronted by adversity—suffering, disappointment, depression, anxiety—we should 'look up'. The natural tendency will be to look down. Dejected individuals, their shoulders sagging, stare at the ground as they walk along. They see only what they feel—gloom. This explains why a bad start to a day often results in everything seeming to go wrong, for we usually find in life what we are looking for, and always see in others an image of our own inner life.

Jesus tells us to look up, to take our eyes away from ourselves, our fears, worries and failings, and to focus them upon God. This will remind us of the triumphant adequacy of our spiritual resources and enable us to see life steady and whole through the eyes of Christ.

LUKE 21: 29-38

'Keep a watch on yourselves; do not let your minds be dulled by dissipation, and drunkenness and worldly cares so that the great Day closes upon you suddenly like a trap' (vv. 34, 35, N.E.B.).

DEGENERATION CAMOUFLAGED BY TAME RESPECTABILITY. 'The final parables of our Lord', old Samuel Chadwick used to say, 'make watchfulness the discriminating mark among those who are in the fellowship of hope. They are distinguished by this one feature: those who watch, and those who do not. The watchers look for Christ's appearing ... They live constantly expecting Him. They are always concerned to be ready for His coming. Because they look for Him coming in glory they see Him everywhere.'

The danger is, of course, that we tend to grow weary in well-doing and allow our diminishing physical resources to excuse our spiritual and mental laziness. Stephen Neill tells of travelling by train with two fellow bishops, and the three of them agreeing that 'the years between forty and fifty are the most dangerous in a man's life'. When only middle-aged, Professor Gilbert Murray confessed: 'The questionings of conscience certainly play a less prominent and disturbing part in my ordinary life than they did in the years between seventeen and twenty-seven.'

Avoiding the folly of morbid introspection, we need, as Jesus said, to keep a watch on ourselves, resisting the easy degeneration of flabby bodies, and dulled spirits, a degeneration which is often camouflaged by tame respectability.

LUKE 22: 1–13

'So Jesus dispatched Peter and John, saying, "Go and prepare the Passover for us to eat"' (v. 8, Moffatt).

ADEQUATE PREPARATION AND FORESIGHT. There are some people who imagine that living by faith means living by chance; they obey the injunction, 'Take no thought for the morrow' by taking no thought. The consequence is unnecessary muddle, inconvenience and inefficiency. Jesus gives the right interpretation to His words about taking no thought by His careful preparation for the Passover feast. His instructions to Peter and John clearly indicate that detailed plans had been made well in advance: the man carrying a water jar would be as noticeable as a modern man carrying a lady's handbag; and the disciples were to follow to a pre-arranged meeting-place, which was 'ready and furnished'.

Confusion and incompetence through lack of method and forethought are inexcusable. The efficiency of some worldlings puts some Christians with their unanswered letters, broken promises and easy forgetfulness to shame.

The Founder of The Salvation Army had a rule about sermon preparation which has a much wider application. 'Prepare as though there was no Holy Spirit; then preach with the conviction that there is.' This is the way for the believer to face every situation—to plan and to pray; to be careful and to be carefree; to make ready for the future and to live in the present.

LUKE 22: 14–23

'Then He took a cup, and after giving thanks He said, "Take this and share it among yourselves" ... And He took bread, gave thanks, and broke it: and He gave it to them, with the words: "This is My body"' (vv. 17, 19, N.E.B.).

ALL LIFE IS SACRAMENTAL. In *Crucified and Crowned* Dr. William Barclay comments on 'This do in remembrance of Me'.

'Does it mean (he asks) that some kind of symbolic action has to be repeated, which is in fact what has happened ... It remains a curious fact that in the gospel narrative there is no definite instruction as to repetition, and from this emerges a possibility of the greatest significance ... The passover meal was a real meal and ... it remains a very definite possibility that Jesus did not intend to institute a symbolic meal, but that He meant that every time bread was broken and eaten, and every time wine was poured out and drunk—that is, at every meal in every house, He was to be remembered.

He may well have meant that every meal was a sacrament, that it should be impossible for any Christian at any time to break bread without remembering Him. It has been said that we are not fully Christian until Christ has become Lord not only of the communion table but of the dinner table ... He was hallowing and sanctifying every common meal so that every meal might become an experience of His presence.' This is the point of view of The Salvation Army, where the daily routine becomes an altar and daily fellowship a holy communion. The onus is on those who hold this view to maintain this standard.

LUKE 22: 24–30

'He who is greatest among you must be like the youngest, and he who is chief like a servant' (v. 26, Moffatt).

THE NATURE OF TRUE GREATNESS. After some three years of intimate fellowship with the lowly Nazarene, the disciples were squabbling about who should be greatest when the Kingdom of God was finally established by, as they still believed, physical force. Jesus told them that true greatness was measured by humility and the spirit of service; not by how much authority a man possessed to order other people about.

The Christian is called not merely to serve, but to be a servant. 'The crucial problem in Christian service', wrote D. T. Niles 'lies not at the point where service is rendered, but at the point where that service is received. No man wants to be served. Any man resents being put under a sense of obligation to someone else. So that, if service is to be truly rendered, and received, it must be made quite obvious that he who serves, serves only because he has already received; and that which he gives he gives not out of his own bounty, but out of the bounty of Him from whom all gifts proceed.'

A self-righteous 'do-gooder' was told by a needy person to 'go and save your soul on somebody else'; she was patronizing and therefore humiliating the intended recipient of her charity; seeking to serve without the spirit of a servant. We must not make the same mistake.

LUKE 22: 31–38

'Sure enough, all that has been written of Me must be fulfilled' (v. 37, Knox).

UNAVOIDABLE CROSS. Before leaving the Upper Room, and the Passover meal which Jesus had longed to share with His disciples, the Master tried to prepare His followers for the ordeal ahead. He was not so engrossed in the fearful prospect of His own sufferings as to forget that His disciples too were facing a shattering experience. Addressing Peter on behalf of them all Jesus spoke of the valley of humiliation through which they must come to a deeper faith. Often in the life of the disciple superficial self-confidence has to be destroyed before we can be of real service in the Kingdom. When we are laid low by failure may we also hear Christ's words, 'I have prayed that your faith may not fail.'

Jesus contrasted the happy days of the Galilean mission, when the disciples could rely completely on kind hospitality, with the hostility which now surrounded them. Now they might well feel they needed both purse and sword. Our Lord's ironic dismissal of the remark that two swords were available is heightened by the reference in v. 37 to Isaiah 53: 12.

Jesus prepared His disciples for His arrest by insisting that the Cross was God's will. From our viewpoint, centuries later, we see that only by suffering could God's love be manifested. William Temple quoted those who say, 'There cannot be a God of Love because if there were, and He looked upon this world, His heart would break.' 'The Church points to the Cross,' wrote Temple, 'and says, "His heart does break."'

LUKE 22: 39–46

'Father, if it be Thy will, take this cup away from Me. Yet not My will but Thine be done' (v. 42, N.E.B.)

THE WEIGHT OF THE CROSS. In the village of Ober-ammergau when the people were making ready to perform the Passion Play which is presented there every ten years, two visitors wandered backstage where actor Anton Lang was preparing to take the tragic journey to Calvary. One visitor tried to get under the cross but found he could scarcely lift it. He asked the actor why it was so heavy. 'I could not play my part', replied Anton Lang, 'unless I could feel the weight of the cross.'

To enter imaginatively into the story of Christ's Passion we need to make the effort to 'feel the weight of the Cross'. What was the the meaning of the dark agony of Gethsemane? The Gospel records indicate that in the garden Jesus plunged into an abyss of mental and spiritual suffering which, in its own way, was as intense as anything endured on Calvary. Here is a mystery we can never fully penetrate, yet it is clear that the horror of Gethsemane was more than fear of cruel death. The traitor's kiss, the judgment which Israel was bringing upon herself, as well as all the pain of unrequited love: these were just a fraction of what was involved in 'the cup' of His Passion.

We can never know how costly was Christ's loving identification with sinful humanity. We can be profoundly grateful that, in the hour of acute agony, He remained willing to pay the price.

LUKE 22: 47–53

'Jesus said to him, Judas wouldst thou betray the Son of Man with a kiss?' (v. 48, Knox).

WHEN TREACHERY CAMOUFLAGES ITSELF. In the ancient world, the kiss in public was a mark of respect and reverence. If a disciple met a beloved rabbi, he would place his right hand on the man's left shoulder, his left hand on the right shoulder, and kiss the teacher's cheek. Judas, encouraged by pious religious leaders, greeted Christ in such a manner, turning what appeared to be an expression of affectionate loyalty into a sign of treachery.

The most unlikely people are sometimes guilty of secret faithlessness, for they are careful always to give the very opposite impression. In his autobiography, A. J. Cronin tells of a patient who was 'unquestionably a virtuous woman' and 'would have scorned the vaguest suggestion that she might be even remotely untrue to her husband'. Yet behind his back she seized every opportunity to make him appear small in the eyes of their children, and was loud in her criticism of his opinions, his dress and much else. To his face, however, she was loving and loyal! Commented Cronin: 'Unfaithfulness is a shoddy business, a despicable betrayal of mutual trust, the meanest sin in the book of human wrong-doing.'

The sin of Judas was treachery with a kiss. Do we ever give Christ some outward sign of loyalty yet in our heart deny Him?

LUKE 22: 54–62

'And the Lord turned His head and looked straight at Peter . . .' (v. 61, J. B. Phillips).

A TEST OF LOYALTY. 'We often dwell upon the Passion of our Lord,' writes J. Alexander Findlay, 'we do not often think of the passion of His friends.' Certainly behind Peter's violent outburst, when he denied his Lord with oaths, there is far more than mere panic. This is the man who courageously resisted the arrest of His Master in the garden (John 18: 10), the man who followed Jesus right into the enemy's camp. He is no coward.

Peter probably felt that Jesus misunderstood him. Some of his most generous actions had met with rebuke. When he urged Jesus to avoid the way of suffering his Master called him 'Satan', when he protested at Christ's washing his feet Jesus warned him, 'If I wash you not you have no part in Me,' and when Peter unsheathed his sword in the garden his action seemed little appreciated. Add to all this the bitterness of having sacrificed everything for an apparently lost cause and we can glimpse what a severe test of loyalty Peter endured.

Though Peter was caught off guard there is no doubt that his love for Christ held firm. One look from Christ broke him down

244

utterly. If this story tells us much about Peter it also conveys a valuable insight into the character of Jesus. Christ sees beneath all our failures and knows when we truly love Him. More than this, His love holds on to us even when our love is proved inadequate.

'From now on the Son of Man will take His seat at the right hand of Almighty God' (v. 69, J. B. Phillips).

POWERFUL IMPOTENCE. As H. H. Farmer has written, 'If we look at the gospel story of the Passion . . . one of the most impressive things in it is the air of strong deliberation and mastery which characterized Jesus throughout those last days. He was not in the least a straw on the stream of events; He was controlling the stream of events.' This was never more evident than when facing the members of the Sanhedrin who had determined, even before the trial, that Jesus must die.

They imagined they were to judge Jesus; in fact, they were being judged by Him. 'From now on,' said Jesus, 'the Son of Man will take His seat at the right hand of Almighty God.' Not, 'when you have done your worst and I have passed out of your hands', but 'from now on'. The battered Prisoner was already Judge.

The story of the trial illustrates the truth of Paul's words, 'the weakness of God is stronger than men'. We read about 'the men who were holding Jesus'. Can men really hold captive He who stilled the storm, forgave sins and cast out devils? But here He is impotent to save Himself. Otherwise He would not have been love, and He would have been powerless to help us in our suffering.

'For all the anguish of the world', wrote William Temple, 'there are three consolations. The Epicurean says, "It is but for a time; ere long we shall fall asleep in the unending slumber"; which is comfort of a sort. The Stoic says, "Rise above it all; to the wise these things are nugatory"; which is no comfort at all if we are not wise. Christianity says, "Christ also suffered"; and that, with the Christian interpretation of "Christ", is real consolation, a human answer to our humanity.'

'Then Herod and his troops treated Him with contempt and ridicule, and sent Him back to Pilate dressed in a gorgeous robe' (v. 11, N.E.B.).

MOMENTOUS DECISION. Pilate could never have dreamed that what he regarded as a disagreeable incident would more deeply engrave his name in history than the names of all the Emperors. How little man is sometimes aware of the significance of his actions. We miss the whole point of the Passion narrative if we imagine that this was true only for the people of Christ's day. Every moral issue is a confrontation with Christ, as is every encounter with human need. Our decisions are often more important than we realize. Pilate, like almost every other person in the drama of Holy Week except Jesus Himself, was motivated by fear. Well as Carl Hilty said, 'A man who holds high public office ... who fears something more than God, is a miserable creature.'

The injustice, contempt and ridicule which Jesus endured is one aspect of His perfect identification with suffering mankind. A group of demoralized prisoners of war, none of them Christians, began to read the New Testament. One of them later wrote: 'In the light of our new understanding, the Crucifixion was seen as being of the utmost relevance to our situation. A God who remained indifferent to the plight of His creatures was not a God with whom we could agree. The Crucifixion, however, told us that God was not indifferent to such suffering. We stopped complaining about our own. Faith could not save us from it, but it would take us through it. We looked at the Cross and took strength from the knowledge that it gave us, that God was in our midst.'

'Once more Pilate spoke to them, offering to set Jesus at liberty; but they continued to answer with shouts of, "Crucify Him, crucify Him"' (vv. 20 and 21, Knox).

OUR KIND OF SIN. It has been said that 'the Cross is the mirror of the world'. All those involved in the Passion story have their true nature exposed. More than this, an imaginative reading of this story forces us to confess that it was ordinary, everyday sins which took Jesus to Calvary. Do we not all try to put off making the right but difficult decision? And is Pilate not the perfect illustration that every moment we delay making the right decision increases the probability that we shall decide wrongly?

Pilate did all he could to evade his responsibility. He sent Jesus to Herod. He tried the old trick of those who aim to manipulate people, trying to convince the Jews that what he wanted was really what they wanted, that he would be doing them a favour by setting Jesus free. He hoped a cruel scourging might allay the crowd's lust for blood. But all in vain. Dare we condemn him? Wrote Helmut Gollwitzer, 'Every refusal of responsibility, however well justified it may be, and apparently reasonable, may today be the reason why, all of a sudden, you begin to behave like Pilate, who was unfaithful to his official duty, ran away from responsibility, and allowed Christ to be nailed to the Cross.

To see ourselves in Pilate and, for that matter, in other 'personalities of the Passion', is a harrowing experience. But it can be a cleansing and revitalizing experience if we allow the same Saviour, by his unquenchable love, to lead us beyond self-despair into a total reliance on His grace.

LUKE 23: 26-31

'Great numbers of people followed, many women among them, who mourned and lamented over Him. Jesus turned to them . . .' (vv. 27, 28, N.E.B.).

A HEART AT LEISURE FROM ITSELF. Imagine the scene! Jesus, crowned with thorns, His back lacerated and His strength gone, collapses under the weight of the Cross. Simon, from Cyrene, now called Tripoli, possibly making his only visit to Jerusalem for the Passover, is compelled to carry the Cross. The Son of Man, racked with pain, blinded by sweat and blood, His every muscle screaming for relief, turns to a group of women and says: 'Weep not for Me, but weep for yourselves.' Pain, like adversity in general, usually tends to make us self-centred and self-pitying.

Today's reading reminds us that those who suffer or face adversity without becoming selfish truly live in the spirit of Christ. The secret of such nobility is illustrated in the life of James Hannington, first Bishop of Uganda. When only thirty-seven years of age, he was seized by the warriors of a suspicious African chief and for his last eight days surrounded by drunken guards and prowling hyenas. Naked and hungry, he suffered from vermin and was delirious with pain. 'I felt', he recorded in his diary, 'that I was being dragged away to be murdered; but I sang "Safe in the arms of Jesus", and laughed at the agony of my situation.' Bishop Hannington knew what it was to have a heart at leisure from itself, to soothe and sympathize.

> Simon, the African, carried His cross,
>   Bore it along on his back,
> Felt its weight, sensed the hate
>   Driving Christ up the sinister track.
> O Simon the African, many a load
>   Your people still carry in sorrow,
> But their care He will share,
>   And redress it, with yours, on the morrow.

LUKE 23: 32, 33, 39-43

'Jesus, remember me', (v. 42, N.E.B.).

THE DYING THIEF REJOICED. We owe to Luke the story of the penitent thief—Dismas his name by tradition—though this description hardly does him justice if we take it to mean that he had been convicted of 'breaking and entering'. More probably he was, like Barabbas, a member of some kind of underground resistance movement against Rome. As world events have repeatedly shown, no holds are barred in such situations and, in contrast to his companion's abuse of Jesus, Dismas turned to the Saviour—first, with an acknowledgment of his guilt. 'We are getting what we deserve' (v. 41, Good News).

In general we are slow to say: I have sinned. The desire to find a scapegoat is as old as time. Sometimes we blame another person. 'The woman gave me . . . and I did eat' (Gen. 3: 12). Sometimes an alleged flaw in our own make-up. 'I suffer from . . .' (fill in as desired). We see ourselves in the role of an unfortunate victim rather than as a responsible person. But with death a certainty, Dismas realized that his hope lay in speaking the truth.

Then came his cry for help—'Jesus, remember me!' A process of elimination left Jesus as his only possible helper. His companions in arms could do nothing for him now. The Jewish priesthood had no saving word for one who, in their views, was forever damned (Deut. 21: 23). That left only Jesus.

To his cry came the swift assurance: 'Today shalt thou be with Me.' And to be with Jesus, in time or eternity, is in itself paradise.

LUKE 23: 34-38, 44-49

'Father, forgive them; they do not know what they are doing' (v. 34, J. B. Phillips).

WHY MEN ARE UNINTENTIONALLY WICKED. What exactly did Jesus mean when He offered this prayer on the Cross? The people most concerned with His death did know what they were doing. Pilate knew! Having preferred safe injustice to dangerous justice, he feebly washed his hands in public to exonerate himself! Caiaphas knew! He first cynically explained how expedient it was that Jesus should die, and then resorted to intrigue to make the necessary arrangements. The common people knew! Having welcomed Jesus into Jerusalem, they chose Barabbas immediately it became clear that Christ was not going to fulfill their hopes in their way. Then what did the Son of God mean when He prayed: 'Father, forgive them; they do not know what they are doing'?

He was surely expressing His belief that men are sometimes wicked because they are spiritually blind. The crucifixion was happening because those responsible did not really know what they were doing. If they had known, known the true identity of the One being crucified, they wouldn't have done it! Characteristically seeing the best in the worst, Christ believed still in the possibility of the very people most responsible for His death becoming obedient children of God.

Incredibly too He still believes in us, even though perhaps, not without reason, we no longer believe in ourselves and have lost the confidence of other people. Take heart! God knows what we are, and yet still believes in what we can become.

LUKE 23: 50-56

'Now a man called Joseph came forward ... he was from Arimathaea, a Jewish city, and was one of those who waited for the Kingdom of God' (vv. 50 and 51, Knox).

WAITING. To all seekers after goodness and truth Good Friday must have seemed the end of the world. It confirmed the most cynical view of human affairs. Into this almost total darkness there comes a faint glimmer of hope in the person of Joseph of Arimathaea. Although a member of the council which had engineered Christ's death he had not consented to their evil scheme. He provides us with a twofold lesson.

Joseph was one of those who 'waited for the kingdom of God'. That is, he did not equate the status quo with the divine will but rested his hope upon God's promise. Of course, the Scribes and Pharisees were also men who 'waited', but they had decided beforehand the shape of the Kingdom. That is why they killed Jesus. Really to wait for God is to recognize that when He comes He may well startle and surprise us. Only those who waited in real openness, willing for God to act as He desires, were able to believe in Jesus. Joseph was such a man.

Joseph of Arimathaea reminds us that human nature is utterly unpredictable. Probably before the Crucifixion he would have been scorned by the disciples because he was a 'secret follower', a man who had not dared to come into the open. Now, when Christ's cause seems utterly lost and the disciples had fled, it is Joseph who risks everything to show his loyalty. Life is continually making nonsense of the labels we place upon people: perhaps it is time we stopped doing it.

LUKE 24: 1–12

'They were quite at a loss what to make of this ... the story sounded like sheer nonsense and they refused to believe' (vv. 4, 11, Barclay).

THE FOUNDATION OF THE FAITH. Professor A. M. Hunter tells the following story. 'I once wrote a book entitled *The Work and Words of Jesus*, whose last chapter deals with the Resurrection. When the Queen (now the Queen Mother) who had asked to see it, wrote to me, she confessed, "I am sorry to say I read the last chapter first, which is, I know, dreadful cheating: but it makes a wonderful and hopeful background to the rest of the book, and I do not regret it at all. What a short time 1900 years is! Perhaps the light of the Resurrection will yet flood the world."'

Christians know that it is only the 'background' of the Resurrection of Jesus that gives meaning to all He did and that makes sense of the Christian Faith and the Christian's claims. Had there been no Resurrection there would have been no Christian Church and no Good News to tell.

It is really quite naïve of people to talk, as some do, about accepting the teaching of Jesus, yet having serious reservations about the Easter story. It is only by the help of a living Christ that

250

the Christian life can be lived. His teaching would be an impossible
ideal were it not that Christ is a present reality, our Contemporary, able and ready to give us His divine support.

LUKE 24: 13-27

**'During their conversation and discussion Jesus Him-
self overtook them and walked beside them, though they
were prevented from recognizing Him' (vv. 15, 16, Moffatt).**

THE UNRECOGNIZED PRESENCE. This story, which
George Eliot called the loveliest in the world, is full of comfort
for every man. Just when these two disciples were plunged into the
deepest distress Jesus was already walking by their side. We
often foolishly associate the presence of Jesus with spiritual
ecstasy and confidence. When we are depressed, or wrestle
as these disciples did with doubt, when the confidence of our
fellow disciples seems 'to be nonsense' (v. 11) and we feel isolated
because we are not so easily convinced, it is then that Christ is
nearer to us than we imagine. From the lives of the saints we
gather that dark moods and periods of spiritual dryness are all a
part of God's education of the human spirit. At these times let us
be assured that Christ is nearer than we imagine.

Not only did Jesus bless these despondent disciples with His
unrecognized presence, He showed God's unrecognized providence at work in what appeared total disaster. That 'the Messiah
was bound to suffer' was consistent with the whole history of
God's people. From the time when God raised Israel out of the
humiliation of Egyptian captivity, to the prophecy of the suffering
Servant who would bring salvation to the Gentiles, God had
attested His ability to bring good out of evil. The Cross was the
supreme instance of this principle. Can we trust God to work the
same miracle in our own lives?

LUKE 24: 28-35

**'He made as if to continue His journey, but they pressed
Him: "Stay with us, for evening draws on, and the day is
almost over"' (v. 29, N.E.B.).**

THE COURTESY OF CHRIST. By the time the two travellers had reached Emmaus the unrecognized Stranger had done
much to revive their faith. Yet the moment of revelation was still
to come and we may well tremble to realize how easily it could

have been missed. With characteristic courtesy Jesus 'made as if to continue His journey'. The disciples had been absent from home for at least several days. Probably the larder was not very full. How easy to let the Stranger pass on His way with only a word of gratitude for the faith and insight He had imparted. But they invited Him in and never wearied of recounting what followed to the end of their days.

It is the very courtesy of God which is the reason why we often miss Him. He comes to us in such unobtrusive ways in the person of someone in need, in the goodness of those we take for granted, in beauty we are too preoccupied to notice, in a quiet moment we are too busy to use. Wrote A. E. Whitham, 'How vulgar seem the loud crash of worlds in their jostlings in space, the shouts of horse-men riding to battle, the pomp of kings and emperors amid their enslaved captives, the pretensions of the rich, the superiorities of the learned, as we stand in the presence of this writhing form, and hear the words, "Father, forgive them, for they know not what they do!"'

Let us beware that we do not become more keenly aware of 'the pretensions of the rich, the superiorities of the learned' than of that quiet unobtrusive Presence which awaits our invitation.

LUKE 24: 36–43

'While they were speaking of this, He Himself stood in the midst of them, and said, "Peace be unto you; it is Myself, do not be afraid"' (v. 36, Knox).

NO APPARITION. Why does Luke place such emphasis upon the bodily form of Christ's resurrection appearances? He is concerned to show that the resurrection had nothing in common with what today is called psychic phenomenon. Jesus was no spirit, nor were the disciples subject to hallucinations. Easter meant far more than an assurance of Christ's survival. It was God's mighty act of vindication, His seal upon Christ's self-offering. What the disciples saw were not ghostly apparitions, but manifestations of the glory of a triumphant Christ.

Writes James Stewart, 'What the Resurrection meant to those men was this: "There is a power in action stronger than the whole hideous alliance of evil forces that crucified our Lord." They now saw that in the age-long terrible conflict of which history was the arena . . . the last word lay with God. They knew now that they were facing a defeated enemy. The power which had taken Jesus out of the grave would yet remake the dark and ruined world, and smite dead hopes with sudden life. The Resurrection is not just a personal survival: it is a cosmic victory.'

This little group of frightened and then radiant disciples, with the risen Christ standing in their midst, constituted the first Christian Church. Despite the manifold variety of its present activities the Church exists to witness to this abiding Presence and, despite its large material resources, this Presence is its only strength.

LUKE 24: 44–53

'They returned to Jerusalem with great joy, and spent all their time in the temple praising God' (v. 53, N.E.B.).

AVAILABLE TO ALL. With that deliberate artistry and sense of composition which is such a marked feature of his writing Luke ends his Gospel where it began, in the courts of the temple. Yet it was with an infinitely enriched faith that the disciples there worshipped God. Their understanding of God had taken on new dimensions because of their companionship with Jesus. The departure of their Master did not leave them feeling bereft but freshly confident.

The ascension meant that Jesus was now in the place of power and authority. The disciples expressed this by saying that Jesus had taken His place 'at God's right hand'. No wonder their worship was revitalized and their approach to God made bold. No longer could they think of God except in terms of Jesus.

The ascension also meant that Jesus 'went from some men's sight to be available to all men's hearts'. The forty days between Easter Sunday and the ascension were a period of spiritual education for the disciples. The resurrection appearances occurred in such a way that they began to feel their Master was never far away. Less and less they depended upon actually seeing Him. More and more they became sure of His abiding spiritual presence. At no date in history is it possible to draw a line and say, 'After this no one any more encountered the living Christ.'

THE GOSPEL ACCORDING TO JOHN
We Beheld His Glory

INTRODUCTION

This was the last of the gospels to be written; R. H. Lightfoot has given the date as 'soon after, if not before A.D. 100'. The purpose of the gospel is that all men 'might believe that Jesus is the Christ; and that believing ... might have life through His name' (20: 31).

Though discussion continues as to the identity of the writer, it will be sufficient if here he is called John, accepting the younger son of Zebedee as the source of this interpretive study of the work and words of his Lord. The inspired insights which came to the Apostle in the maturity of age have resulted in his own comments being woven so closely into the story of Jesus that at times it is hard to tell where the one begins and the other ends.

The gospel writers have been symbolically represented by the four creatures around the throne (Rev. 4: 7), with the fourth of them—'like a flying eagle'—traditionally associated with John. Just as the eagle can peer undazzled into the sun, the beloved disciple gazed at length and in love into the eternal mystery of the Incarnation, and Christian people in all ages have been enriched beyond words by his understanding of Him who was 'full of grace and truth'.

'So the Word became flesh; He came to dwell among us, and we saw His glory, such glory as befits the Father's only Son, full of grace and truth' (v. 14, N.E.B.).

THE DOMINANT THEME. Stanley Jones told the story of a little boy who, gazing at a photograph of his absent father, sighed, 'I wish father would step out of the picture.' Before the birth of Jesus men had composed many pictures of God, with varying degrees of truth or falsity. But how often the most earnest among them had longed that God would 'step out of the picture'. Christians believe this is precisely what happened in the life, death and resurrection of Jesus Christ. And this belief is the dominant theme of the fourth gospel.

The first eighteen verses of this book form a prologue. As a musical overture introduces themes which are later developed in full, so does the evangelist in this passage. In the case of the Gospel these themes are: (1) Jesus Christ is the full revelation of God; (2) the work of Jesus is to impart life; (3) this life is given to men by union with Christ.

In order to introduce his dominant theme John writes about 'the Word'. Jewish readers would remember that it was by His word that God created the world, inspired the prophets and moulded history. But the term was also meaningful to Gentiles. Both in the schools of philosophy, and in more popular thought, 'the word' referred to the divine agent through whom God made, sustained and governed the universe. 'The word was made flesh' is one of the simplest but most profound phrases in the Bible; it is also the very heart of the Christian faith.

'Out of His full store we have all received grace upon grace' (v. 16 N.E.B.).

BOUNDLESS MERCY. God's coming to mankind in Jesus went unnoticed by the majority, as yesterday's reading made clear. But there were some who both recognized and welcomed Him. These received a continual stream of unmerited blessings—'grace upon grace'. One commentator writes, 'As one wave follows another from the depths of the ocean, so there flows from Christ's fulness wave upon wave of grace.' Similarly, in one of his sermons on the grace of God, J. H. Jowett said, 'Grace does not flow from a half reluctant and partially reconciled God, like the scanty and uncertain movements of a brook in time of drought. It comes in oceanic fulness.'

The phrase 'grace after grace' (v. 16, Moffatt) contains a further suggestion. Not only are we to think of one grace heaped upon another, as waves rolling on to the shore. We are to remind ourselves that it is as we receive and use each grace given to us that further understanding and strength becomes available.

We may revel in all the light shed on our way from the life and character of Jesus, but unless His pardon makes us more forgiving and His patience teaches us long-suffering, then we prevent further grace from coming to us. If we long for further spiritual enrichment we should ask ourselves: How much of the gospel am I already translating into daily life?

JOHN 1: 19–28

'He told them, "I am what the prophet Isaias spoke of, the voice of one crying in the wilderness, Straighten out the way of the Lord"' (v. 23, Knox).

A VOICE. One of the lesser aims of this Gospel is to clarify the relationship between John the Baptist and Christ. During the first century a sect of the Baptist's followers became widely established (Acts 19: 1–7). Some even claimed that the rugged prophet of the wilderness was superior to Christ, on the grounds that Jesus had submitted to his baptism. Certainly the evangelist loses no opportunity of stressing the Baptist's subordination to Jesus (1: 6, 19, 34; 3: 13; 1: 4).

When the Baptist replied to the Jerusalem deputation that he was nothing more than 'a voice crying aloud in the wilderness' they naturally challenged his right to baptize. John pointed out the limited aim of his baptism. It was (as R. Y. S. Tasker has pointed out) 'negative rather than positive; it cleansed but it bestowed no gift by which the cleansed could remain clean.'

In his humble witness to his Master the Baptist is an example to every Christian. Our task too is to point men away from ourselves to Jesus. Although this may not always be done verbally, indeed, it will be done best by the lives we live rather than what we say, there is a time when silence is sinful. 'The Church owes the world its Gospel,' writes Douglas Webster. 'It is in debt to Christ and repays that debt only by sharing His love with all mankind. . . . It is as criminal to keep men in ignorance of this love as it is to keep a child, as the press recently reported, locked up in a cellar for the first five years of its life in ignorance of daylight. Presumption lies not in proclaiming the gospel but in withholding it.'

JOHN 1: 29-34

'On the following day, John saw Jesus coming towards him and said, "Look, there is the Lamb of God Who will take away the sin of the world!"' (v. 29, J. B. Phillips).

LAMB OF GOD. To the deputation from Jerusalem the Baptist spoke of the greater One who was already 'among' them. Next day, probably to his own disciples, he identified Jesus, acclaiming Him 'the Lamb of God who takes away the sin of the world'. To the Baptist's first hearers, and to later Jewish readers of this gospel, the title 'Lamb of God' was rich with meaning. It spoke of the passover lamb which symbolized salvation from destruction: perhaps also of the figure of the Suffering Servant, who bore himself as 'a lamb that is led to the slaughter' (Isa. 53: 7).

But what of we modern readers? Sacrificial terms fall strangely on our ears. Yet we are not strangers to the experience which gave rise to the Old Testament sacrifices. We too have felt the gulf of separation caused by our guilt, and have lamented our powerlessness to bridge that gulf. When the ancient Jew came to God with his sacrifice he recognized the gravity of sin, and acknowledged that it was God who provided healing and reconciliation. For the sacrificial system was not man's invention, but God's gracious provision.

To recognize that Jesus is the Lamb of God means seeing that all the alienation and estrangement of human life—including our own self-hatred—has been dealt with by God. What a strange paradox this is, that a Cross of agony should become a Cross of healing! But, in so far as we take seriously the love manifested at Calvary, reconciliation and healing become glorious and deepening realities.

'Jesus looked steadily at him and said, "You are Simon, the son of John. From now on your name is Cephas"— (that is, Peter, meaning "a rock")' (v. 42, J. B. Phillips).

OUR POSSIBILITIES. There is so much food for meditation in this passage: the Baptist's selflessness in pointing his disciples away from himself to Christ; Andrew's immediate impulse to share his spiritual discovery with his brother; Christ's first recorded word in this gospel, a word He addresses to every would-be follower, 'What are you looking for?' Space compels us to focus on one aspect of this story: the new name Jesus gave to Simon.

Jesus valued Peter, not only for what he was, but for what he could become. Long before he had earned the right to be regarded as a man of rock, Jesus gave him a name that would ever remind him of the Master's faith in him. So it is with ourselves. 'Often I am haunted by the memory of what I have been,' wrote Francis James, 'and often tortured by the knowledge of what I am. Yet there is something that I would be, something far different. I can find deep comfort in the thought that this is also known to God; it is to this that His merciful eyes turn most of all.'

Years ago in France they held an election to decide who was the most distinguished Frenchman. They chose Louis Pasteur, one of the founders of modern medicine. Yet a school teacher's report on Louis as a boy read: 'He is the meekest, smallest, and least promising pupil in my class.' God does not make this kind of superficial assessment of us. He is more hopeful for us than we are for ourselves. 'Not what thou art, (wrote the unknown author of *The Cloud of Unknowing*) nor what thou hast been, beholdeth God with His merciful eyes; but what thou wouldest be.'

JOHN 1: 43-51

'In truth, in very truth I tell you all, you shall see heaven wide open, and God's angels ascending and descending upon the Son of Man' (v. 51, N.E.B.).

THE SIN OF PREJUDICE. The first three gospels portray the disciples' faith in Christ maturing slowly during a fairly long period: here in this gospel we find a new disciple proclaiming Jesus the Son of God at his first encounter. Some scholars suggest that the evangelist, writing after many years of meditation and

I

spiritual communion, has telescoped events, seeing in early intimations the strong convictions of later days. However this may be, Nathaniel's conversion to Jesus has a valuable lesson for us.

Prejudice almost robbed Nathaniel of the greatest privilege of his life. His caustic comment, 'Can anything good come from Nazareth?', has been echoed in varying forms whenever men with closed minds have refused to look at the evidence. Fortunately, his prejudice was not obstinate or he might never have come to Jesus, or coming, he might have seen only what he previously expected.

Nothing distorts our vision like prejudice. H. E. Fosdick describes a pamphlet written by a man who passionately believed in the segregation of the races and claimed support for his policy from the gospels. 'The conclusion is inescapable,' read the pamphlet, 'that both in principle and practice Jesus was the most consistent and rigorous Segregationist of whom we have authentic information.' If prejudice can so terribly distort a man's vision of Jesus we ought frequently to ask ourselves whether we are seeing Christ clearly. Or do we see in the life and character of the Master only what we want to see?

JOHN 2: 1–11

'Everybody I know puts his good wine on first and then when men have had plenty to drink, he brings out the poor stuff. But you have kept back your good wine till now' (v. 10, J. B. Phillips).

A NEW JOY. In this gospel the mighty works of Jesus are not called 'miracles', but 'signs'. They are acted parables, whose meaning is far greater even than the meeting of the human need. So in the story of the water turned to wine we have, 'not a purposeless exhibition of supernatural power, but a teaching miracle of deep significance'. The water was contained in stone waterjars of the kind used for Jewish rites of purification. The miracle is a sign that Jesus transforms the insipid religion of Jewish legalism into the active ferment of a joyful relationship with God.

It has been said that a man can live at one of three levels—instinct, conscience or grace. He can follow his impulses, or he can try to obey the moral law, or he may enter a relationship with God in which both instinct and conscience find their rightful but subordinate place. Life then becomes far more than the satisfaction of our desires, but also much more than striving to be good. It becomes what Augustine meant when he urged, 'Love God and do what you will.'

Our self-centredness makes it easy for us to seek for the wrong thing even in our religion. For instance, we may seek personal cleansing only in order to rehabilitate our pride. This is what motivated so much religion in Christ's day. But this quest is self-defeating because it is still basically self-centred. To be brought into a loving, confident relationship with God succeeds where much moral striving fails. This is why the gospel of Jesus is infinitely more than good advice, it is good news.

JOHN 2: 12–17

'His disciples recalled the words of Scripture, "Zeal for thy house shall destroy me"' (v. 17, N.E.B.).

THE WRATH OF THE LAMB. That the story of the changing of water into wine should be followed by the cleansing of the temple may seem strange, especially when we recall that the other three gospels place the temple cleansing almost at the end of Christ's earthly ministry. But remembering this evangelist's method of probing the inner meaning of events we see that both stories contrast the old religion with the new gospel. Time after time in these early chapters, the evangelist returns to this theme of new things: a new temple, the new birth, a new worship.

The cleansing of the temple shows a much neglected aspect of Christ's character. There is no need to imagine Jesus using physical violence to oust the money changers. Jewish tradition held that the Messiah would bear a lash for the punishment of sinners, so that the scourge may be regarded as an emblem of authority rather than an offensive weapon. Nevertheless, there was a passion exhibited on that occasion before which men quailed. J. S. Stewart writes, 'There is a type of religion which sings, with suitable emotion, the love songs of the church, without ever so much as giving a thought to what an old saint once called "the stormy north side of Jesus Christ".'

What was it which aroused this fierce anger in the heart of the gentlest of men? It was an exploitation of the poor carried on under the cloak of religion, a selfishness which made impossible the true worship of God. The spirit of Jesus will always oppose those who erect barriers between their fellows and God.

260

'"Destroy this temple," Jesus replied, " and in three days I will raise it again"' (v. 19, N.E.B.).

A NEW TEMPLE. Challenged to show His authority for His attack upon the temple commerce, Jesus replied in an enigmatic phrase which the Jews thought was either absurd or blasphemous. This claim was widely circulated and inaccurately quoted at His trial. The disciples later understood these mysterious words to refer to His resurrection and also to that new temple, the Christian Church, in which purer worship would be offered to God.

The Church has received so much criticism in recent years that Christians themselves are tempted to undervalue its usefulness. When a man told D. L. Moody that he could be just as good a Christian outside the Church as within it, the famous evangelist said nothing. He stepped over to a brightly blazing fire, picked out a piece of coal with the tongs and laid it on the hearth. The two men silently watched it smoulder and go out. Next Sunday that man went to church.

Just because the Church is no longer exempt from public criticism it is faced with a great opportunity. As the Body of Christ on earth it should not expect to be cushioned against opposition; should know, in fact, that the time of rejection can be the moment of greatest triumph. Raymond Efemy, an Anglican parson, writes, 'The Church has reached its nadir in the eyes of the world; if it has the gumption to understand the first thing about its own belief this is just the point when it should be flinging its cap in the air.'

'In truth, in very truth I tell you, unless a man has been born over again he cannot see the Kingdom of God.' (v. 3, N.E.B.).

A NEW BIRTH. Gilbert Russell, a Christian psychotherapist, once told the story of a man of fifty, intellectual, conscientious to a fault, but in despair about his marriage. After a suicide attempt he came for analysis. He then dreamt that he left a bookshop where it seemed he had worked for years and began working at Kew Gardens as a boy. He had to turn from his one-sided intellectual approach to life, symbolized by the bookshop, to begin again in the place where things grow, symbolized by his working as a boy in Kew Gardens.

This kind of psychological rebirth throws light upon the spiritual rebirth about which Jesus spoke to Nicodemus. Here was a Pharisee of the best kind, a man in whom there was much to admire. Yet a radical change of outlook was required before he could even glimpse the Kingdom of God. He had to abandon the attempt to earn God's favour by his own efforts and receive the grace of God as a free gift.

The error of the Pharisees is the religious failing of the natural man. It is man's pride exercised, not in revolt against God, but in the pretence that he can make himself worthy of God's love, that he can get out of God's debt. Such a man has to start again as a child, simply accepting the fact that he is loved and accepted, not because of what he is, but because of who God is.

JOHN 3: 13-21

'For God loved the world so dearly that He gave up His only Son, so that everyone who believes in Him may have eternal life, instead of perishing' (v. 16, Moffatt).

GIVING AND SUFFERING. Condensed in these few verses are several of the major themes of this gospel: Christ alone is the full revelation of God and it is in His Cross that redemption is accomplished; Christ's coming is for man's salvation but results also in judgment. As these great themes are developed Nicodemus disappears from the picture, for the evangelist is concerned with what these truths mean for all men and not just for this one seeker. What we later learn about Nicodemus (7: 50 ff.; 19: 39) suggests that he may have accepted the revolutionary teaching which he heard from the lips of Christ on that night.

God's love is manifested both in the coming of Jesus (v. 16) and in His Cross (v. 14). That is, in giving and in suffering. 'God is love' is a precious truth, asserted William Temple, but it is not the heart of the Gospel, for it affirms 'no divine act for our redemption'. 'God so loved ... that He gave', this is the heart of the Gospel. God's love is the model of all true love—it is expressed in self-giving, and it is prepared to suffer.

'If Christ had not suffered,' wrote James Reid, 'there is something in God which would never have been known.' Likening the Cross to a crystal which breaks up the light passed through it into its component colours, he added, 'The Cross of Christ ... breaks up the light of uncreated love, and lets us see the myriad-coloured glory. But for the suffering of Christ we had never seen into the wonder of that love.'

JOHN 3: 22-30

'It is the bridegroom who possesses the bride, yet the bridegroom's friend who merely stands and listens to him can be really glad to hear the bridegroom's voice. That is why my happiness is now complete' (vv. 2, 9. J. B. Phillips).

THE HUMILITY OF STRENGTH. We usually picture the Baptist in terms of rugged strength and moral toughness. This view is confirmed by his memorable words, 'He must grow greater and greater and I less and less' (v. 30, J. B. Phillips). Only a man of real maturity could, with such grace, rejoice in the success of another.

The evangelist records this event because, as we have already noted, this gospel was written at a time when the disciples of John the Baptist were claiming priority for their master. These claims had no foundation in the life of the Baptist himself who clearly saw his own role as herald and forerunner, or as the 'best man' at a wedding. For us the story provides a valuable lesson in humility.

Healthy self-effacement lies on the far side of true self-appreciation. There is, of course, a neurotic self-effacement. This is either a defence mechanism in what appears to be a dangerous world ('if I make myself small enough nobody will notice me and I will be safe'), or a perverted form of self-aggrandisement ('See how humble I am'). The humility of the mature person is impossible while we are anxious about our own value. This is why it is wrong to expect too much in the way of humility from growing teenagers. The Baptist could afford to be humble—he had a truly significant role to play in the drama of redemption. We too can afford to relinquish self-aggrandisement—if we have first recognized our value and our place in the purposes of God. As Thomas Merton has said: 'Humility is the surest sign of strength.'

JOHN 3: 31-36

'He who puts his faith in the Son has hold of eternal life, but he who disobeys the Son shall not see that life; God's wrath rests upon him' (v. 36, N.E.B.).

VITAL CHOICE. This gospel often reports a historical incident and then, sometimes imperceptibly, the words of one of the characters merge into the comment of the evangelist. Today's passage is the gospel writer's comment upon the witness which John the Baptist made to Christ. Although the forerunner had an important assignment he could never fully reveal the nature of God; only the Son of God could do that.

Jesus being the perfect revelation of God, faith in Him is a matter of life and death. To interpret this as meaning that no Hindu or Buddhist, living according to the highest ideals he knows, can know God would be a denial of the love of God. A great proportion of the human race has either never heard of Jesus or encountered only a distortion of His gospel. We must remember that this evangelist sees the historical Jesus as being the incarnation of that 'light which enlightens every man' (1: 9). What matters is our response to Christ (if we have heard the Gospel truly preached), or our response to that light which we have and which proceeds from Him (even if we have never heard of Jesus).

Rejection of Christ exposes us to 'wrath'. Stephen Neill has written that it is hard for us to imagine wrath which is entirely free from the personal elements of malice or vindictiveness, and therefore we misconstrue the wrath of God. ... His wrath is no more than the clear shining of His light, which must go forth implacably to the destruction of all darkness.'

JOHN 4: 1–15

'Whoever drinks of the water I will give him will never be thirsty again. For My gift will become a spring in the man himself, welling up into eternal life' (v. 14, J. B. Phillips).

GOD'S BEST GIFT. This story of a noontide encounter between Jesus and the Samaritan woman is so familiar to us that we fail to see its strangeness. Superficially the most staggering thing was that a Jewish Rabbi should address a Samaritan woman, and even at that level it has much to teach us. Alan Richardson has pointed out that Judaism is the most masculine of all the world's religions; a Jew thanked God daily that he was not born a woman and the rabbis used to debate whether women had souls. That the disciples had gone to the town to buy food shows that they also shared Christ's rejection of Jewish conventions, according to which 'to eat the bread of a Samaritan is as eating the flesh of swine'. Jesus repudiated conventions which erected barriers to human fellowship. Do we share His impatience? Or are we complacent about barriers which are to our advantage?

At a deeper level this encounter was even more unusual. Thinking she was face to face merely with a very unconventional rabbi, the Samaritan woman was in fact confronting the One who offered unfailing spiritual life. The rabbis identified the water of life with the Law, to which the Samaritans also professed loyalty. This gospel likens the Holy Spirit to the water of life. The Law leaves man inwardly unchanged, perhaps even in despair. But the believer who is open to receive God's greater gift of His Spirit knows an unfailing source of renewal and strength. 'The Holy Spirit does not abolish the old Law, the exterior command', wrote Thomas Merton. 'He makes that same Law interior to ourselves, so that doing God's will becomes now no longer a work of fear but a work of spontaneous love.'

JOHN 4: 16–26

'The woman answered, "I know that Messiah ... is coming. When He comes He will tell us everything." Jesus said, "I am He, I who am speaking to you now."' (vv. 25 and 26, N.E.B.).

THE ALL-IMPORTANT DECISION. To be fully certain of the undertones of this dialogue we would need to hear the inflexion in the Samaritan woman's voice, and see the expression in her eyes. When she asked Jesus to give her 'living water' to save her coming "all this way to draw', was she being a little slow or merely flippant? And when Jesus probed her failure to establish a loving marriage relationship was her question about rival places of worship a theological diversion, or a sincere quest for truth? Her statement that the Messiah would one day reveal everything certainly seems an evasion of issues too challenging and disturbing. But escape was impossible for, in one of the most dramatic disclosures recorded, Jesus made His claim, 'I am He.'

In our decision about Jesus all the issues touched upon in this conversation are involved—the question of where to find satisfaction, the quality of our personal relationships, our approach to God. In accepting Christ's claims the Samaritan woman made a decision which would open up to her vast inner resources of refreshment, graciously permeate all her relationships and vitalize her worship.

Why does our faith in Jesus sometimes leave us joyless, impoverished in our relationships, lethargic in our worship? Perhaps because our faith is not true commitment, but merely an assent to certain doctrines about Jesus. But also we must recognize, for our comfort, that Christian discipleship is a progressive experience in which deeper and deeper areas of our personality are influenced by our increasing understanding of Christ.

JOHN 4: 27-34
'Jesus said, "My food is to do the will of Him who sent Me, and to accomplish His work"' (v. 34, Moffatt).

EAGER OBEDIENCE. After the Samaritan woman had left Jesus, her water jar forgotten in her excitement, the disciples returned with food from a nearby town. There followed a conversation recorded in a way so typical of this gospel. Jesus made a symbolic statement; this was taken literally by His hearers; then a clarification from Christ disclosed the deeper meaning of His words. In this instance the disciples learned that, for their Master, doing the will of His Father was His very 'meat and drink'.

Eager obedience to the will of God, free from all sense of constraint and burden, has marked all who followed Christ closely. A Catholic priest who had been confined in prison and in labour camps for many years for his Christian witness was told that at last he could meet his family again. He was dizzy with joy and anticipation. Yet on the evening when he received this wonderful news he prayed specifically that God's will should be done. He writes, 'I deliberately didn't pray that I should see my sister, but only that I would do what was His will and what was for the best. In all my excitement and enthusiasm I didn't want to begin interfering with His providence.'

Is such heroic dedication to God's will far beyond us? Then we must follow the advice of the Quaker, Thomas Kelly, who wrote, 'Begin where you are. Obey now. Use what little obedience you are capable of, even it it is to be like a grain of mustard seed. . . . Live this present moment, this present hour . . . in utter, utter submission and openness toward Him.'

'We no longer believe in Him simply because of your talk we have now heard for ourselves, and we know that this really is the Saviour of the world' (v. 42., Weymouth).

PERSONAL ASSURANCE. Resulting from the Samaritan woman's account of her meeting with Christ, many of her friends and neighbours made their way to Jacob's well. Perhaps it was the sight of them, streaming along the road from the town, which prompted Christ's words, 'Look round on the fields; they are already white, ripe for harvest.' The Samaritans pressed Jesus to stay with them and out of this closer association their belief in Him became personal.

William Temple rightly observed that faith in Christ must develop 'from a state of dependence upon authority to an assurance arising out of experience'. All Christians accept Christ first of all because of another's witness, whether that other be a parent, friend, colleague or simply the written testimony of the gospel-writers. But faith which remains at that stage is perilously insecure.

Shortly before his death, the famous psychotherapist Carl Jung was asked whether he believed in God. He replied, 'All that I have learned has led me step by step to an unshakable conviction in the existence of God. . . . I do not take His existence on belief. I know that He exists.' Commenting on this Margaret Isherwood wrote, 'Certainly we would be wise to give attention to his message that there is a vision at the end of the road, but if we want to see it we must make the same "step by step" journey into life. For religious knowledge is of a different order from factual knowledge. It cannot be handed on; it can only be won.'

JOHN 4: 43-54

'Jesus said, "Return home; your son will live." The man believed what Jesus said and started for home' (v. 50, N.E.B.).

FROM FAITH TO FAITH. The writer of this gospel is often at pains to show that there are many degrees of faith. Belief on a fairly superficial level can be occasioned by a woman's story, 'He told me everything I ever did' But if this initial trust is deepened by commitment and fellowship it becomes the confidence of that disciple who, without seeing the risen Christ, but gazing only at the empty tomb, 'saw and believed' (20: 8). Our task is to ensure that our faith goes 'from strength to strength'.

When Jesus asked, 'Will none of you ever believe without seeing signs and portents?', He was not rebuking the distraught father, but the people as a whole. This man had precisely the faith Jesus looked for. He was willing to go home without seeing even such a sign as Christ's willingness to accompany him. Consequently, his faith received further confirmation—'he and all his household became believers'.

Faith is deepened every time we exercise it. We must use what faith we have, not waste time regretting its limitations. Robert Youngs tells the story of Leslie, a twenty-year-old girl stricken by disease, but still happy and enthusiastic about life. When asked for her secret she said, 'It takes faith.' 'Then how does one get this faith?' she was asked. 'You don't get it,' she replied, 'until you need it.' We could also add: 'You don't get it until you use what you have.'

JOHN 5: 1–9

'When Jesus saw him lying there on his back—knowing that he had been like that for a long time, He said to him, "Do you want to get well again?"' (v. 6, J. B. Phillips).

LIFE AFFIRMING. Disease is sometimes an unconscious flight from the responsibilities and difficulties of daily life. Leslie Weatherhead writes of a woman whose case was diagnosed as inoperable cancer but she was later informed that this was a mistake. She refused to leave hospital and was more distressed at being told she was well than that she was dying. 'I cannot bear the thought of facing life again,' she said. The question of Jesus, 'Do you want to get well again?', is one we should all consider in relation to our own illness, emotional handicaps and spiritual failings. The last thing we should try to do is to assess the possible motivation behind other people's weakness.

We cannot remind ourselves too often that Jesus was life-affirming, not life-denying. People sometimes retreat into weakness and even sickness because they have been taught to suspect happiness and to see suffering as the will of God. One patient, the daughter of a 'saintly Christian', said to her psychotherapist, 'There must be something satisfying in failure. If things had gone right for me as a child, I don't think my father would have accepted me any more. If I suffered by failure or misfortune, then I was able to stand alongside him and be a fellow-sufferer. It made us closer.'

Another reason for unconscious retreat into weakness is that sympathy can become a substitute for love. Let us affirm and re-affirm: God wills us to be strong and to enjoy fulness of life. He is continually at work in us to this end.

JOHN 5: 10–18

'Jesus' answer to them was this, "My Father is still at work and therefore I work as well"' (v. 17, J. B. Phillips).

WORK AND REST. No one can read the fourth gospel without noting the difference of tone between the controversies there recorded and Christ's teaching in the other gospels. One reason for this is that the fourth gospel is Jerusalem-centred and therefore describes the clash between Christ and the religious authorities. These arguments, carried on after the fashion of rabbinic discussion, sound arid to the modern ear. We must recognize that Jesus was meeting His opponents on their own ground and seek for the timeless truth behind these debates.

Today's reading is a perfect example of this. In contemporary Judaism the rabbis often tried to reconcile God's continued activity with His Sabbath rest. Obviously, God did not cease working in the literal sense or the world would cease to exist. One rabbi solved the problem by saying, 'May not a man wander through his own house on the Sabbath? The house of God is the whole realm above and the whole realm below.'

Jesus claimed that just as God pursued His loving activity on the Sabbath—so must He. With God, rest and work are not separate and alternative modes, they are one. Being true Man, Jesus needed to rest from work. Yet there was a tranquillity and a noticeable absence of frenzy even about His work. Accomplishing more in His brief ministry than any man who has ever lived, He yet called men to share His rest.

Wrote Henry Drummond, 'Christ was never in a hurry. And if God has given us anything to do for Him, He will give time enough to finish it with a repose like Christ's.' Christian activists should remember the saying of Jacob Boehme: 'Let the hands or the head be at labour, the heart ought nevertheless to rest in God.'

'In truth, in very truth I tell you, a time is coming, indeed it is already here, when the dead shall hear the voice of the Son of God, and all who hear shall come to life' (v. 25, N.E.B.).

THE 'NOW' OF THE GOSPEL. Replying to the charge of Sabbath breaking Jesus had claimed that—like God—He could not suspend His work. This, of course, was to claim a unique relationship with God, as the Jews were quick to see. This relationship is made more explicit in today's passage where it is affirmed that two activities, usually regarded as the special prerogative of God—raising men from the dead and judgment—are also the work of the Son. In the New Testament there is no rigid distinction between the work of the three Persons in the Trinity. And the Church early affirmed that 'the whole Godhead is active in the work of each Person of the Trinity'.

The more practical truth contained here is this. Resurrection and judgment are usually considered as final things. But in Jesus Christ men and women are faced with these last things now. He who listens to Christ and puts his trust in God who sent Him 'has hold of eternal life'. Christ's power to raise the dead is not something held in reserve for the consummation of all things. 'The hour is coming, and now is', when those who hear His voice find newness of life (v. 25). Nor is judgment merely a future event which, by a later change of heart, we may hope to avert. By our response to Jesus Christ we are all the time forming our characters, and so passing judgment upon ourselves. Similarly, eternal life is not something we can only hope for. In Christ it is offered now.

JOHN 5: 31-40

'You study the Scriptures diligently, supposing that in having them you have eternal life; yet, although their testimony points to Me, you refuse to come to Me for that life' (vv. 39 and 40, N.E.B.).

ESCAPE OR ENCOUNTER. The claims Jesus made in this episode were staggering, but they did not stand unsupported. For instance, Scripture bore witness to Christ. Yet here is one of the supreme ironies of the gospel narrative. The most diligent students of the Scripture were the ones who rejected Jesus. They failed to recognize that no book – not even one divinely inspired—could impart life.

The purpose of Bible reading is to make us more sensitive to God who meets us in the whole of life. At times the Bible has been used as an evasion. An evasion of the need for hard thinking, when ready-made solutions for all problems are sought in its pages. An evasion of God Himself, when we imprison Him firmly in the past.

A Japanese woman who had lost her husband sought healing for her broken heart. One day a school girl brought her a grubby little pamphlet, and said, 'I found this in the street. Somebody must have dropped it. I read it. There is a wonderful story in it of a Man who helps whose who are unhappy. I thought of you. It might do you good.'

The pamphlet was a copy of Luke's gospel. She not only read it through but found her life changed by the Christ to whom it witnessed. Is this what our Bible reading does for us? Is it an escape or an encounter?

JOHN 5: 41-47

'How on earth can you believe while you are forever looking for each other's approval and not for the glory that comes from the one God?' (v. 44, J. B. Phillips).

STUMBLING BLOCK. John Oman, one-time principal of Westminster College, Cambridge, claimed that 'we have no right to believe anything we can avoid believing, granting we have given it entire freedom to convince us'. He also affirmed that we have no right to exhort other people to believe. We can only 'present what is true in such a way that nothing will prevent it from being seen except the desire to abide in the darkness'. We can also help people to faith by pointing out 'what they are cherishing that is opposed to faith'.

This is precisely what Jesus did in today's passage. He was far too loving, and sympathetic with human weakness, to demand the impossible. And it is impossible to force oneself to believe. Jesus pointed out that the Jews rejected Him, not because they failed to see the truth, but because they were unconcerned about the truth. 'They are loyal to their tradition,' William Temple commented, 'but they wish to be praised for their loyalty. So in fact they are only loyal to that in it which their comrades value.'

The desire to be well thought of is natural enough. Indeed, the person who cares nothing for the opinion of others is something of a monster. But when thirst for human praise becomes insatiable we end up by sacrificing all that is noble and worthwhile. To hold only convenient convictions, to voice only acceptable views, is to place an insurmountable stumbling-block in our own pathway, to ensure that we will never wholeheartedly believe anything.

JOHN 6: 1–15

'Then Jesus, realising that they were going to carry Him off and make Him their King, retired once more to the mountain quite alone' (v. 15, J. B. Phillips).

A MORE SUBTLE REJECTION. As we shall see later in this chapter, the feeding of the multitude was far more than a miracle of multiplication. It was a 'sign' conveying the deepest spiritual significance. Unfortunately, the Galileans saw only the miraculous provision of physical sustenance and wanted to make Jesus a political leader. Here is the double tragedy of Christ's rejection. The religious authorities in Jerusalem had already rejected Jesus as a lawbreaker and blasphemer (5: 16 and 18); the ordinary people of Galilee accepted Him but on their own terms. Yet to accept Jesus only on our terms amounts to a rejection.

Do we want from religion only the satisfaction of our needs? Or do we see it as entering a harmonious relationship with a God whose purposes far transcend our personal desires? Is the purpose of our prayer that God should help us to achieve our aims, or that we should discern God's? Because our basic self-centredness can don a thousand disguises we must never feel superior to facing these questions. We are saddened by those who utterly reject Christ. Could we be guilty of the more subtle rejection of wanting to use Him only for our own ends?

JOHN 6: 16–21

'They were terrified, but He called out, "It is I; do not be afraid"' (v. 20, N.E.B.).

IN THE STORM. When John Coleridge Patteson—pioneer missionary to the Melanesian Islands—was a boy, he came down to breakfast one morning to hear his mother read a letter she had received from her cousin who was a missionary bishop in the West Indies. The letter vividly described a hurricane which has swept the district. 'Well, Coley,' his mother asked, noticing that the boy was deeply stirred. His reply was swift. 'I'll be a bishop; I'll have a hurricane.' Later, at the age of forty-four, he became a martyr for Christ.

Few have the audacity to choose a 'hurricane', but many Christians testify to the presence of Christ in life's storms. This is the point of today's reading. No doubt the writer, who wishes to emphasize the divinity of Jesus, wants his readers to note the power of Jesus over the winds and the waves. This demonstrated that unique relationship of Christ with His Father which is one of this Gospel's major themes. But that is not all. The story also reminds us that in the darkest hour the Risen Lord comes to His followers, calming their fears and bringing them to their spiritual destination.

To practise the presence of Christ in the calm periods of life is the best way to become sensitive to His presence in the storm. True, some who neglected prayer have suddenly been made aware of the divine presence in a crisis, but we should never count upon being exceptions to a general rule.

JOHN 6: 22-27

'You should not work for the food which does not last but for that food which lasts on into eternal life' (v. 27, J. B. Phillips).

IMPERISHABLE FOOD. When Jesus saw the crowd which had followed Him to the other side of the lake, He recognized that it was no spiritual quest which brought them. They were there, not because they saw the signs (v. 26)—that is, the inner significance of this miracle—but because they had eaten the food.

The Christian faith is by no means indifferent to man's material needs. Right at the heart of His model prayer Jesus placed the petition, 'Give us this day our daily bread.' Yet it is also true that 'Man shall not live by bread alone.' If the people of Christ's day had to be rebuked for their obsession with bread, what would Jesus say about our preoccupation with gadgets, amenities and status symbols?

Material possessions cannot satisfy the deep hunger of the soul. In *Boldness be my Friend*, Richard Pape says that to the soldiers who fought in the war the loyalty of their womenfolk was utterly essential. Any doubt about this led to rapid deterioration. 'The love of wife or sweetheart,' he writes, 'was the food that fed their hearts.' Yet some are too busy even to give and receive the sustenance of family affection, too preoccupied to seek quietness, too ambitious to drop out of the race for success in order to give priority to more lasting values. The result is a gnawing dissatisfaction, and, in the end, disillusionment.

JOHN 6: 28–40

'Jesus said to them, "I am the bread of life. Whoever comes to Me shall never be hungry, and whoever believes in Me shall never be thirsty"' (v. 35, N.E.B.).

GOD'S GIFT. We noted yesterday that man's spirit needs its own form of nourishment. Material possessions and worldly success cannot satisfy. Yet it is also true that human love, beauty and the quest for truth can leave men spiritually hungry. Christ is uniquely the bread of life, who satisfies our hunger and thirst for God and for true life. Christ's claim is most emphatic. The negatives, as William Temple pointed out, are the strongest in the Greek language, 'Whoever comes to Me shall never be hungry . . . never be thirsty.'

Here is a forceful reminder of our spiritual dependence. Evelyn Underhill writes, 'We accept our constant dependence on physical food as a natural and inevitable thing. Yet it is not necessarily so: there are creatures which are free from it for long periods of time. . . . But perhaps because of his border-line status, his embryonic capacity for God, man is kept in constant memory of his own fragility, unable to maintain his existence for long without food from beyond himself; his bodily life dependent on the humble plants and animals that surround him, and his soul's life on the unfailing nourishment of the life of God.'

Here also is a reminder that spiritual life is God's gift. The Jews had no conception of this. 'What must we do if we are to work as God would have us work?' they ask, still thinking in terms of the performance of religious duties. But this gift is received by 'coming' and by 'believing': by a personal closure with Christ, not a frenzied attempt to become worthy, which still holds Christ off at arm's length. As the Swiss theologian, Godet, wrote: 'Faith is the highest kind of work, for by it a man gives himself, and a free being can do nothing greater than to give himself.'

'Is not this Jesus, the son of Joseph, whose parents we know? How can He say that "I have come down from Heaven"?' (v. 42, J. B. Phillips).

MISUNDERSTANDING THE INCARNATION. The Jewish rejection of Christ's claim has been echoed through the centuries. Surely, says the critic, we can account for Jesus in terms of human history: there is no need to see in Him the coming of God to man. Two misunderstandings in particular lead men to reject the Christian claim that Jesus is divine.

Men stumble over the truth of the incarnation when they over-spiritualize God. Howard Williams has a humorous illustration of this error. When Edward VII was a young Prince his mother, Queen Victoria, was very particular about the people with whom he talked. She disliked, for example, his speaking with the barber, so arranged that his directions to his barber should be conveyed through a valet. But Queen Victoria was still disturbed that, although the young prince did not speak with the barber, he did speak with someone who spoke with the barber! If we picture God as too remote and too 'spiritual' to have direct dealings with His world we shall never accept John's tremendous affirmation, 'The Word was made flesh'.

Men stumble over the truth of the incarnation for a further reason. They imagine that Christians claim, not only that God is uniquely present in Jesus, but that God is only present in Jesus. This completely distorts the Christian faith. Faith in Christ does not blind us to goodness and truth evidenced, for instance, in other religions and in the lives of unbelievers. Rather it helps us to see the source of that goodness in the one God who is also the Father of our Lord Jesus Christ.

'Even as the living Father sent Me and I live by the Father, so he who feeds on Me will also live by Me' (v. 57, Moffatt).

OUR FELLOWSHIP WITH CHRIST. We have already noted the way in which Jesus is often misunderstood in this gospel, His words being taken literally when they should be understood spiritually. The central meaning in this passage is our utter and complete dependence upon Christ. Our communion with

Him must be so close that the very life of Christ becomes our own. Nothing else can keep the Christian strong. No merely mechanical reception of the sacrament will produce spiritual life—nor can the Quaker or Salvationist take a purely negative attitude to the sacrament. What matters is that, whether sacramentalist or non-sacramentalist, we do indeed 'feed upon Him in our hearts'.

In one of his sermons John Baillie affirmed the absolute priority of this fellowship with Christ, this attention to His word and receiving of His life. He told the story of a man on the North West frontier of India leading a fine horse richly caparisoned. One band of robbers seized the horse but let the man go. Later a further troop of robbers robbed him of a gold chain concealed in his turban. At last he reached his destination wearing only a ragged loincloth. But to his master's son he presented the real present he had been assigned to convey: a great pearl which he had hidden in his armpit. 'So let us if need be,' said John Baillie, 'surrender all other things, but hold to the one thing needful.'

JOHN 6: 59–71

'Simon Peter answered Him, "Lord, to whom shall we go? Your words are words of eternal life. We have faith, and we know that you are the Holy One of God"' (vv. 68 and 69, N.E.B.).

PUZZLED BUT LOYAL. Most of His hearers found the words of Jesus about eating His flesh and drinking His blood intolerable. Few passages in the gospel are more sad than this: 'From that time on, many of His disciples withdrew and no longer went about with Him' (v. 66, N.E.B.). How grateful we are for Peter's passionate affirmation of loyalty. He, for one, was not prepared to turn his back upon his past experience of Christ's saving help.

Leslie Weatherhead suggests that Peter and the other loyal disciples 'put Christ's words away in their minds as one might put into a drawer a letter from a dear friend who wrote in a foreign language which one could not understand, to take it out when an interpreter turned up who would reveal its meaning'. So it must be with the reading of the Bible. We must not be impatient with those parts we cannot understand, nor on the other hand should we become obsessed with the mysterious and symbolic. As Morgan Derham has said, 'we must let what is clear and plain be the key to what is obscure and difficult.'

There came a time when the disciples were well able to understand these words of Christ. Some facets of Christian truth light up with significance only as our experience of life and fellowship with God make them meaningful. This is one reason why we must never limit the gospel to our own present understanding of it.

JOHN 7: 1–13

'"Since you are doing these things, let the whole world know about You!" ... Jesus said to them: "The right time for Me has not yet come"' (vv. 4, 6, Good News for Modern Man).

CREATIVE INDEPENDENCE. The truly great personalities of history have exhibited a rare degree of independence and freedom from the pressure of other people's opinion. Carl Rogers, the American psychotherapist, illustrates this from the lives of three creative giants. El Greco might easily have looked at his work and said, 'Good artists do not paint like that.' Ernest Hemingway was surely aware that 'good writers do not write like this'. Albert Einstein might well have been daunted by the recognition that good physicists did not think his kind of thoughts. Yet each man was true to his own vision and consequently enriched immeasurably the sphere in which he worked.

In the moral and spiritual realm Jesus showed this same freedom to a unique degree. This is seen on almost every page of the gospel story. In today's reading His brothers tried to persuade Him to go to the feast and exhibit His miraculous powers, so fulfilling popular messianic expectations. But He refused to go at their bidding. When His 'hour' was come He would manifest His power and glory in the holy city—on a cross.

Christ's freedom was the result of His single-minded devotion to His Father's will. We can share His freedom only if we are willing to share His single-mindedness. We can be independent of external pressures as we yield to this inner divine constraint.

JOHN 7: 14–24

'Whoever has the will to do the will of God shall know whether My teaching comes from Him or is merely My own' (v. 17, N.E.B.).

TRUE WISDOM. The note of authority in Christ's teaching

was a source of constant bewilderment to the religious leaders of His day (see also Mark 6: 2). 'How is it that this untrained man has such learning?' they asked. Jesus replied that His teaching was given Him by God: anyone whose heart was set on the divine will would recognize its truth.

At this time in history, when man's knowledge is growing at an unprecedented speed, we need to remind ourselves that knowledge is not the same as wisdom. According to the theological standards of His day Jesus was apparently 'untrained', but His words have for centuries been a life-giving fountain. To recognize this is not to become anti-intellectual: it is to admit the limited influence of factual knowledge upon life and character. Writing of those he called 'spiritually established men', Thomas Kelly, himself a university professor, said, 'where pride in one's learning is found, there they are not. For they do not confuse acquaintance with theology and church history with commitment and the life lived in the secret sanctuary. ... They have found the secret of the Nazarene, and, not content to assent to it intellectually, they have committed themselves to it in action, and walk in newness of life in the vast fellowship of unceasing prayer.'

Growth in spiritual wisdom and perception depends upon obedience to God's will. Insight cannot be divorced from action. Recognizing moral and spiritual truth has far more to do with character than brains.

JOHN 7: 25-31

'I have not come of My own accord. I was sent by the One who truly is, and Him you do not know' (v. 28, N.E.B.).

FALSE EXPECTATIONS. A common Jewish belief at the time of Jesus was that the Messiah already existed—either as a heavenly man or living a human life somewhere in disguise—and would remain hidden until the appointed time. This was sufficient grounds for some to reject Jesus, whose origins were quite well known (v. 27). Others accepted Him, but for the wrong reason! He fulfilled their expectation of a Messiah who would perform miracles (v. 31), but their faith would soon wither when He allowed Himself to die on a Cross.

We must always guard against the temptation to make Christ fit into our expectations. 'Woe betide the man who tries to fit this Man into any political or humanitarian slot!' J. B. Phillips writes. Describing his experience of translating the gospels this writer continues, 'What I am concerned with here is . . . to set down my witness to the continued shocks which His words and deeds gave me as I approached the gospels uninsulated by the familiar cover of beautiful language. The figure who emerged is quite unlike the Jesus of conventional piety, and even more unlike that imagined hero whom members of various causes claim as their champion. What we are so often confronted with today is a "processed" Jesus. Every element that we feel is not consonant with our "image" of Him is removed, and the result is more insipid and unsatisfying than the worst of processed food.'

Do we picture Jesus according to our own tastes and desires or do we try to conform to His?

JOHN 7: 32–36

'Then Jesus said, "For a little longer I shall be with you; then I am going away to Him who sent me . . . Where I am, you cannot come"' (v. 33 and 34, N.E.B.).

WHO IS HE? These words of Christ completely mystified the Jews, as they must also mystify us if we see Jesus only in human terms. Yet the Jews were unable to shake these words off. They had a vague sense that there was in them 'some unfathomed meaning' (Westcott). So they interpreted them in terms of a possible mission to the Gentiles. And, as so often in this Gospel, they made an unwitting prophecy. The death of Jesus would in fact result in the Gentiles being brought into the people of God.

The uniqueness of Christ's relationship with God is hinted at in His words, 'Where I am, you cannot come'. William Temple commented, 'It is not merely where He will be that they cannot come, but where He is now, that is in the bosom of the Father (1: 18). When He came down out of the heavens (6: 38), He did not leave heaven, but all the while is in heaven (3: 13)'. To ponder this truth is no mere speculation: Jesus invites those who believe in Him to share something of His intimacy with the Father.

The mystery of Christ's relationship with God must not be lost sight of as we attempt to communicate with modern man. Such a phrase as 'the Man for others' is both illuminating and inspiring. But it does not plumb the depth of the New Testament teaching about Christ. If we were forced to make a choice then, as Douglas Webster has observed, 'perhaps we would do less harm by presenting to men the full Christ of the biblical revelation, even if the linguistic vessel were gravely inadequate, than a diluted or anaemic Christ in readily understood language but without any mystery and no longer One to be worshipped and adored.'

JOHN 7: 37-44

'If any man is thirsty, he can come to Me and drink! The man who believes in Me, as the Scriptures said, will have rivers of living water flowing from his inmost heart' (vv. 37 and 38, J. B. Phillips).

UNFAILING REFRESHMENT. At the feast of Tabernacles, celebrated in the autumn and one of the three great festivals of Judaism, a golden pitcher filled with water from Siloam was poured out each morning as a libation in the temple court. Probably with this in mind Jesus made His claim to be the source of unfailing refreshment to the spiritually parched. Like other rabbis, Jesus usually sat to teach. But, such was the importance of this proclamation, it was made standing. The gospel writer saw the fulfilment of these words in the outpouring of the Holy Spirit which followed Christ's exaltation.

It is important to note that Jesus here carried His teaching about living water (i.e. the indwelling Spirit) a stage further than in His conversation with the Samaritan woman. Much more than a perpetual source of refreshment is offered. This is an outflowing which refreshes others.

We can never accurately assess our own spiritual progress. For the most part we will do better to keep our eyes firmly fixed on Christ. But if we are occasionally to attempt some self-evaluation, we would do better to ask ourselves, not 'Am I conscious of spiritual enrichment?' but 'To what extent are the lives nearest to me enriched by my living?' This is a far better test of the presence of the Spirit, even though we never have sufficient evidence to answer the question with any finality.

JOHN 7: 45-53; 8: 1

'Nicodemus, the same man who came to Jesus by night ... asked, "Is it the way of our law to judge a man without giving him a hearing first, and finding out what he is about?"' (vv. 50 and 51, Knox).

A PASSION FOR TRUTH. The temple police, who had been

sent to arrest Jesus, returned to the chief priests empty-handed, so fascinated had they been by the matchless power of Christ's teaching. In pleading for a fair hearing for Christ, Nicodemus invited the withering scorn of His colleagues. But how refreshing, in the midst of prejudice and emotional reaction, to find one who is loyal to truth and justice.

Prejudice nearly always leads to injustice. After years of courageous struggling with physical handicap Evelyn Ayrault at last became a teacher. She was almost shattered one day when she heard a fellow-teacher remark to another staff member, 'A teacher who is handicapped is just not good for the children. I must speak to the Superintendent of schools about replacing her.' Few of us are entirely free from prejudice. Let us beware lest we add to this the sin of injustice. The two evils are bosom companions.

Prejudice also causes impoverishment to ourselves. 'When I was a small boy,' wrote F. W. Boreham, 'I dreaded the policeman; when I grew older I feared the bookseller.' This, he explained, was because the bookseller who knows us well continues to press upon us the books which confirm our prejudices, the books we least need to read. How cabined, confined and restricted we all are by our prejudices! We need a new passion for truth wherever it may be found.

JOHN 8: 2–11

"Neither do I condemn you," said Jesus to her. "Go home and do not sin again"' (v. 11, J. B. Phillips).

CHRIST AND THE MORALIZERS. We are fortunate indeed to have this story, for it had no fixed place in the ancient texts. In some manuscripts it is omitted, in some it appears after Luke 21: 38, in one after John 7: 36 and in others after John 21: 24. A piece of floating tradition, it nevertheless bears all the marks of authenticity. How typical of Jesus the story is, and how well it defines the Christian attitude to wrongdoers.

The moralizing and loveless Pharisees were quite shameless in exploiting a woman's failure in order to score a point. They cared nothing for her rehabilitation. As a person she scarcely existed for them, and in this they were probably much nearer than they imagined to her partner in sin. Their lack of self-knowledge is also staggering. Not until they had looked into the angry eyes of Christ did they recognize that an almost unconscious enjoyment of sin can disguise itself beneath excessive condemnation.

Jesus refused to act as judge or rake over the past. He recognized the woman's own self-condemnation. What mattered was the future. If she was crushed by the condemnation of others genuine repentance would be impossible. What she needed was forgiveness and acceptance. Can we be as positive as this in our attitude to the wrongdoing of others? For that matter, do we adopt a positive attitude about our own failures? God is not well pleased by the constant recital of our shortcomings. He would rather we accepted His pardon and met the future creatively in His strength.

JOHN 8: 12–20

'I am the Light of the world. The man who follows Me will not walk in the dark but will live his life in the light' (v. 12, J. B. Phillips).

DARKNESS DISPELLED. During the feast of Tabernacles the Jews recalled, in the ceremony of lighting a golden candelabra, the time when their nation was led across the desert by a pillar of fire by night. This is the background to Christ's claim to be the light of the world. In a sermon on this text Harry Williams, Dean of Trinity College, Cambridge, suggests the following application.

In a world that is hostile and often threatening, Christ assures us of the love of God. Sometimes it seems as though some malignant fate is attacking us or those we love. Or, on the other hand, the darkness may be within our own hearts, the darkness of guilt or depression. But, in the darkness, Christ brings us light. 'He assures us that whatever else may be against us, even if we are against ourselves, God, the most real of all realities, is on our side, not condemning us but taking our part and seeing us through.'

The light of Christ dispels not only the darkness of our hostile world, but also 'the treacherous shadows of our illusions'. Most of us at times long for a magician God—one who, in return for our worship and respectability, will save us and ours from pain and suffering. The life and death of Jesus shatters this idol, for His path was neither smooth nor easy. The light of Christ illuminates human suffering, not by saving us from it, but by assuring us of God's love and showing how even evil is redeemed.

'"The difference between us," Jesus said to them, "is that you come from below and I am from above. You belong to this world but I do not"' (vv. 23 and 24, J. B. Phillips).

CONTRASTING VIEWPOINTS. The controversy here recorded between Jesus and the Jews was conducted at cross-purposes because the viewpoint of both was so different. Jesus put His finger on the cause of the confusion when He asserted, 'You come from below and I am from above.'

It is sometimes claimed that this kind of spatial imagery—above and below—is only a hindrance to modern man who has outgrown a primitive 'three decker' view of the universe. Alan Richardson points out that such language is not particularly Greek or Hebrew but is the universal language of religion—'it could be paralleled in Norse saga or Japanese Buddhism'. Similarly, E. N. Ducker, a Christian psychotherapist, claims that this way of viewing spiritual reality is basic to the human mind.

What, then, was the difference between Jesus and His antagonists? Certainly not that He was an other-worldly visionary and they practical men of affairs. He was so sociable that they called Him a glutton and a winebibber: His parables showed keen observation of everyday life. He was 'from above', not only because He came from God, but because He lived in constant fellowship with His Father. God's purposes were central to Him. Their own ends came first with the Jews, even in their religion.

Man, as Evelyn Underhill often insisted, is meant to live an 'amphibian' existence. He is a creature of time but also of eternity. If this world becomes an end in itself we lose our spiritual vision and life itself lacks deep significance and value.

'If you dwell within the revelation I have brought, you are indeed My disciples; you shall know the truth, and the truth will set you free' (vv. 31 and 32, N.E.B.).

TRUTH OR ILLUSION. Jean Jacques Rousseau began a famous treatise with the assertion, 'Man was born free, but he is everywhere in chains.' His own programme of liberation was an abysmal failure, as his *Confessions* shows. T. R. Glover was nearer the heart of the matter when he pointed out that a person with an eye defect 'must get the glasses that will show him the real world, and he is safe, and free to go and come as he pleases. See the real in the moral sphere, and the first great peril is gone. It is our illusions that keep us in bondage, and not the least of these is the one which imagines we are free when we are not.'

This is clearly illustrated in today's reading. The Jews were blinded to the truth about themselves by thinking only in religious clichés— 'We are Abraham's descendants; we have never been in slavery to any man.' Refusing the truth about themselves they were incapable of 'seeing straight' on any issue.

Jesus claimed that those who 'dwell' within the revelation He brought would know the truth. This applies equally to the truth about God and about ourselves. The saints continually remind us that we progress in both simultaneously. Can we face the truth about ourselves undismayed unless at the same time we see the truth about God?

JOHN 8: 42–50

'Jesus told them, "If you were children of God, you would welcome Me gladly; it was from God I took My origin, from Him I have come"' (v. 42, Knox).

WHEN RELIGION OPPOSES GOD. We noted above that the Jews who rejected Jesus refused to face the truth about themselves. Their enslavement to sin was disguised beneath the claim to be 'Abraham's descendants'. They were also incapable of recognizing the new truth about God which Jesus brought. Thus they falsified their own claim to be Abraham's spiritual heirs. Abraham welcomed the divine messengers sent to him (Genesis 18: 2 ff.), but they sought only Christ's death. And this rejection was made in the name of religion.

When does religion become the enemy of Christ—of God? Not simply when the ideas it presents of God become inadequate. All our pictures of God are inadequate—and always will be. After a lifetime of thinking and writing about God, Thomas Aquinas saw a vision which made him confess, 'I have seen that which makes all that I have previously taught and written seem as chaff to me.'

Religion becomes the enemy of Christ when its picture of God ceases to grow and expand. We must beware of worshipping a god who is simply the guardian of all we cherish, the justification of all our ways of life and the protector of our group. 'When we are confident we know the absolute truth of God,' R. S. Lee writes, 'confident to the degree of dogmatism, our prayers become drugs to take away our powers to respond to life, that is, to God. Instead of promoting growth they will arrest it.'

JOHN 8: 51–59

"'I tell you in solemn truth," returned Jesus, "before there was an Abraham, I AM!"' (v. 58, J. B. Phillips).

A TREMENDOUS CLAIM. Only rarely do we read of Jesus making verbal claims about His own nature. Usually He left men to arrive at the truth about Him from His character and actions. And there was plenty in His ministry which left men no option but to believe in His uniqueness or regard Him as an impostor. Did He not forgive sins, reinterpret the ancient Mosaic law and invite men to come to Him for peace of soul? In closely argued debate with the religious authorities, however, it was impossible for Jesus to maintain this verbal reticence—'If I said that I did not know Him I should be a liar.' So the present controversy ends with the tremendous claim, 'before Abraham was born, I am'.

Ultimately we assent to, or repudiate, this claim of Jesus in our own daily experience. It is not primarily a question of theology. Mervyn Stockwood writes, 'As a boy I accepted the divinity of Jesus as I accepted the arrival of William the Conqueror. It was inevitably secondhand. When, as I grew older, I examined my beliefs I found that I was becoming personally involved. In the first instance it was respect. Here was a man who exemplified excellence and set the pattern. The time soon came when the word "man" proved inadequate to describe my reactions to the compelling qualities of His character. More important still, the compulsion derived not from a mere historical figure but a living person. The Jesus of Palestine was the Christ of today.'

JOHN 9: 1–12

'While daylight lasts, we must be busy with the work of Him who sent Me: night comes, when no one can do any work' (v. 4, Moffatt).

MORALITY AND MORALISM. The disciples betrayed their Jewish training when, faced with a blind man, they immediately began to ask questions about guilt. It was typical of Jesus that, looking upon the same man with deep compassion, He saw an opportunity to reveal the love and power of God. How is it that morality, which is an essential part of all true religion, can become moralism, which was one of the foes that hounded Christ to death?

Genuine morality recognizes the solidarity of mankind in sin, and acknowledges our personal responsibility. When a young man exploits a girl and produces an illegitimate child after a long period of gloating over pornographic magazines, who has sinned? asks Raymond Efemey. 'The young man? The publishers? The newsagent? The girls who posed? The society which permits the dissemination of such material?' True morality acknowledges our shared responsibility. Moralism, however, is concerned only to load the young couple with guilt.

Secondly, true morality aims at giving helpful guidance in the present situation. This is so because it is love-directed. Moralism is obsessed with 'picking at the past', usually other people's past. This is because its unconscious motivation is the achievement of moral superiority. Jesus' attitude to sick and sinners alike was always, 'Where do we go from here?' His offer was one of loving acceptance, liberation from the past, and a new future.

JOHN 9: 13-25

'"Whether or not he is a sinner, I do not know," the man replied, "All I know is this: once I was blind, now I can see"' (v. 25, N.E.B.).

IRREFUTABLE EVIDENCE. In face of the Pharisee's attempts to discredit Jesus the healed man's reply is a model testimony. He refuses to be carried out of his depth by doctrinal theorising, but repeats the unvarnished tale of his healing. This cannot be refuted.

In his book, *The Last Enemy*, Richard Hillary describes a railway journey he made with Peter Pease, a fellow-pilot who was a Christian and the best man Hillary had ever met. Determined to destroy Peter's faith he glared at him and said, 'Your religion is a fake—a hereditary hangover, a useful social adjunct and no more.' Peter stammered a few protests and then fell silent before his opponent's arguments. But Hillary knew he had lost the argument, for Peter's character was more powerful than all his dialectics. It was a testimony that could not be refuted.

The witness of our lives is undoubtedly the most important. But there are occasions when words are called for. Then our lips are sometimes sealed because we cannot give the impressive witness we have heard others make. Yet we can all say, 'This is what Jesus Christ means to me.' And, when our lives are consistent with our words, that is the most powerful testimony we can give. As Dean Inge once rightly observed: 'You cannot confute a person.'

JOHN 9: 26-34

'That a man should open the eyes of one born blind is something unheard of since the world began' (v. 32, Knox).

WHAT PRICE THE TRUTH? In Bernard Shaw's play *Saint Joan*, King Charles says of the maid, 'If she would only keep quiet!' And so say all those who wish to silence the voices which do not accord with their own beliefs. This was why the Pharisees expelled the man born blind from the synagogue. His taunts, heavy with sarcasm, roused them to fury. We may condemn their blindness in saying, 'We know that God spoke to Moses, but as for this fellow, we do not know where he comes from.' But let us admit one fact. It is always easier dogmatically to assert that God spoke in the past, in such and such a way, through this person or that, than to hear His word from our contemporaries.

All men are tempted to follow the Pharisees in silencing the disquieting voice, dismissing the contrary evidence. So the materialist puts forward cheap explanations of spiritual experiences which have transformed human lives. So the narrow-minded believer refuses to recognize the activity of the Spirit in non-Christian saints. In the interests of maintaining our neat and tidy theories about life we are all tempted to toy with the evidence. Yet this is a betrayal of which no follower of Christ need be guilty. He who is the truth would have us courageously face the truth, even that which may seem to deny Him. Such a way of living brings deepening confidence that Christ can be trusted utterly.

JOHN 9: 35-41

'Then Jesus said, "I have come into the world to find that I judge it—those who cannot see have their eyes opened and those who think they can see become blind"' (v. 39, J. B. Phillips).

BLINDNESS AND VISION. The closing verses of this chapter

make it clear that the healing of the man born blind is recorded primarily as an acted parable of faith and unbelief—a sign. The controversy which follows it concerns spiritual vision and blindness. Although the purpose of Christ's coming was the salvation of men it also resulted in judgment. In His presence those who claimed to have spiritual insight, but had closed their minds to new truth, were separated from those who were conscious of their blindness, but willing to receive the light.

The Pharisees stand as a perpetual warning against the cocksure attitude which 'knows it all'. Writes the Swiss psychiatrist, Paul Tournier, 'I have noticed more and more how dangerous it is for us to be right. The most fruitful hours in life are those of humiliation, when we see our sins and wrongs, and when we are upset by them. Just as long as we zealously uphold a cause in which we know ourselves to be right, however, we remain inaccessible to any such inner feeling.'

Does this mean we must be forever uncertain, hesitant and without confidence? Certainly not. Strong convictions need not imply a closed mind. The danger signs to watch for in ourselves are a belligerent attitude to the opposite point of view, an inner panic when our convictions are questioned. These are the signs of the closed mind and have no place in the humble seeker after truth.

JOHN 10: 1–10

'I am the door; anyone who comes into the fold through Me shall be safe. He shall go in and out and shall find pasturage' (v. 9, N.E.B.).

SECURITY WITH ADVENTURE. The imagery in this passage is highly compressed. The first picture is of many flocks sheltering for the night in one fold. In the morning the various shepherds call their sheep, using their own peculiar call, and the sheep infallibly follow their own shepherd. So those who belong to Christ have a perceptiveness and discrimination which enables them to recognize what is spiritually authentic. This is not developed without much listening to the voice of the Shepherd.

When Jesus goes on to say, 'I am the door' the picture seems to change. But in the East sheep were often gathered into a rough enclosure, the entrance to which was merely a gap in the wall. In this gap the shepherd would lie at night beside a blazing fire. The sheep could rest in complete safety. Their shepherd was *also* the door.

Christian discipleship combines spiritual security with the spirit of adventurous exploration. The sheep will 'go in and out and shall find pasturage'. Said the Swiss guide to a party of frightened tourists during an Alpine storm, 'These hands have never yet lost a man.' Christ is equally reassuring to those who commit themselves to Him. But, together with the spiritual security, He offers a wide ranging freedom of thought, and calls us to adventurous service. The sheep are grateful for the fold, but they do not spend their lives there.

JOHN 10: 11-21

'I have also other sheep—which do not belong to this fold. Those also I must bring, and they will listen to My voice; and they shall become one flock under one shepherd' (v. 16, Weymouth).

A UNIVERSAL SHEPHERD. The figure of David, the Shepherd-King, who once risked his life to save his sheep, and later rescued his countrymen from their enemies, played a prominent part in Jewish thinking. Israel looked for a new David who would save and rule the flock of God. So this passage presents Jesus as the One who fulfils the nation's highest hopes. Yet Jesus is much more than a national deliverer of the Jews. There are 'other sheep' who will be included in the one flock, for Christ is the Saviour of the world.

Much more than moral goodness is implied in the term 'the good shepherd'. The adjective carries the sense of 'beautiful' or 'attractive'. Is this not the very quality that makes Jesus a universal Shepherd? As Leslie Weatherhead has said, 'There is not one nation that feels He is a foreigner, that His ideas and ideals are out of harmony with its own. ... Mohammed has made no conquests in the far north, the far south, the far east, the far west. Hinduism spreads hardly at all. Confucianism makes little appeal to the west, and Esquimaux and Hottentots make little of the Buddha. Christ has disciples who would die for Him in every country under heaven.' Culture often divides men, so does theology, but all men respond to the appeal of Christ's character —for in Him goodness is supremely attractive.

'My sheep listen to My voice, and I know them ... they shall never perish, nor shall any one wrest them from My hand' (vv. 27 and 28, Weymouth).

A SHEPHERD'S PROTECTION. Urged to declare Himself clearly, Jesus affirmed that He had already done this—for those who could hear His voice. His own sheep already acknowledged that He was indeed the Good Shepherd. To them would be granted eternal life and the security of the Shepherd's protection.

What kind of security is offered here? Certainly not protection from physical ill or sorrow. 'Where is your God?' asked the old men of an Indian penal settlement of Solomon Smith, a Salvationist missionary. Solomon's three children had died of smallpox— despite the earnest prayers of the Christians. 'Your God did not hear,' claimed the old men. Alone in the jungle Solomon fought his doubts and won through a faith deeper than that based on fortunate circumstances.

The security Christ promises to His followers is nearer that described by Rupert Brooke, soldier-poet of the First World War. 'Safe shall be my going,' he claimed,

> Secretly armed against all death's endeavour;
> Safe though all safety's lost; safe where men fall;
> And if these poor limbs die, safest of all.

Christ does not promise protection from pain (how could He, who went to a Cross?), but He does save us from the despair of meaningless suffering. He does not promise we shall be spared from bereavement, but He does rescue us from the ultimate loneliness of a godless universe. He does not promise we will never know disappointment, but He guards us against the bitterness which poisons the soul.

'If I fail to do what My Father does, then do not believe Me. But if I so do, even though you have no faith in Me personally, then believe in the things that I do' (vv. 37 and 38, J. B. Phillips).

ACTIONS SPEAK LOUDER. Here is another example of that

K

involved Rabbinic debate into which Jesus was drawn, particularly in Jerusalem. The most immediately helpful aspect of this for our purpose is the willingness of Jesus to be judged, not by His words, but by His deeds.

The absolute consistency in Christ's life was one aspect of His radiant holiness. His deeds harmonized with His words: His life perfectly reflected His faith. How different it often is with us! How tragically divorced are our ideals from our achievements, our profession from our accomplishment!

If we are ever to share something of the unity and integrity of our Lord's character we need to act upon two related truths. Because human nature exhibits this divorce between thought and deed it is by examining our conduct that we gain self-knowledge. We must ask ourselves, not 'Do I feel loving?', but 'Do I act lovingly?' In the sphere of thought and feeling the human mind has an infinite capacity for self-deception. But we cannot refute the evidence of our actions.

On the other hand, the divorce between thought and deed can sometimes be healed by giving priority to action. 'It is sometimes easier,' E. Stanley Jones wrote, 'to act your way into right thinking than to think your way into right acting.'

JOHN 11: 1-10

'Therefore, though He loved Martha and her sister and Lazarus, after hearing of his illness Jesus waited for two days in the place where He was' (vv. 5 and 6, N.E.B.).

AGONIZED WAITING. Although Lazarus has not previously appeared in the Gospel narrative it is clear that he was a close friend of Christ's. The repeated references in this chapter to Christ's love for him (vv. 3, 5, 11 and 36) have even led some Bible scholars to suggest he is 'the disciple whom Jesus loved' and the author of this Gospel. More important for our purposes is to recognize this story as a 'sign'—in fact, the last and greatest of the seven signs recorded in this gospel. Jesus raised Lazarus not only out of sympathy with Martha and Mary, or merely because Lazarus was specially dear to Him, but in order to manifest Himself as 'the resurrection, and the life'.

The two days' delay before Jesus answered their summons must have seemed totally inexplicable to Mary and Martha. They had to learn, as have all followers of Christ, that even the most intimate communion grants us no rights to dictate when and how the

Lord shall help us. John Baillie writes, 'In the last resort Christian prayer has always left it to God's own wisdom to decide what precisely He is to do about our need. ... If I thought that God were going to grant me all my prayers simply for the asking, without ever passing them under His own gracious review, without ever bringing to bear upon them His own greater wisdom, I think there would be very few prayers that I should dare to pray.'

JOHN 11: 11–19

'Thomas (known as the Twin) then said to his fellow disciples, "Come on, then, let us all go and die with him!"' (v. 16, J. B. Phillips).

GRIM LOYALTY. Whether or not the reputation of Thomas for chronic pessimism is deserved it is hard to say. Certainly, in this passage, he sees more clearly than his fellows the grim possibilities of their return to Judaea. But his foreboding was not so far wide of the truth. What is wholly admirable is his loyal adherence to Christ even in face of danger. It is one thing to be brave when one is almost blind to the possible consequences: quite another order of courage is required to go open-eyed into danger.

Is it not possible to glimpse a deeper meaning in the loyal cry of Thomas, 'Let us all go and die with Him'? Christ's call to take up the cross can mean nothing less than an invitation to death—a death to the values and standards of a godless world, a death to our own selfishness and egotism. Dietrich Bonhoeffer, who was to drink to the dregs the cup of suffering for Christ's sake, wrote, 'The cross is laid on every Christian. The first Christ-suffering—which every man must experience is the call to abandon the attachments of this world. It is that dying of the old man which is the result of his encounter with Christ ... the cross is not the terrible end to an otherwise god-fearing and happy life, but it meets us at the beginning of our communion with Christ. When Christ calls a man, he bids him come and die.'

JOHN 11: 20–27

'I am the resurrection and I am life. If a man has faith in Me, even though he die, he shall come to life; and no one who is alive and has faith shall ever die' (vv. 25 and 26, N.E.B.).

PUTTING DEATH IN ITS PLACE. When Jesus arrived in

Bethany Martha greeted Him by repeating what the sisters had been saying to each other since their brother died—'If Jesus had been here this would not have happened.' The assurance of Christ that Lazarus would rise again was taken to refer to the last day and was only a partial comfort. As R. V. G. Tasker has said: 'In times of bereavement present sorrow dims the prospect of future bliss; and when the imagination is overwrought, death, not life, is apt to seem the ultimate reality.'

The dialogue between Jesus and Martha leads up to the tremendous affirmation of Christ—of which the raising of Lazarus will be the sign—'I am the Resurrection and the Life.' Jesus is the giver of life upon two levels. To those who believe in Him He grants eternal life now. But also He is the promise and assurance of life beyond the physical death we all, even Lazarus whom He is soon to raise to life, must eventually face.

This twofold emphasis makes impossible any morbid obsession with life after death on the one hand, or the fear that death is the absolute end on the other. Christ puts death in its place, but He also fills with significance this earthly life. Those who follow Him may emulate Edward Wilson, Scott's companion on that last dreadful journey in the Antarctic. No one had a greater relish for life than Edward Wilson, yet when he faced death his eyes had 'a comfortable blue look of hope'.

JOHN 11: 28-37

'Seeing her wailing, and the Jews in like manner wailing who had come with her, Jesus, with deep emotion and greatly troubled, asked them, "Where have you laid him?"'.
(vv. 33 and 34, Weymouth).

THE CONQUEROR PREPARES FOR BATTLE. 'No fire, no heroism, no intensity of thought and feeling can preserve an individual life beyond the grave,' claimed Bertrand Russell "All the labours of the ages, all the devotion, all the inspiration, all the noonday brightness of human genius, are destined to extinction in the vast death of the solar system.' Perhaps it was the utter hopelessness and meaninglessness that this view engenders that so disturbed Christ when He pondered the death of His friend. Not His own private grief, but the thraldom death holds over the human race deeply agitated His spirit. The Greek text indicates indignation and even anger.

B. B. Warfield's beautiful comment on this passage is worthy of note. 'It is death that is the object of His wrath, and behind it him who has the power of death, and whom He has come into the world to destroy. Tears of sympathy may fill His eyes, but this is incidental. His soul is held by rage; and He advances to the tomb, in Calvin's words, "as a champion who prepares for conflict" ... Not in cold unconcern, but in flaming wrath against the foe, Jesus smites on our behalf. He has not only saved us from the evils which oppress us; He has felt for and with us, in our oppression, and under the impulse of these feelings has wrought out our redemption.'

JOHN 11: 38–44

'He raised His voice in a great cry: "Lazarus, come forth"' (v. 43, N.E.B.).

A PRELIMINARY ADVANCE. How typical of our human fluctuations between faith and doubt are Martha's reactions. At first she says to Christ, 'Even now I know that whatever you ask of God, God will grant you,' but later she fearfully protests against the opening of the tomb. On the other hand, note the calm confidence of Christ's prayer—'simple words of thanksgiving, as if already Lazarus was restored'.

As we have repeatedly noted, each miracle in this gospel is a 'sign'. Much more than the restoration of a man to his family is involved here. In any case Lazarus would still have to die eventually. What is vital is the manifestation of Jesus as the Conqueror of death. Here we witness a preliminary advance, prior to that complete conquest over the grave on Easter Day.

In terms of the believer's own experience this means that death is stripped of its more fearsome aspects. 'I have a fair summer religion,' confessed John Wesley a few months before his conversion. 'I can talk well while no danger is near. But let death look me in the face and my spirit is troubled.' Shortly afterwards, in a terrifying storm at sea, he watched admiringly as a group of Moravians calmly sang a psalm while the mainsail split in pieces above them and water poured in between the decks. 'Were you not afraid?' he asked one of their number later. 'I thank God, no,' was the confident reply. Dag Hammarskjöld's comment is to the point: 'In the last analysis, it is our conception of death which decides our answers to all the questions which life puts to us.'

'You do not realize that it would be a good thing for us if one man should die for the sake of the people—instead of the whole nation being destroyed' (v. 50, J. B. Phillips).

FOR OTHERS. In the view of this gospel writer Jesus signed His own death warrant by raising Lazarus from death. The other gospels see the cleansing of the temple as the act which finally sealed His fate. But in both instances it was not just the deed, but the claim which lay behind it, which was intolerable to the Jewish authorities. In one way or another Christ threatened to disturb the *status quo,* and leaders are always prone to imagine that their own best interests are identical with the interests of the people they lead. So, asserted Caiaphas, Christ must die.

The High Priest's cynical comment that it was necessary for one man to die for the people was an 'unconscious prophecy'. It also reflects a principle which is written into the very constitution of the universe.

James Stewart comments, 'It is expedient—it always has been and always will be expedient—that one man should die for the people. David Livingstone, dying on his knees in darkest Africa; the X-ray pioneer losing limb or life for the advancement of knowledge and the relief of suffering; the Headmaster of an English school who during an air-raid marshalled his pupils into the shelters and then, going back to make sure that none had been left behind, was himself caught by a bomb and instantly killed— "one man dying for the people". This is the cosmic principle of life, the cruciform pattern on which life itself is built, the ground-plan of the universe.'

JOHN 12: 1-11

'Then Mary brought a pound of very costly perfume, oil of pure nard, and anointed the feet of Jesus and wiped them with her hair, till the house was filled with the fragrance' (v. 3, N.E.B.).

LOVE RECIPROCATED. This beautiful account of a woman's uncalculating devotion had at least a twofold significance in the life of Jesus. Undoubtedly, it was associated with His coming death, as the words of Jesus show, but it also symbolized His messiahship. The word 'messiah' or 'Christ' means 'the anointed one'. Recorded here, immediately prior to the triumphal entry into Jerusalem, John sees the anointing as much in terms of a 'coronation rite' as a 'funeral rite'. C. H. Dodd claims that the gospel writer also associates the incident with the saying of Jesus, recorded later in the chapter, about the buried seed (v. 24).

Mary perfectly typifies the true Christian disciple. Her gift, equivalent to an unskilled labourer's wage for three hundred days, expressed whole-hearted response to Christ's love (which also was extravagant and, to worldly eyes, wasteful).

Writing in *The Friend* Reuben Shapcott describes a couple behind whom he sat on a bus. The girl kept pressing her cheek against the man's shoulder with great tenderness. He only yawned. 'She gave: he took—without visible response'. Were they, Shapcott asked, 'unequal in loving'? For equality in loving is rare and this is why love is so closely linked to pain. Rare, too, is it for Christ's love to be returned with the fierce intensity shown by Mary.

> Lord, it is my chief complaint
> That my love is weak and faint;
> Yet I love Thee, and adore;
> O for grace to love Thee more!

JOHN 12: 12–19

'Jesus found a donkey and mounted it, in accordance with the text of Scripture: "Fear no more, daughter of Zion; see, your king is coming, mounted on an ass's colt"' (vv. 14 and 15, N.E.B.).

LONELY IN A CROWD. What mixed feelings Jesus must have had about His triumphant entry into Jerusalem! He gladly accepted the enthusiastic praise of His sincere followers and rebuked those who would have silenced the excited Hosannas (Luke 19: 40). Yet He knew that genuine adulation was mixed with many false hopes. A great part of the crowd saw Jesus merely as a nationalist leader. Once before, when a crowd had wanted to make Him a king, He had escaped from them (6: 15). Escape was now impossible. Reasoned instruction about the nature of His kingship was equally out of the question. But in His choice of a donkey on which to make His entrance, Jesus disclaimed all military ambition. He came in fulfilment of Zechariah's prophecy of a peaceable king.

As well as gladly accepting the praise of His followers Jesus must have experienced the keenest pangs of loneliness. He was alone in a crowd—always the most poignant form of loneliness. He had chosen a way that not even His dearest friends approved— and a way which would turn the nationalistic fervour of others to furious resentment.

H. H. Farmer speaks for all of us when he says, 'The seeds of virtue in my soul need a little social warmth to make them germinate; let there be no frost of unappreciation, please, if you want them to thrive.' Without any human support Jesus chose to be the kind of king whom the Jews would inevitably reject.

JOHN 12: 20–26

'I tell you truly that unless a grain of wheat falls into the earth and dies, it remains a single grain of wheat; but if it dies, it brings a good harvest' (v. 24, J. B. Phillips).

AN ETERNAL PRINCIPLE. The inquiry of the visiting Gentiles who wanted to see Jesus was addressed to Philip. He had a Greek name and probably spoke Greek. To Christ these men were representatives of the wider world which desperately needed a Saviour and which would hear the gospel only through His Cross and Resurrection.

The principle which Jesus here aid down stands for all time. Floyd Filson has rightly said: 'Life selfishly preserved and protected is barren; only life given in sacrifice and death yields the harvest'. This was true not only for Jesus, but for all who would follow Him (v. 26).

Courageous self-giving is possible only in those persons who experience a basic security. The child who knows he is loved and and accepted can be more outgoing and self-forgetful. The man who is sustained by the affection of his wife can undertake the more demanding task. The mystic or saint who has the keenest awareness of God's love can be self-giving to a degree that is almost miraculous. The life of sacrifice is energized by the life of communion.

The time-lag between the death of the seed and the harvest may be prolonged. Charles de Foucauld laboured for years in North Africa, won only one convert, and was murdered by an Arab raiding party. Fifty years later his life and Christian witness is stimulating the Church to a new conception of evangelism. In this life we may never see our sacrifice bear fruit. We may be called upon to make that same act of faith which Jesus made when He went to the Cross.

JOHN 12: 27–36

'Now comes My hour of heart-break, and what can I say, "Father save Me from this hour"? No, it was for this very purpose that I came to this hour' (v. 27, J. B. Phillips).

HUMAN STRUGGLE. John's gospel omits Christ's agony at Gethsemane, but this passage describes a similar experience. In Mark 14: 35 Jesus prays that 'this hour might pass Him by' (N.E.B.): here He questions whether to pray, 'save Me from this hour'. On the whole this gospel is so concerned to emphasize the divinity of Christ that there are fewer examples of His very real humanity than in the synoptic gospels. To get a true picture of Jesus we need all four Gospels. However, this evangelist also affirms that the Word was truly 'made flesh'.

Nels Ferré, the American theologian, describes the shock which a student's essay brought to his professor, Daniel Evans. The professor loved to dwell upon Christ's continual serenity, assurance and confidence. The student, however, gathered together all those instances in the gospels where the human struggles of Jesus rose to the surface. He found that Jesus groaned within Himself, wept over Jerusalem and at the tomb of Lazarus, complained of tensions until He could accomplish His mission, was tempted in the wilderness, agonized in Gethsemane, and cried out in lonely dereliction from the Cross. Reading the student's paper the professor almost choked, 'You might as well have kicked my grandmother in the teeth as written this paper for me.'

Like Daniel Evans, some believers are blind to the true humanity of Jesus. But their misunderstanding places Christ on a plane where He can no longer help us. It was through Christ's real humanity that God was revealed: it was in the midst of genuine conflict that victory was achieved.

JOHN 12: 37–50

'I have come to save the world, not to pass sentence on the world' (v. 47, Knox).

SALVATION AND JUDGMENT. The Church has never

found it easy to combine the picture of Christ as Saviour with that of Christ as Judge. The medieval pictures of Christ, advancing with clenched fist to divide the nations, portray a very different person to the Jesus who died for sinners upon the Cross. The repressed desire that others shall pay in full for sins we would like to have committed is often at the bottom of a distorted presentation of judgment.

This gospel, as we have seen, has much to say about judgment. It affirms that judgment is a present reality, not just a future event. But it repeatedly claims that salvation, not judgment is Christ's prime mission (3: 17; 8: 15; 12: 47). C. H. Dodd suggests that John highlights this truth as a protest against crude ideas of judgment current in his day.

In presenting Jesus as the light, the fourth gospel perfectly harmonizes the themes of salvation and judgment. Christ comes only to bring illumination and healing. In His life we are assured that God is pure love. Yet just because God is love He seeks our free response and refuses to coerce. We can turn from the light, and then that very light exposes our sin, becomes in fact the source of judgment.

Christ the Saviour will not undergo some mysterious change before He becomes Christ the Judge. His compassionate heart cannot harden. He is love unchanging. It is when we reject His way and turn our backs upon the light that we pass sentence upon ourselves.

JOHN 13: 1–11

"'If I do not wash you," Jesus replied, "you are not in fellowship with Me"' (v. 8, N.E.B.).

PETER'S NEED—AND OURS. The washing of the disciples' feet by Jesus was far more than a lesson in humble service. Such cleansing was always performed before a meal. This act was imbued with profound significance by being enacted during or after the supper. The writer of this gospel sees the incident on the same level as the cleansing of the temple or the triumphant entry into Jerusalem. He deliberately links the act with Christ's awareness of His divine authority and vocation. It was when He knew 'that the Father had entrusted everything to Him, and that He had come from God and was going back to God', that Jesus undertook the service of a slave.

Peter's first refusal of Christ's service is typical of our human pride. He would much rather wash Christ's feet than allow His Master to wash his own feet. And this pride is more basic than the passing embarrassment of this occasion. The writer uses the same word to indicate that Jesus 'laid aside' His garments and that the Good Shepherd 'lays down' His life for the sheep. The feet washing points forward to the Cross. Are we not, like Peter, reluctant to admit our need of Christ's cleansing ministry?

Christ's statement that Peter's refusal would exclude him from fellowship was no arbitrary ruling. Unless Peter recognized his own deep need of cleansing, and unless he was willing to see lordship in terms of humble service, his pride would forever be a barrier between him and Jesus.

JOHN 13: 12-20

'I have set you an example in order that you may do what I have done to you' (v. 15, Weymouth).

THE SERVANT. We noted above that the evangelist saw much more in the feet washing than a lesson in humble service. Yet the deeper symbolism must not blind us to the more obvious meaning. In the fourth gospel the narrative often moves on two levels: we must try not to miss either.

Although facing His most momentous task—which would be accomplished in direct pain and suffering—Jesus did not miss the chance to perform a menial service. Indeed He made the lesser task a foreshadowing of the greater. Dag Hammarskjöld, one-time Secretary General of the United Nations, noted in his journal that the 'great' commitment can all too easily shut our hearts to the more ordinary, everyday acts of service. Indeed, 'a willingness to make the ultimate sacrifice can be associated with, and even produce, a great hardness of heart'. This was certainly not so with Jesus.

Following Jesus on this path of humble service requires the sacrifice of all arrogance and pride. Douglas Webster writes, 'The Church sometimes talks about humility as if it were a tame domestic virtue, easily cultivated and with which we can be quite at home. But is this the humility of the feet-washing and of Calvary? Von Hügel taught that "there is no humility without humiliation". Humiliation is being brought low, being cast down, usually in public. This is what Jesus accepted. And through all the ages His servants, like most others in the servant class, have smarted under humiliation. Yet this was the form He himself chose for His incarnate life on earth, and it was the servant-form He prescribed for His disciples and His Church.'

JOHN 13: 21-30

'Jesus exclaimed in deep agitation of spirit, "In truth, in very truth I tell you, one of you is going to betray Me"' (v. 21, N.E.B.).

MAN'S TREACHERY AND GOD'S LOVE. Today's reading confronts us with three mysteries, one of which is relatively unimportant. In this passage we are first introduced to the figure of 'the beloved disciple'. Church tradition since the latter half of the second century has identified 'the beloved disciple' with John the son of Zebedee. Many still hold this view on the grounds that the fourth gospel does not mention John by name but links Peter and 'the beloved disciple' just as Peter and John are linked in the synoptics. However, as this gospel nowhere names 'the beloved disciple' there will always be some conjecture as to his identity.

A more relevant mystery, because it touches our own moral struggles, is the enigma of Judas' treachery. That one who had experienced intimate fellowship with Christ, and had received the divine commission (Luke 9: 1 ff.), could turn traitor is inexplicable. Or is it? The anxious questioning of the disciples, recorded in Matthew's gospel (26: 22), 'Lord, is it I?', suggests that more than one had doubts about his absolute loyalty. The story of Judas is not an invitation to indulge in moral superiority: it is an exhortation to watchfulness.

The third mystery here is that of Christ's infinite compassion. The offering of a special morsel from the common dish to a particular guest was a sign of special favour. Jesus met the hostility of Judas with unrelenting love. So does the love of God hold on to us despite all our ingratitude and failure.

JOHN 13: 31-38

'Now the Son of Man is glorified, and in Him God is glorified' (v. 31, N.E.B.).

WHAT IS GLORY FOR US? At the beginning of this gospel it is declared that, because the Word became flesh, we beheld 'His glory' (1:14). In the Old Testament the glory of God was the manifestation of His nature and presence, in a way men could apprehend, usually as a radiance of dazzling light.

How significant then, that at that moment when Judas left the upper room to set in motion those forces which would bring about Christ's death, Jesus should declare, 'Now is the Son of Man glorified.' In one sense when Judas went out, 'it was night'. But in a deeper sense the true light of God's love was now beginning to shine in all its splendour. The fourth gospel emphasizes that for Jesus glory and victory lay not on the far side of Calvary, but in the very Cross itself.

Since for Jesus glory lay in the uttermost self-giving, His disciples dare not seek it elsewhere. Karen Horney, an American psychotherapist, described one of the compulsive urges which drive neurotic people to seek a solution of their emotional problems as 'the search for glory'. Ambition, domination over others, lust, power, success: these can all provide temporary alleviation for insecurity. Few are entirely free from the attractions of these pseudo-glories. Dare we place our ambitions and desires beside the glory which Jesus sought and achieved? As Thomas à Kempis wrote: 'God weigheth more with how much love a man worketh, than how much he doeth. He doeth much that loveth much.'

JOHN 14: 1–14

'You must not let yourselves be distressed—you must hold on to your faith in God and to your faith in Me' (v. 1, J. B. Phillips).

DESTINATION AND ROUTE. A few months before he was murdered, Charles de Foucauld, who for many years maintained a lonely witness among the Moslems of North Africa, wrote, 'How good God is to hide from us the future. What a torture life would be if this were known. And how good of Him, too, to show us so clearly His future in Heaven which will follow these earthly trials.'

To disciples who were understandably distressed by their Master's words about His 'going away', Jesus pointed to the ultimate goal of the Christian life. There are times when nothing less will serve to strengthen us. Nor need we be disturbed by the scoffer's jeer about 'pie in the sky'. To limit one's perspective to this life alone is inevitably to become confused by its apparent meaninglessness. Only 'the eternal dimension' makes sense of the suffering inherent in our present life.

The Christian, however, is not unhealthily obsessed with heaven. For this life he knows he needs guidance, direction and strength.

The truth of Christ's claim—'I am the Way, the Truth, and the Life'—can be proved only in experience. We begin, H. H. Farmer said, with 'the soul's surmise' that these words were trustworthy. Then, just as it is necessary to treat a man as a friend if we sense he is capable of friendship, so we must commit ourselves to Christ's way of life. As a result, what began as 'the soul's surmise' becomes the soul's deepest conviction.

JOHN 14: 15-21

'I will ask the Father, and He will give you another to be your Advocate, who will be with you for ever ... I will not leave you bereft; I am coming back to you' (vv. 16 and 18, N.E.B.).

NO MERE COMPENSATION. The Holy Spirit is both other than Christ and also the way Christ's presence is manifested following His ascension. This is the inescapable paradox of this passage where Jesus speaks of asking the Father to send 'another to be your Advocate', but also asserts, 'I am coming back to you.'

This means that we who never companioned with Christ in the flesh are by no means spiritually 'underprivileged'. We understand the feelings of the children's hymn writer: 'I wish that His hands had been placed on my head ...' But by His Spirit Christ is as truly present with us today. The Holy Spirit, J. E. Fison writes, 'is no mere compensation for what we have not got, and need, whether that be happiness or a clear conscience or friendship of the Lord Jesus Christ Himself. He does not make up for the absence of Christ: He is the way to the presence of Christ.'

The experience of Christ's presence will come to different people in different ways. Simone Weil, the French mystic who died at the age of thirty-four, claimed that during prayer, 'Christ is present with me in person, but His presence is infinitely more real, more moving, more clear than on that first occasion when He took possession of me.' Yet most of us, for most of the time, lay hold of Christ's presence by faith rather than by feeling. And this is by no means to be regarded as a spiritual second-best.

JOHN 14: 22-31

'Peace is my parting gift to you, my own peace, such as the world cannot give' (v. 27, N.E.B.).

WHAT KIND OF PEACE? One writer urged that we should

take care to understand what we are asking when we repeat that ancient prayer, 'Lamb of God, that takest away the sins of the world, grant us Thy peace.' For if it is indeed Christ's peace we are after, this was certainly not the peace of a quiet and tranquil existence.

This was well illustrated by Henry Drummond when he described two artists who each painted a picture to portray his conception of rest. 'The first chose for his scene a still, lone lake among the far-off mountains. The second threw on his canvas a thundering waterfall, with a fragile birch tree bending over the foam; at the fork of the branch, almost wet with the cataract's spray, a robin sat on its nest. The first was only stagnation; the last was rest. . . . Christ's life outwardly was one of the most troubled lives that was ever lived; tempest and tumult, tumult and tempest, the waves breaking over it all the time. But the inner life was a sea of glass. The great calm was always there. At any moment you might have gone to Him and found rest.'

As we have recently noticed, this peace of Christ was certainly not the absence of pain or even conflict. Yet beneath the level of stress and turbulence there was the peace of single-minded devotion to God's will, and implicit trust in God's love. This peace can be ours today, provided we are also willing to take the path of discipleship.

JOHN 15: 1-10

'The branch that does not live on in the vine can yield no fruit of itself; no more can you, if you do not live on in Me' (v. 4, Knox).

NO ROOM FOR SELF-SUFFICIENCY. 'The Christian is one who has forever given up the hope of being able to think of himself as a good man.' These words of Lesslie Newbigin, at first glimpse so startling, reflect the same truth expounded in this important passage. The branches of the vine are not self-sufficient: they have no source of life within themselves. There is plenty of room for effort in the Christian life, but that effort is primarily directed to maintaining our union with Christ.

Faced with insuperable difficulties in her work Florence Nightingale confessed, 'The very vastness of the work raises one's thoughts to God, as the only One by whom it can be done.' Similarly, the Christian, confronted by the example of Jesus, knows that only the Spirit of Christ within him can transform his life into the likeness of his Master.

Fruitfulness of Christian character can result only from a consistently maintained union with Christ. 'There are some people who visit Christ,' wrote J. H. Jowett. 'There are others who abide in Him.' The merits of a health resort, claimed this great Congregational preacher, cannot be experienced by the day-tripper, but only by those who live continually in the clean, invigorating air. Spasmodic bursts of spiritual zeal cannot produce likeness to Christ. But carefully to guard our links with Jesus, expressed and deepened by prayer, worship, fellowship and quiet meditation—this is to ensure that we remain fruitful branches of the Vine.

JOHN 15: 11–17

'This is My commandment: love one another, as I have loved you' (v. 12, N.E.B.).

THE TRANSFORMING FRIENDSHIP. 'How can I possibly keep such a commandment?' asked H. H. Farmer in one of his sermons. 'Shall I on my knees register a solemn vow of obedience, such a vow as must always lie near the heart of genuine dealing with God, and then go forth to fulfil it?' The preacher then emphasized what we all recognize sooner or later: much more is needed, if we are to fulfil Christ's commands, than to 'wave the airy wand of resolution' over our natures. We would add to this the inevitable artificiality of any 'love' which is given by command.

But of course, Jesus does not merely say, 'Love one another.' He says, 'Love one another, as I have loved you.' He also offers us His undying friendship (v. 14). How astonishingly consistent this is with the most modern insights of psychology. The experience of being loved is always prior to the experience of loving. The child deprived of affection becomes emotionally stunted. Being able to love others is closely linked with being loved and, indeed, with being able to love ourselves in a healthy way. As Shakespeare said, 'Love, loving not itself, none other can.'

The Christian is free to grow in love to the extent that he repeatedly realizes the unfailing love of Christ for him. Communion with Christ, what has been called 'the transforming friendship', is no mere private spiritual indulgence. It is the dynamic of loving service and self-giving. Of St. Francis, Bonaventura said that 'he heard the Lord speaking with him by night, as with a friend.'

JOHN 15: 18–27

'When the truth-giving Spirit, who proceeds from the Father, has come to befriend you, He whom I will send to you from the Father's side, He will bear witness of what I was' (v. 26, Knox).

HOLINESS AND TRUTH. These words of Jesus about the Spirit of truth warn us against two errors into which Christians have often fallen. The first is to divorce the quest for holiness from the quest for truth. Of course, new truth is often disturbing and may threaten long-held views. But God and truth are never enemies.

Suppressing truth in what we believe are the interests of God's Kingdom may well have disastrous effects upon the very cause we seek to serve. Welcoming truth, even when it is disturbing, will eventually lead to deeper faith and a more adequate conception of God. Said William Harvey, in his historic book *The Circulation of the Blood*, 'It is never discreditable to desert error, even though error be sanctioned by the highest antiquity.' Of course, we shall not be so foolish as to promote every latest fancy into the category of truth. But we shall follow after truth, as after holiness, knowing that the Holy Spirit is equally our helper in both quests.

The other error against which these words warn us is to imagine that truth can be contained in a series of propositions. Jesus said of the Spirit of truth, 'He will bear witness to Me' (N.E.B.). The deepest truth is personal. It cannot merely be carried in the head. It calls for a total response from the whole person. This is why Christians find the ultimate truth, not in scientific statements about the universe, not yet in theological statements about God, but in a living encounter with Jesus Christ.

JOHN 16: 1–15

'There is still much that I could say to you, but the burden would be too great for you now' (v. 12, N.E.B.).

PROGRESSIVE UNDERSTANDING. Jesus promised that the Holy Spirit would lead His disciples into understanding which was quite beyond them at present. For our capacity determines our grasp of God's revelation. Let us relate this fact both to the way we teach our children (and others), and our own spiritual quest.

We must ensure, as far as possible, that the religious teaching we give to children never needs to be unlearned. True, it will later need expansion, but it should never need expulsion. For the disciples, there was no going back upon the truth given them by Jesus—only a subsequent deepening and widening of that truth. Careless and makeshift teaching of the young cannot be excused on the grounds that later years give opportunity for correction.

For ourselves, we must recognize that the Spirit will carry us forward into new understanding only as we patiently and watchfully heed His movements in our hearts. Reminding his readers that the Spirit is frequently likened to wind, a leader writer in *The Friend* wrote, 'A man who takes up dinghy sailing does not know immediately where the wind is coming from . . . winds do not blow steadily; they freshen and die away and then come in from a new quarter . . . he has to haul his sheet a little when the wind moves aft, and sometimes change direction when faced with a calm patch.' So must the believer watch for the movements of the Spirit among his fellows and in his own heart if he would be carried forward progressively into truth.

JOHN 16: 16–24

'Up to now you have asked nothing in My Name; ask now, and you will receive, that your joy may be overflowing' (v. 24, J. B. Phillips).

JOYFUL CONFIDENCE. In these chapters Jesus is preparing His disciples for the hostility they will face after His ascension. Yet Christ does not envisage a gloomy future for them. On the contrary, they will know radiant joy. The sources of this joy are twofold: the resurrection of Christ and a confident relationship with God in prayer. These two were linked. The disciples' approach to God contained a new boldness because Christ was at 'God's right hand'.

What does this promise mean that prayer made in Christ's name will be answered? Misunderstood, these words can have disastrous results. One minister records how, as a child, he prayed 'in Christ's name' that he would pass a school examination. His faith took a hard knock when he failed.

In Bible times a person's name and character were linked. So to ask in the name of Jesus is to ask according to His nature, to pray in fact as He would pray. 'Asking what Jesus would ask,' writes

Peter Coleman, 'may seem a rather frightening rule to guide our prayers and somewhat contradictory of the liberty we have reckoned to be ours until we realize the enormous scope of Christ's own prayer.' Too much of our praying falls into the category of the child's prayer that he should pass his exam—it seeks to use God for our ends; it hopes for exemption from pain and striving. Prayer 'in Christ's name' offers our minds, wills and sympathy as channels through which God can fulfil His purposes.

JOHN 16: 25–33

'In the world you will have trouble. But courage! The victory is mine; I have conquered the world' (v. 33, N.E.B.).

WHAT TO EXPECT. 'God hath called you to Christ's side,' said Samuel Rutherford in a time of persecution, 'and the wind is now in Christ's face in this land; and seeing ye are with Him, ye cannot expect the lee-side or the sunny side of the brae.'

In similar terms Jesus promised His disciples trouble and persecution. A world which had rejected Him and was in fact planning His death was unlikely to welcome His disciples with open arms. Neither can we expect exemption from either persecution or, what is often the modern world's equivalent, scorn and derision.

Jesus knew that persecution was not the only threat to the disciples' faith. Their own failure could have an even greater demoralizing effect. So He told them of their coming desertion, not to unnerve them, but in order to steady them. 'The fact that He had forseen their failure (wrote Floyd Filson) will convince them that He is superior to their failures and fickleness and that he loves them in spite of their need for His forgiveness.'

Whether we are distressed by the world's scorn, or by our own weakness, we can find fresh courage by contemplating the victory of our Master. As the English mystic, Julian of Norwich, wrote: 'He said not: "Thou shalt not be tempested, thou shalt not be travailed, thou shalt not be afflicted"; but He said: "Thou shalt not be overcome."'

JOHN 17: 1–10

'When Jesus had said these words, He raised His eyes to heaven and said, "Father, the hour has come"' (v. 1, J. B. Phillips).

PRIESTLY INTERCESSION. The one long continuous

prayer of Jesus recorded in the gospels is found in this chapter. It is called the 'high priestly' prayer because in it Jesus intercedes for His followers, and consecrates Himself to the sacrifice of the Cross.

Each verse of this prayer provides rich material for meditation. Let us concentrate, however, on the fact of Christ's intercession. For while we have no other lengthy record of this ministry we know that Jesus often prayed for His disciples (Luke 22: 32), and the New Testament asserts that He continues to intercede for us in heaven (Heb. 7: 25). As an underground stream gushes out of the rock, to delight the eye before being lost to sight again further on, so the intercessory ministry of Jesus comes to the surface in this wonderful chapter.

This will mean little to us if we hold the widely accepted, but quite erroneous, view that intercession is telling God what He already knows, or asking God for favours He is reluctant to bestow. Intercession is one way in which divine energies are released into the world, one method, which we by no means fully understand, by which man co-operates with God. That Christ intercedes for us is a thought of infinite encouragement: that our own intercessions are linked with His can keep us faithful in the place of prayer.

JOHN 17: 11-19

'For their sake I now consecrate Myself, that they too may be consecrated by the truth' (v. 19, N.E.B.).

PRIEST AND SACRIFICE. We saw yesterday that in His high priestly prayer Jesus made intercession for Himself and His followers. But a priest offered sacrifice as well as intercession, and in today's reading Jesus dedicates Himself for this purpose. 'He consecrates Himself both as priest and victim' (Alan Richardson). His intercession would culminate in arms stretched out upon a Cross.

What does it mean that Jesus offered Himself as a sacrifice for sinners? The modern mind tends to reject sacrificial ideas because of their primitive associations. Ancient man often aimed at placating an angry deity. Some Christians have presented the death of Jesus in these terms. So John Nicholas Grou, often a wise spiritual guide, wrote, 'Through the Cross, Jesus Christ repaired the glory of His Father, appeased His anger, and reconciled Him with the world.' But is this not the very opposite of what Paul

says—'God was in Christ reconciling the world to Himself'
(2 Corinthians 5: 19)?

The sacrifice of Jesus was offered by God. It revealed 'the price
of sin'—the pain borne by a loving God because of man's rebellion. It bridged the gulf between God and man—and this was
always the purpose of sacrifice—from God's side.

We must not limit sacrifice to what it meant to primitive man.
Sacrifice is a universal principle. Jean Henri Fabre declared that
the more he studied nature the more he was convinced that 'all
life, however unconsciously, was obedient to a sublime law of
sacrifice'. What this naturalist saw in creation, Christians see
also in the Creator.

JOHN 17: 20-26

**'I am not praying only for these men but for all who will
believe in me through their message, that they may all be
one' (v. 20, J. B. Phillips).**

THE UNITY OF CHRIST'S FOLLOWERS. It is with
quickened interest that we reach the point in Christ's intercession
where He prays 'for those also who through their words put their
faith in Me' (N.E.B.). Here Jesus prays for us. He prays that His
followers may share the unity He experiences with His Father.
Is this prayer now being answered in new ways as the churches
draw together? Certainly this prayer is quite specific—the world
will believe only when the Church manifests its unity (vv. 21 and
23). Christians hold different views concerning the ways this
unity will be expressed but there can be no question of its importance.

Roger Schutz, the founder of the Taizé Community, suggests
five principles which should guide the search for unity. First, we
should learn to listen to our fellow-Christians. 'Instead of deliver-
ing long monologues in which we hear only our own voice we
must learn to listen in order to understand and appreciate from
the inside the thought and position of the man with whom we are
speaking.'

Secondly, says Roger Schutz, we must come together with pure
motives. 'We are together because God has called us and not because we are to convert one another.' Prayer and patience are
two further requirements. Apparently insurmountable barriers
can be overcome by those who, with these two tools, work with
God in God's way and at God's pace. Lastly, we must be

sensitively aware of the love and devotion which inspires our
fellow-Christians, sometimes to acts we find strange. There may
seem a wide gulf between the incense-swinging deacon at the altar
and the timbrel-playing Salvationist lassie—but God recognizes
the praise-filled heart.

JOHN 18: 1–11

'Jesus said to Peter, "Sheathe your sword. This is the cup
My Father has given Me; shall I not drink it?"' (v. 11,
N.E.B.).

TWO KINDS OF ACTION. The Passion of Jesus occupied a
central place in the preaching of the early Church. Therefore, it is
likely that this part of the gospel narrative was the first to achieve
a settled form. All four evangelists give a similar sequence of
events, but the way these are treated reveal the special interests of
each writer.

For instance, John is concerned to show that Jesus was no mere
passive victim of circumstances. He is actively in control of
events. The initiative is with Christ, not with His enemies. It is
they who are really unfree, mere puppets directed by evil powers.
So, in this passage, Jesus does not wait beneath the shade of the
trees to be hunted out. The calm dignity with which He presents
Himself to His enemies fills them with awe and throws them into
confusion.

In the Passion Jesus is active—not passive. Yet His action is
totally different from that of Peter who courageously, but mistakenly, lashes out with his sword. Christ's action is that of close
adherence to the will of God, discovered in the place of prayer
and spiritual struggle. Peter's is an all too instinctive and un-
considered reaction.

Writes Fulton Sheen, 'The Divine work is best done away from
the periphery and close to the centre. We do not need an activism
which, like Peter's, neglects the quiet task of watching and
praying, in favour of swinging swords because our enemies
swing them.'

JOHN 18: 12–18

'Then the guard, with its captain and the Jewish officers
took hold of Jesus and tied His hands together, and led
Him off to Annas' (vv. 12 and 13, J. B. Phillips).

THE WEAKNESS OF GOD. With the arrest in the garden it appears that Christ's last chance of freedom has vanished. Astonishingly, with hands tied together and wholly at the mercy of His captors, Jesus now begins His greatest work. Men could bind Him with cords, or nail Him to a Cross, but they were impotent to quench His love, lessen His resolution or deflect His loyalty. No wonder Paul later affirmed, 'Divine weakness is stronger than man's strength' (1 Cor. 1: 25, N.E.B.).

One outstanding impression gained from the life of Jesus is that He was extraordinarily free. Martin Conway claims this was a two-fold freedom. Negatively, Jesus was free from 'personal anxiety and insecurity, from the social patterns and restraints of the prevailing ... culture—free from anything that stood in the way of His living in the way He thought He was meant to live'. Positively, Jesus was free for 'His neighbours ... for the calling and purpose He knew to be supremely urgent and important'.

When we are tempted to feel robbed of our liberty by outward circumstances we should ponder the freedom of Christ—especially the freedom of the bound and crucified Christ. The Indian poet, Tagore, illustrates the paradox of true freedom by describing a piece of catgut which he picked up. Hanging between his fingers it appeared free but was quite useless. Fitted into his violin, bound at both ends and drawn taut, it became free to sing. If we would know the freedom of Christ, we must seek it in singleminded love, not in the absence of pain and suffering.

JOHN 18: 19–27

'Then one of the High Priest's servants, a relation of the man whose ear Peter had cut off, remarked, "Didn't I see you in the garden with Him?" And again Peter denied it' (vv. 26 and 27, J. B. Phillips).

DRAMA ON TWO STAGES. The story of the Passion is the most complete exposure of human sin and folly. Only because it is, at the same time, the most complete revelation of God's unswerving love can we dare to face its implications. Today's passage, for instance, has been likened by one commentator to 'a drama being performed on a double stage'. We witness two scenes: the trial of Jesus before the high priest and the denial by Peter of His Master in the nearby courtyard.

Here is supreme irony. The man who was supposedly God's

representative is confronted by God Incarnate, the Hope of Israel. He utterly rejects Him. Confident of his own wisdom and grasp of spiritual truth the priest sees Christ as a mere impostor. How different it might have been if, like Nicodemus, the high priest had dared to question his own prejudices! Lack of humility leads men into all kinds of sin, including the rejection of God Himself when He comes to us in some unexpected form.

A different form of pride led to Peter's downfall. The disciple was no coward, as his entry into the enemy's camp shows. Perhaps it was the form of the question, 'Surely you are not another of this man's disciples?' which caught Peter off guard. It was the kind of question which positively invites the answer 'No'. As when we are challenged, 'You surely don't believe that?'. And we, if we don't deny Christ like Peter, for the danger is not so great, start apologizing for our faith.

JOHN 18: 28–40

'Jesus said, "Is that your own idea, or have others suggested it to you?"' (v. 34, N.E.B.).

SECOND-HAND OPINION. Early in the morning Jesus was taken from the high priest's palace to Pilate. The Jews refused to enter the Governor's residence because they were anxious to avoid ritual defilement. Scrupulously careful about ceremonial purity they were totally indifferent to justice. Their refusal, however, enabled Pilate to interview Jesus privately. This interview, recorded at length in the fourth gospel, is full of subtle contrasts between two types of kingship.

How surprised the Governor must have been when his first question drew from his Prisoner simply a further question! This Man seemed to be making no effort to escape the awful fate which awaited Him.

The question Jesus put to His earthly judge—'Is that your own idea, or have others suggested it to you?'—is timeless. In so far as it represents Christ's passion for reality, His hatred of insincerity, it can as well be applied to ourselves. No toying with second-hand opinions will lead us to truth.

Walt Whitman described his visit one night to an astronomy lecture. The hall was stuffy and the lecturer dull. At last he could stand it no longer. Leaving the hall, he wandered out into the night, and stood gazing up at the stars themselves! So must we seek the truth from Christ Himself if ever our religion is to be based on more than hearsay.

JOHN 19: 1–7

'The soldiers put on His head a crown which they had woven out of thorns, and dressed Him in a scarlet cloak' (v. 2, Knox).

PERFECT MANHOOD. Pilate made repeated attempts to evade condemning Jesus to death. One of these consisted in trying to turn the crowd's hatred into pity. The Governor had Jesus flogged, and a Roman flogging was such torture that men sometimes died as a result. The soldiers responsible for this indulged in contemptuous mockery, dressing Jesus in a purple robe and crown of thorns. Pilate then presented Jesus to the people, hoping that He would present so ridiculous and pitiful a figure that their malice would be satisfied. How did Pilate voice those memorable words, 'Behold, the Man'? Was it with contempt—'Look at the poor fellow'—or with growing admiration? Certainly we have here another of the evangelist's 'double meanings'. The record of the trial has several such and we shall consider a further example below.

Whatever Pilate meant, the gospel writer intended these words to convey one tremendous truth. Jesus is the perfect Man, and never more so than at that moment when He bore scornful abuse without resentment and rendered to His Father a perfect obedience.

It is interesting to see that in different epochs and in different lands men hold varied ideals of human nature. At one time it is the soldier who is everyone's ideal, at another it is the artist. In the East the mystic is still widely revered—in the West it is the technician who is most admired. Where do we find our model of true manhood? Among the giants of an acquisitive, luxury-loving society? Or in the Man who risked everything in love for men and loyalty to His Father?

JOHN 19: 8–16

'Pilate now said to the Jews, "Look, here's your king!" At which they yelled, "Take Him away ... crucify Him!"' (v. 15, J. B. Phillips).

JUDGE AND JUDGED. We saw above that although we

cannot be certain with what tone of voice Pilate uttered the memorable words, 'Behold the Man!' we can recognize John's underlying meaning. His narrative so often moves simultaneously on two levels. Today's passage is a further example of this. We are told that Pilate took his seat on the tribunal (v. 13). Now in the original Greek that could equally well read that he sat Jesus on the tribunal. In fact, that is what two early authorities say he did. If so, he was continuing the mockery of his own soldiers.

C. K. Barratt suggests that John is being deliberately ambiguous in his narrative, leaving us to read it either way. This, to emphasize the truth that Jesus, not Pilate, was the true judge on that momentous day. 'Behold, your King!' was spoken in mocking irony. In fact, it was the sober truth. To all except a few classical scholars, Pilate's name is known only because of his connection with Jesus and he is remembered for his weakness. Well may we ask: Who of these two men was judge and who was judged?

We live at a time when the Church and the Christian faith is constantly under fire. We cannot be indifferent to what is sometimes perfectly fair criticism. God has often addressed His people through their enemies. But we need be little disturbed by men who imagine they can similarly judge the Church's Lord. History will prove that it is Christ who passes the verdict.

JOHN 19: 17–30

'When Jesus took the vinegar, He said, "It is finished," bowed His head, and gave up His spirit' (v. 30, Moffatt).

ACCOMPLISHED! Let us heed the advice of A. E. Whitham and be unconcerned about our emotions. Nothing can move a man to the depths of his being as can a visit to Calvary. But we are saved by the Cross, not by our emotions. To seek for the right emotional response is the best way to inhibit it. Let us rather keep our eyes fixed upon Christ, so that a deeper understanding of His passion may be given to us.

All the synoptic gospels record that, just before His death, Jesus gave 'a loud cry'. John alone records that before yielding up His spirit, Jesus said 'It is finished!' In the Greek this is one word— 'Accomplished!' Probably this was the 'loud cry' of the Synoptics, a shout of triumph and victory. Again we are reminded that Jesus was no passive victim. While men imagined they were working their evil designs upon Him, He was completing His work of redemption, offering the perfect sacrifice that would reconcile men to God, defeating the powers of evil, manifesting the unquenchable love of God.

'Those devils and weaklings who met at Calvary', wrote W. E. Sangster, 'would have said, "We did it." He cries from His Cross, "I did it! It is finished!" If they were right, the Cross would be a gibbet, a symbol of shame, something to hide and speak of only by compulsion and with bated breath. In point of fact, we placard it to all the world. ... It is His message, not theirs, which it bears at the last.'

JOHN 19: 31–42

'Now at the spot where He had been crucified there was an orchard, and in the orchard a new tomb ... they put Jesus there' (vv. 41 and 42, Moffatt).

TERMINUS AND BEGINNING. As the Sabbath began at sundown, there could be no delay in taking the bodies of the crucified men from their crosses. The legs of the criminals were broken to hasten death. As Jesus was already dead a soldier pierced His side with a lance. That blood and water flowed from this wound was obviously highly important to the evangelist, as showed by his reference to an eyewitness. Why this emphasis upon what may appear to us a detail?

Some suggest the blood and water were seen as important confirmations that death had taken place. The risen Christ was no weak, sickly figure who somehow survived the torture of the Cross as some enemies of the Church suggested. For us, this emphasizes, as Neville Clark has written, that 'The Cross is a terminus. It is set starkly in the path of all natural expectations, and on its cross-beam is inscribed the caption: "No through road" ... Only a new act of God, a light which is divine, can turn night into day, and make of the terminus a fresh beginning.'

Remembering John's love of symbolism, we may also recognize that outpoured blood was an essential part of true sacrifice. Water, in this gospel, symbolizes the new life of the Spirit (4: 14, 7: 38 and 39). Although the Cross is 'a terminus' and only God's new act can create an Easter Day, it is also true that the Cross immediately begins to win its victories, as in the lives of two 'secret' disciples who now find the courage to declare their loyalty by caring for Christ's body.

'Then the other disciple ... went in, and when he saw the inside of the tomb he was convinced' (v. 8, Barclay).

THE INSIGHT OF LOVE. It is noteworthy that it was to Peter that Mary hurried with the news that the sepulchre where the body of Jesus had been laid was disturbed. Though dawn was hardly breaking she could see that something seemingly untoward had happened, and her first conclusion was that the enemies of Jesus, not content with His death, had sought to dishonour Him further by stealing His body (v. 2). So Peter, still apparently the leader of the stricken band of disciples, and John ('that other disciple' of v. 3) hurried to the tomb. Though the younger man outstripped the elder, he did no more than 'peer in' (v. 5, N.E.B.). The big fisherman, impulsive as ever, went inside and noted the details itemized in vv. 6 and 7.

Luke (24:12) says that Peter then went home 'wondering in himself at that which was come to pass'. John then entered the sepulchre and, though he only saw what Peter had seen, with the instinct of love 'believed'.

Love has its own insights and its own fierce loyalties. Of all the friends of Jesus the forgiven Mary was first at His tomb. She could not have visited the sepulchre on the Sabbath because that would have been to break the Sabbath law. But she was there first thing on our Sunday morning, and the disciple whom Jesus loved was the first to believe. To our prayer for an increase of faith, we can add a petition for the increase of love.

'Mary of Magdala went to the disciples with her news: "I have seen the Lord!" she said, and gave them His message' (v. 18, N.E.B.).

A PRESENT EXPERIENCE. 'There were no Christians before Easter,' claims one writer. For although the disciples made personal sacrifices to follow Christ, on the night of His betrayal 'they all forsook Him and fled'. It took the Resurrection, and Pentecost, to make them as fearless as their Master.

The Resurrection of Christ is the very heart of the gospel. The saintly Indian Bishop Azariah was asked, 'If you were in a village where they had never heard of Christ, what would you preach about?' Without hesitation he replied, 'The Resurrection.' Concerning the way in which this happened there is room for differences of opinion for the Resurrection is an unrepeatable mystery. But that it happened is what changes Christianity from a moral code to a moral dynamic. The Resurrection not only lifts our horizons, enabling us to live in 'the eternal dimension', it assures us that goodness ultimately triumphs.

Usually, the further removed we become from an event through the passing of time, the less thrilled we are by it. We need the photographs of last year's holiday to recapture even a little of its pleasures. The very opposite was true for the disciples with the Resurrection. After many years their letters throbbed with the joy of Easter, for the risen Christ was still their Companion.

JOHN 20: 19–25

'Then He showed them His hand and His side, and the disciples were overjoyed when they saw the Lord' (v. 20, J. B. Phillips).

BEHIND CLOSED DOORS. We do not begrudge the disciples those barred doors. Had we been there, we should have been as anxious as anyone to test their security. The fact remains that Jesus came to them on that never-to-be-forgotten evening to impel them to abandon the safety of closed doors. 'As the Father sent Me, so I send you' (v. 21, N.E.B.), was His charge to them. And that commission has never been withdrawn, no matter how much a hostile, cynical or scornful world may tempt us to retreat into comfortable separation.

Taken alone, nothing could be more daunting than this commission of Christ to His Church. But we must not take it so. First of all, the risen Christ greeted His disciples with the old familiar salutation, 'Peace be with you!' 'Its use conveyed in a moment to the disciples that their faithlessness had not destroyed that relationship of confidence and love which they had enjoyed with their Master', writes Leslie Cooke. 'He loved them still, and was ready to trust them again.' Nothing less than this constantly renewed forgiveness can strengthen us to continue an undertaking in which we so often fail.

Jesus not only assured His disciples of His forgiveness, He imparted to them His spirit (v. 22). This gospel sees the giving of the Spirit as the immediate outcome of Christ's death. For our reassurance we can remember that Jesus does not give us any task without also supplying the resources.

JOHN 20: 26–31

'Jesus said, "Because you have seen Me you have found faith. Happy are they who never saw Me and yet have found faith"' (v. 29, N.E.B.).

THE WOUNDED GOD. The first draft of this gospel may well have ended with this reading, and what a powerful conclusion! The final picture is of the risen Jesus confronting His once doubting disciple. The gospel has repeatedly touched on the theme of 'seeing and believing'. The Jews had seen Christ but had not believed. The disciples, and now Thomas, had seen and believed. The rapturous affirmation of Thomas, 'My Lord and My God!' marks the climax of the gospel. But we are not left there. In what has been called 'the last and greatest of the Beatitudes' (Westcott) Jesus points foward to those who will not see, but will still believe.

Let us take a further glimpse at what the evangelist first intended to be his final picture. Jesus shows to Thomas the nail prints. These are much more than a means of identification. Whatever they meant to Thomas, they remind us that to all eternity the risen Christ is also the crucified Christ. The wound prints tell us that in Jesus God had borne, and still bears, our suffering and our sin. This is well expressed in the poem *The Prayer of a Modern Thomas* by Edward Shillito:

> If Thou, O God, the Christ didst leave,
> In Him, not Thee, I do believe;
> To Jesus dying all alone,
> To His dark Cross, not Thy bright Throne,
> My hopeless hands will cleave.

> But if it was Thy love that died,
> Thy voice that in the darkness cried,
> The print of nails I long to see,
> In Thy hands, God, who fashioned me
> Show my *Thy* piercéd side.

JOHN 21: 1–14

(Just as dawn began to break, Jesus stood there on the beach, the disciples having no idea that it was Jesus' (v. 4, J. B. Phillips).

INDESTRUCTIBLE LIGHT. We do not know how soon after completing the first twenty chapters of his gospel the evangelist added this final postscript. We are very grateful that it was added for it contains a very beautiful account of Peter's complete restoration.

A. B. Starratt wrote an allegory which may help some readers to grasp the transformation which the Resurrection produced in the outlook of Peter. There was once a race of men who were constitutionally unable to lift their eyes above the horizon. Aware of the presence of light in the daytime, they argued long and passionately about its source. Eventually the sun, which stands in this allegory for a benevolent God, decided to show them the source of the light. This he did by creating a lens or magnifying glass through which his own rays were focused.

Men were amazed and attracted by this intense light. Others considered it a threat and succeeded in breaking the magnifying glass. Those who loved the light were heartbroken. One of them, named Peter, was by the sea shore when the sun in the sky gave him power to lift his eyes above the horizon and see the sun itself. At once he knew that the light he had loved in relation to the magnifying glass was the light of the sun, the source of all the light men had ever known, and that breaking the magnifying glass could not destroy that light.

'In Him was life; and the life was the light of men. ... That was the true Light which lighteth every man that cometh into the world' (1: 4 and 9).

JOHN 21: 15–25

'There is much else that Jesus did. If it were all to be recorded in detail, I suppose the whole world would not hold the books that would be written' (v. 25, N.E.B.).

TOGETHER AT THE END. As William Temple concludes his *Readings in St. John's Gospel*, this is pardonable exaggeration for 'to tell the whole story of Jesus' love and power would exhaust the capacities of the universe.' We may be grateful, however, that as Peter and John are together in the opening chapter of this gospel, they are together at the end.

Contrasted in temperament, they were one in their love. At the Last Supper one of them leaned on Jesus' breast; the other tried to prevent the Master washing his feet. As has been noted above, at the tomb it was John who believed though Peter went in first. At the lakeside it was John who first recognized Jesus though it was Peter who swam ashore first. The Church of Christ has ever had both types of men—and needs them still. All believers are not intended to be cast in the same mould, nor to think the same as one another, not to copy each other's actions. The fellowship which Jesus offers has room for all sorts and conditions of men. The word to the sinner is 'whosoever', and the word to the saint is the same.